Garabandal

Message of Hope

Translated from *Garabandal, Mensaje de Esperanza* (2015).

First English Edition: June 2016.

Second English Edition: March 2017.

Legal Deposit: SA-77-2015

ISBN:978-84-606-5504-6

Garabandal
Message of Hope

José Luis Saavedra

"No one but the holy hierarchical Mother Church may give us complete certainty about the religious significance of San Sebastián de Garabandal; we, with well intentioned efforts [of study], may open and facilitate the way towards the Hierarchy's decision."

José María Alba Cereceda, *Report on Garabandal*, Barcelona, 1962.

Table of Contents

PART I · "The Facts"

What happened in Garabandal?

PART II · "The Doctrine"
Why did Garabandal happen?

PART III · "The Fruits"
What happened with Garabandal?

PROLOGUE

This is the first time that I have written a Prologue for a book the fundamental content of which proceeds from a Licentiate Thesis. In effect, this book is the result of months of intense work culminating in José Luis Saavedra's obtainment of the title of Licentiate in Theology.. All of this was accomplished under the direction of the Department of Historical Theology of the Faculty of Theology at the University of Navarre. This is by no means frequent; normally these studies are not published as a book until the termination of the Doctoral Thesis. There are exceptions, but very few. I recall academic legends that speak of it having happened "once upon a time," but such exceptions are extremely rare. Among them may now be numbered this work of the licensed José Luis Saavedra. His thesis joins him to that small legendary group of scholars whose Licentiate Theses have found interested publishers. The result is the present study of the apparitions of the Virgin Mary in San Sebastián de Garabandal (Santander).

My relation with José Luis Saavedra, the author, has been close and easy during the time of the work. Of course, there is only one author of the thesis and of this book: he himself. But I may well be the person who has followed most closely this investigation as the content extended, its ideas matured, and its structure became more solid. I can say that Saavedra's work has improved each time new parts were completed and added for my revision. And I think that I should say that the work has been completed within deadlines, often at the very last moment because the author, as well as attending classes for the Licentiate in Theology and writing the thesis, never ceased to tend with true zeal and enthusiasm to his numerous parishes scattered among the foothills of Pamplona. But all of this is now ended. The book is finished and if you are reading the Prologue, it is in your hands.

This book about the Virgin will help readers who seek to get closer to Her, to contemplate Her, and to pray. But it is also, principally, an academic study of an extraordinary event in which some girls from a small village in Santander lived the most special relationship with the Most Holy Virgin. We could say that these girls were chosen. Without wanting it, without remotely expecting it, they became the protagonists of these events. Furthermore, a very great number of other people shared their experience of those events. At the very beginning there were just a few others, and then the number grew with the passing of time. Many people in the most varied life situations gathered around the children and around the apparitions, which for all except the four children were invisible. Yet many received very intimate and special favors, felt the action of grace in their souls, converted and returned to God. Independently of whether or not these apparitions are officially approved by the Church, there is one question that interests us: how does the fact that the Virgin appears to men and speaks to them affect Catholic theology? Does theology have something to say in response to the messages of the Virgin in the approved apparitions? Or do these belong to a different world that has nothing to do with the reflections of theologians?

There are diverse attitudes inside and outside of the academic world towards the subject of supernatural manifestations, concretely towards the apparitions of the Blessed Virgin. Some, without possession of the facts, simply say: "No, that is

8

impossible," and look the other way. Others say: "Yes, that is surely true," and succumb to an interest closer to idle curiosity about strange novelties than to true piety. Others, however, when they consider it opportune, are not afraid to approach the facts, to read, to investigate, to consult informed authors, to seek out sources, to compare, to be well informed, and then they elaborate a real history, with its pros and cons. This is what José Luis Saavedra has procured to do in his thesis and now in this book about the apparitions of Garabandal. Without drawing conclusions that do not correspond to me, I simply ask: what would have happened in other great occasions if nobody had pursued this third way, which demands constancy, work and effort. What would have happened with the apparitions of Lourdes, Fatima, the Miraculous Medal of the Rue du Bac, Guadalupe and so many other cases? The decision of the authority of the Church is one thing, towards which this work has nothing but respect and obedience, yet another thing is the interest of the historian and theologian who seeks to comprehend the event without preconceptions, and to make the facts known.

The fact that the origin and end of this book are academic has its advantage; the reader will not find any illusory considerations here, or any emotive affirmations of the author intended to move the sentiments, targeting enthusiasm rather than the intelligence. We fully hold in common what Rémi Brague has written in his recent book *In the Middle of the Middle Ages*, when he speaks of the great number of false legends about the medieval world, saying: "If the commercial motivation of the so-called *"intellectual"* consists of repeating the dominant opinion and being *"politically correct,"* the duty of the University scholar is above all to re-establish what he believes to be the truth, regardless of whether or not people find it pleasant." One of the main characteristics of the work of academics is that we are obliged, gladly obliged, to tell the readers the truth. Unlike the writer of fiction or even the essayist or ideologue, who analyzes things in his own favor, the academic author works within limits that he does not wish to breach: that which is proven, that which has been discovered whether he likes it or not, and nothing more. His universitary intellectual identity is manifested precisely in working under the governance of the truth; and this implies that statements without foundation will not be made, the reader will find nothing that cannot be proven, corroborated by witnesses, by confirmed sources, etc. Each reader may then draw his own conclusions from the evidence impartially presented.

Despite the fact that this book originated in a work of investigation under "the vigilance," so to speak, of the academic norm, José Luis Saavedra has artfully softened its language to convert it into an attractive book, easy to read and understand, which will offer the reader much veridical information about the facts of the not yet officially approved apparitions of the Most Blessed Virgin in Garabandal. Furthermore, many serious and interesting positions are to be found in the book concerning what spiritual theology and the recent magisterium of the Church have said about mystical phenomena, and especially about the apparitions of the Virgin. I believe I should add that the author has studied the principal theologians who have addressed these questions in recent times. José Luis Saavedra's personal work is bolstered by consultation of the most solid theologians who have written about the nucleus and the periphery of the subject under consideration.

A closing word concerning approval by the Church. There is no question here of wishing to point an accusatory finger. We are confronted with marvelous events that may in time be recognized as authentic apparitions of the Blessed Virgin and celebrated by great multitudes of people. However, even though quite a number of years have passed since their occurrence, the events are still very recent. This book has been written without any spirit of undue haste, without any desire to accelerate processes unwisely. It is a work of historical theology that seeks to contribute order and clarity concerning events that occurred in a small village of Santander in the latter half of the 20th Century. If it were to have the indirect effect of serving those whose task it is to form an authoritative judgment in relation to the facts, this would be beyond the scope of our author. Like any good historian, the author simply asks: how did it all begin? What happened there during those years? Who were those children and what were their families like? How did the Virgin appear to the children and what did She say to them? In that region, what was the social and religious environment like? Who came from other regions when they learned of these events, and with what intentions? What testimonies do we have from medical personnel, priests, theologians, agents of public order, ordinary people who witnessed the apparitions or conversed in some way or another with the seers? What has happened since the apparitions ended? What has the authority of the Church said up to this point? And like any good historian he has responded to all of this and more with all of the information he has been able to gather.

M. Lluch

Miguel Lluch Baixauli,
Director of the Department of Historical Theology
of the University of Navarre, Spain.
Pamplona, 8 November 2014.

I

Introduction

The Place of Marian Apparitions in Contemporary Theology

Benedict XVI, in the Apostolic Exhortation *Verbum Domini* (2010), affirmed the value of *private revelations*, among which are included the *Marian apparitions*.[1] The Catechism of the Catholic Church (1992) explains the function of said private revelations: to recall the definitive revelation of Christ (public Revelation), helping to "live more fully by it in a certain period of history."[2] Public and private revelations are clearly different. Effectively, public Revelation is self-proposing (Cf. Jn 10:35; Lk 24:44). Private revelations, on the other hand, are always dependent upon and referenced to public Revelation.

From this, important consequences may be drawn: the book that proceeds from the pen of the sacred writer (public Revelation) is, without doubt, the *Word of God* and must be received as such; everything that is taught therein is guaranteed by the testimony of God and demands our theological faith. This does not occur in the case of private revelation. Here, the prophet does not have the charism of inerrancy, and therefore, the fidelity

---

[1] Cf. BENEDICT XVI, Apostolic Exhortation *Verbum Domini*, Rome, 2010, 14.
[2] *Catechism of the Catholic Church*, Rome, 1992, 67.

of his expression is never divinely guaranteed. His utterances are subject to error. Moreover, according to Saint Thomas, it can happen that he continue to prophesize in good faith, after the prophetic light has been extinguished in him.[3] In this case, therefore, discernment is required, since private revelation is an instrument that is *vulnerable by its very nature*. However, its fruits have been bountiful in the history of the Church, beginning with the Sacred Scriptures.

Private revelations abound in Sacred Scripture; throughout the entire Bible—Old Testament and New—we find that "God speaks and appears to the patriarch Abraham, to Moses and the prophets, to Jesus Christ, to the apostles Peter and Paul and to other Christians in the Acts of the Apostles."[4] It is true that the Sacred Scriptures denounce the false prophets, but it is equally the case that they denounce the repression of authentic prophecy (Am 2:11-12; Is 31:10, Jer 11:21; Zach 1:5; Neh 9:30), which attempts to extinguish the prophetic vision and function among God's people (Lam 2:9-10; Ez 2:26). In fact, the gift of prophecy is promised in the restoration of Israel (Is 59:21; Os 12:10; Joel 3:1). In the New Testament the prophetic function, like extraordinary mysticism, holds an equally important place in fundamental moments: in the Incarnation, Gethsemane or Pentecost, where, as well as the visible Gift of the Holy Spirit, the Apostle Peter celebrates the fulfillment of a prophecy (cf. Acts 2:17). So, it is clear that in the Sacred Scriptures, prophecy, with its extraordinary manifestations, merits an important place.

---

3 SAINT THOMAS AQUINAS, *Summa Theologiae*. II—II , q.171, a.5.

4 "Dieu parle et apparait au patriarch Abraham, à Moïse et aux prophètes, à Jésus—Christ, aux apotres Pierre et Paul et à d'autres chrétiens dans le Actes des Apotres" LAURENTIN, R. — SBALCHIERO, P. (dir.), *Dictionnaire des apparitions de la Vierge Marie: Inventaire des origins à nos jours: Méthodologie, bilan interdisciplinaire, prospective*, Paris 2007, 15.

"Consequently—Benedict XVI concludes in *Verbum Domini*—it [private revelation] *should not be treated lightly."*[5]

With these words, *"ideo non est neglegendum,"* Benedict XVI expresses a peculiar tension typical of private revelations; they have a genuine value, so that, although not an indispensable means, *they are not merely dispensable*. The Latin phrase employed (the periphrastic passive, composed of the gerundive of the verb *neglego*—to discard, to despise—and the verb *sum*), expresses obligation, an imperative "ought," meaning here that private revelations *may not, must not* be despised. This is because to do so would be to despise thereby their very author, who in the final analysis, in the case of Marian apparitions, is God Himself.

After all, Javier Paredes, Chair of Contemporary History in the University of Alcalá (Madrid), expresses perplexity towards the academic void regarding concrete apparations today. In abstract or when already approved, they are accepted; but apparitions, prior to their approval, are often simply silenced. However, it is worth mentioning that *Marian apparitions* never take place with prior approval of the local Ordinary. The apparition always happens without asking permission, without giving anybody prior notice. It belongs to the Church to go where there appear to be solid indications of supernaturality and to evaluate them. The work of the scholar will always be united with discernment, which forms part of the nature of this matter. The Church finds herself in a difficult situation when an apparation starts happening: "because it is not a question of minorities—writes Paredes—; because this has moved milliones of people. Well then—logically— let us see what is there, what it consists in, what is going on. But, it is that, besides, as a Catholic... it interests me very much. Above

---

5 BENEDICT XVI, Apostolic Exhortation *Verbum Domini*, Rome, 2010, 14.

all, because St. John Paul II said that 'Jesus Christ is the *Lord of History.'"[6]* That is how it is: sure apparitions, besides their religious finality, constitute a historical fact that enlightens the life of man.

Effectively, private revelation is "a valuable aid for better understanding and living the Gospel at a certain time."[7] In order to avail of this *aid*, a rigorous study of possible cases that arise is required.

These criteria of discernment have important consequences. It is of course true that apparitions are useful "for directing human conduct," (*ad directionem actuum humanorum*), as St. Thomas affirms,[8] but it is also true that, on occasions, it is possible that "the subject [visionary] may have added—even unconsciously—merely human elements and even some error of a natural order to a true supernatural revelation."[9] For this reason, prior to proposing apparitions to the consideration of the faithful, the Church must study them and approve their content.

To this effect, the Congregation for the Doctrine of Faith published in 1978 the *Norms regarding the manner of proceeding in the discernment of presumed apparitions and revelations*. All apparitions have to be studied, evaluated and sanctioned *a posteriori* by the Hierarchy of the Church, which bears the responsibility in this area.

"...*May not be despised.*" The saints and mystics are a precious gift for the Church, a supernatural indication of the path to be

6 PARADES, J., "*Importancia de las apariciones de la Virgen*," en ATANEO DE SANTANDER, *Presentatción del Libro "Madre de Dios y Madre Nuestra,"* Santander, October 7, 2013.
7 *Ib.*, 14.
8 SAINT THOMAS AQUINAS, *STh*, II—II, q.174, a.6, ad.3.
9 CONGREGATION FOR THE DOCTRINE OF FAITH, *Norms regarding the manner of proceeding in the discernment of presumed apparitions and revelations*, Vatican, 1978, I.2. Hereafter cited as CDF, *Norms for the discernment of presumed apparitions*, 1978 with section and number.

followed in the present. This supernatural light does not constitute a way that is independent of or parallel to the way of reason; rather it is joined to that way inseparably.[10] For this very reason private revelations may be studied by the Hierarchy, with the light and guidance of theology, oriented by the Holy Spirit and reason, discerning the charisms—including *Marian apparitions*—for the service of the Church.

The study of the experience of the saints and mystics is relevant for theology, as is the consideration of the possible apparitions and revelations. This is true especially in those cases with contents that point in the best direction, given that true revelations have constituted—for the good of the whole Church—a "valuable aid for better understanding and living the Gospel at a certain time."[11]

The Phenomena of Garabandal

Between the years 1961 and 1965, thousands of people testified to having witnessed extraordinary phenomena connected with four girls in a Cantabrian village. *These visionaries*, between 10 and 12 years of age at the beginning of the phenomena, are the subjects of events that, even for numerous physicians who performed rigorous studies *in situ* of the events, are inexplicable from the scientific point of view. Many theologians agree with these conclusions. Since that time, conversions associated with Garabandal and cases of instantaneous and lasting healings have multiplied throughout the world, occurrences which several physicians have not hesitated to refer to as *"miracles."*

---

[10] LUBAC, H., *Paradoxes et Mystère de l'Église*, Paris, 1967, 32 (quotation translated from the Spanish edition: *Paradojas y Misterio de la Iglesia*, Salamanca, 2002).
[11] BENEDICT XVI, Apostolic Exhortation *Verbum Domini*, Rome, 2010, 14.

However, these phenomena are lacking in solid studies that might permit the Hierarchy to pronounce judgment thereon. This may be gleaned from the words of Archbishop Carlos Osoro Sierra, when, in 2007, as Apostolic Administrator of Santander, the diocese of the *"apparitions,"* he affirmed:

> *I am sure that the next Bishop will promote investigations, so that the events of Garabandal may be examined with greater profundity...*
>
> *I have known authentic conversions connected to the apparitions* [of Garabandal]. *In the face of such events, how can we not feel the need to open our heart always to Mary our Mother to tell her that we need her protection, her help, her encouragement, her enthusiasm, her faith, her hope and her love.*
>
> *I encourage you to maintain this devotion to our Mother.*[12]

These words form part of what is, to date, the most recent episcopal utterance on the events of Garabandal. On this occasion, as in others, the Hierarchy of the Church has expressed interest in the phenomena. This book hopes to respond to the desire expressed by Archbishop Osoro (*"that the events of Garabandal be examined with greater profundity"*) and thereby to perform a service to history and theology. This work shall be done by means of a rigorous approach that might facilitate discernment of this case which, as may be gleaned from the words of Osoro, even to this day, fifty years after the facts, has not yet been the subject of a study of sufficient *"profundity"* to provide the foundations for the necessary judgment that corresponds solely to the Hierarchy.[13]

---

[12] OSORO SIERRA, Carlos, *"Letter to Edward Kelly* (May 7, 2007)" en GARABANDAL JOURNAL, Minnesota, 2007, V—VI, 5; LANÚS, S., *Madre de Dios y Madre Nuestra. Fátima, Ámsterdam y Garabandal,* Madrid, 2013, 174.

[13] Cf. CONC. EC. VATICAN II, Dogmatic Constitution *Lumen Gentium,* AAS 57 (1965) 12; Cf. CDF, *Norms for the discernment of presumed apparitions,* 1978, III.1.

Those phenomena, according to Rolando Cabeza Fuentes, Pastor of the parish church of Garabandal at the time of writing, have been a sign of hope for millions of people throughout the world;[14] their approval would open up that apostolic efficacy to many more souls. This presupposes a serious discernment with rigorous documentation. And the Church, in Vatican Council II, encourages this task, because:

These charisms, whether they be the more *outstanding* [e.g. apparitions] or the more simple and widely diffused, are [all] to be received with *thanksgiving* and *consolation* for they are perfectly suited to and useful for the needs of the Church (cf. 1 Corinthians 12: 11; 7:7).[15]

The Council, which will lead the Church towards a *"new Pentecost,"* invests all its hope in the Virgin. Benedict XVI affirms as much when he adds that, in fact, in the first Pentecost:

The presence of the Mother of God with the Eleven, after the Ascension, then is not just a historical record of a past thing but takes on a meaning of great value ... the Apostles and the Church gather with Mary to await with her the gift of the Holy Spirit, without whom one cannot become witnesses... If there is no Church without Pentecost, there is no Pentecost without the Mother of Jesus..."One cannot therefore speak of the Church unless Mary, Mother of God is present... The Church of Christ is where the Incarnation of Christ from the Virgin is preached."[16]

The story of Garabandal is precisely about this presence of Mary in today's Church, among her children; that is why it is so relevant and interesting.

---

14 Cf. CABEZA FUENTES, J. R., *"Un antes, un después y un hoy"* en http://www.garabandalparroquia.com (September 8, 2013).

15 CONC. EC. VATICAN II, Dogmatic Constitution *Lumen Gentium*, ch. I, *AAS* 57 (1965), 12.

16 BENEDICT XVI, General Audience, March 14, 2012; St. Chromatius of Aquileia, Sermon 30, 1: *SC* 164, 135.

PART I

"The Facts"

What happened in Garabandal?

II

"The Beginnings"

Garabandal from June 18 to July 2, 1961

In these matters, the origin is of paramount importance when it comes to judging whether there has been deceit or whether they [the apparitions] really are due to something external [supernatural] and unforeseen.[17]

June 18, 1961. It is Sunday, and four girls are playing in the plaza of San Sebastián de Garabandal, a small village in the Peaks of Europe. They do not suspect that this same evening there would take place what the eldest of them, Conchita González— then 12 years old—would later describe as *"the biggest event of my life."*[18] Even greater events would later occur; *the apparitions of the Virgin, the locutions,* the levitations, dramatic healings, radical conversions... But it all began that 18ᵗʰ of June. On that day began the extraordinary phenomena that would mark their lives and the

---

[17] GARCÍA DE PESQUERA, E., *Se fue con prisas a la montaña. Los hechos de Garabandal (1961-1965)*, Pamplona, 2004, 121. Cited hereafter as PESQUERA, 2004, with page number added.
[18] CONCHITA GONZÁLEZ, *Diario de Conchita de Garabandal*, Lindenhurst-Nueva York, 1967, 15. Cited hereafter as *Diario de Conchita* with page number.

lives of many more people. That day saw the beginning of the apparitions of *San Sebastián de Garabandal.*

An Unknown Village

Garabandal, with its scarcely 300 inhabitants who work the surrounding fields and flocks, had been until that day a small and forgotten village. Huddled among the final foothills of the Peaks of Europe, at an altitude of 497 meters and some 90 kilometers southeast of Santander, Garabandal possesses nothing that might attract attention. It is simply and solely a mountain village. Situated in an enclave somewhat protected from the wet Cantabrian climate, its skies are not always gray, and yet the life of its inhabitants is rather gray and monotonous: the cows, the harvest, the meadows, the barns... in the perpetual rotation of the seasons, life unfolds between the kitchen chatter, the warmth of the home, the fire and the family.

During the years of *the apparitions,* San Sebastián possesses "two official schools, one for boys and one for girls, with fewer tan twenty children in each one... Attendance at class was not greatly enforced. Religious instruction was given in the school itself and completed in the family;"[19] focusing solely on the most elemental questions. The parish priest tends to the village from his residence in the neighboring village of Cosío. His name is Valentín Marichalar and he visits the village on horseback almost every Sunday evening, celebrating Mass and hearing some confessions. "I had known the girls and their families well for quite some time."

---

[19] LAFFINEUR, M. - LE PELLETIER, M.T., *La estrella en la montaña,* Tielt, 1967, 27.

Father Valentín would follow the events surrounding *the apparitions* with great doubts and perplexity.[20]

The physician only visits the village when there is a real need; and then *he comes on foot*. Access by automobile was difficult, since the only road leading to the remote village was not asphalted at the time. The boys who did not climb to the high pastures to take care of the animals either emigrated or worked in the city. Without grocery stores, telephones, radio transmitters or, in the majority of cases, automobiles, it took an hour-long hike to reach Cosío, from whence all provisions were brought on the back of a donkey; bread included. The village lived in authentic isolation. In fact, many homes did not even have running water.[21]

The village depends on the Town Council of Río Nansa. The chief of the Civil Guard in the area, Brigadier Juan Álvarez, graphically describes the village in the days in which our story commences:

> The customs of its inhabitants are primordially religious. They never forget, for example, to pray the *Angelus*, as soon as the bell rings at twelve noon. In the afternoon they always pray the Holy Rosary in the church. In the evening, Simon's wife (mother of Jacinta, one of *the visionaries*) walks around the village with her lantern and a little bell to invite the neighbors to pray for the dead among their closing prayers of the day. On Sundays, after attending Holy Mass, the young people gather together under porches or out in the open and they sing or play to the beat of the tambourine.[22]

This is the scenario in which those *extraordinary events* would unfold throughout the following four years, events that gave rise to so many pilgrimages, so many conversions... and so many

---

[20] ANDREU, R. M., *Nota 9* en CONCHITA GONZÁLEZ, *Diario de Conchita*, 20; Cf. PÉREZ, R., *Garabandal. El pueblo habla*, Burgos, 1991, 27. Hereafter cited as PÉREZ, 1991 with page number.
[21] Cf. LÓPEZ DE SAN ROMÁN, J. L., *La verdad sobre Garabandal*, Valladolid, 2012, 2.
[22] BRIGADA ÁLVAREZ SECO, J., *"Informe sobre Garabandal"* in PÉREZ, R., 1991, 369.

questions among witnesses, who often waver between curiosity and fervor. In fact, no one will remain indifferent in the face of what is about to occur.

A Clap of Thunder on a Sunny Day

The story commences on a sunny day. Conchita González González leaves the plaza where the village children are playing and walks away from the village in the company of another girl, Mari Cruz González Barrido. Conchita is 12 years old and the youngest of four siblings. Her older siblings are all boys, but she is not the little princess of the house. Her mother, Aniceta González, was widowed at a very young age, and, with four children in the home, everyone had to work hard to help the family to get by, Conchita included; in any case, it was normal for all the children in the village to help their families by working in the fields.

Mari Cruz, Conchita's friend, is only 10 years old, but still only one year younger than Conchita since her eleventh birthday is just around the corner, on the 21st of June; just three days away. Mari Cruz will be the youngest of *the visionaries*, one year younger than her companions, but she is as tall as the others. Her parents are Escolástico and Pilar, and her family is perhaps the least fervent of the four. This would be a cause of suffering for Mari Cruz. Conchita recorded in a *Diary* the events of those days:

> *Mari Cruz and I had the idea to go pick some apples and we headed towards the orchard without saying anything to anybody.*[23]

So they leave the grown-ups and the other girls playing in the plaza, and head towards the teacher's orchard in the outskirts of the village, thinking that nobody would notice them: "*We went to pick some apples,*" Conchita confesses. But they were not long

---

[23] *Diario de Conchita*, 15.

alone; two other girls have followed them, Mari Loli and Jacinta. The group of *the four visionaries* is now assembled.

Jacinta González González is the eldest after Conchita. She is only two months younger, born on April 27, 1949; she too is 12 years old. Her parents, Simón and María González, are very religious, and have seven other children. With Jacinta comes María Dolores Mazón González, the fourth *visionary*; she too is 12 years old and is just four days younger than Jacinta, born on May 1, 1949. She is called *Loli*, or *Mari Loli*, and is the second of the six children of Ceferino and Julia. Her father is the village mayor. Apart from a small plot of land, he also has a small tavern in San Sebastián de Garabandal.[24]

Conchita and Mari Cruz, standing on the tips of their toes to reach the apple tree, hear a noise. They try to hide, but it is too late. Suddenly, *Loli exclaims: "Don't run, Mari Cruz; we saw you, we're going to tell the owner."* All of them run away together. Then, all together, they decide to go back:

After second thoughts, the four of us went back to pick apples... [And] when we had filled our pockets we ran off to eat them without fear of being disturbed in... the Calleja.[25]

In spite of what Conchita writes, those apples, rather than sating their appetite, must have been a source of diversion for the girls on a boring Sunday afternoon. They were not devoured with gusto; rather, they ended up falling to the ground with just a few bites taken. In effect, in early June the apples of Garabandal, even in those years when everything turns ripe *"before their time,"* are never much more than poor half-ripe fruits, bitter, without juice and perfectly designed to put one's teeth on edge. They would

---

[24] Cf. LAFFINEUR, M. - LE PELLETIER, M.T., *La estrella en la montaña*, Tielt, 1967, 28-29.
[25] *Diario de Conchita*, 16. *La Calleja* is a stony path that goes from the village to a small cluster of pine trees.

certainly not be as appetizing as the apples of *Eden*, but even so, they have an incredible seductive power over these *village-girls*, who scarcely ever see any other fruit than those brought to them annually by the trees of their village.[26] Suddenly, with no connection whatsoever to what has occurred up to now, something happens that grabs the attention of all four girls: *"While busily eating, we heard a loud noise like thunder."*[27]

All at once the girls raise their heads to see where the thunderclap came from... They look first towards Peña Sagra, so often crowned with dark rain-clouds, and then towards the nearer peaks, towards the West, a frequent source of storms, but they detected nothing threatening on the horizon. They are unsettled by this strange thunderclap.

A moment later, as they stood there disconcerted and pensive, Conchita exclaimed: *"Lord, what have we done! Now that we've taken those apples, that weren't ours, the devil is happy, and our poor guardian angel is sad!"*[28] The girls immediately recognize the wrong they have done and are moved to repentance: "The reaction of the girls," Brigadier Juan Álvarez narrates, "was to blame the devil for what they had done; and, filled with indignation, they picked up stones, throwing them towards a corner with all their might," "thinking the devil was there laughing at them."[29] The mysterious thunder awakens their abhorrence of sin. And this is just the beginning.

---

[26] Cf. PESQUERA, 2004, 22.
[27] *Diario de Conchita*, 17.
[28] *Ib.*
[29] BRIGADA ÁLVAREZ SECO, J., *"Informe sobre Garabandal"* in PÉREZ, R., 1991, 369.

The Echo of a Mysterious Thunderclap

There are mysterious resonances in the commencement of the events of Garabandal. The apparitions of Fatima began in a similar way, with a blinding flash of lightning in the middle of a sunny day. On the 13th of May 1917, moments before the first apparition of the Blessed Virgin, the three little shepherds experience *"a searing flash of lightning that suddenly wounds their eyes."*[30] *Lucia's* cousins were frightened; it was the middle of the day and the skies were clear. And yet, they are startled again by *"another flash, more dazzling than the first one." Francisco and Jacinta* are now even more frightened and wish to flee... Then the Lady appears, smiling. And with a gesture She invites them to approach her and says to them: *"Don't be afraid; I will do you no harm."* Later on, Lucia herself, in an attempt to describe this phenomenon, would write: *"They weren't exactly flashes of lightning; they were more like reflections of a light that was getting nearer...."*[31] In other words, they find themselves in the presence of a mystery.

A similar phenomenon presents itself in the beginnings of *Lourdes. Saint Bernadette Soubirous*, a humble 14-year-old girl, semi-literate, provides an all-too-brief account that records the events but leaves much to the imagination:

> One day I went to the bank of the Gave River to collect wood with two other girls. Suddenly, I heard *a noise. I looked towards the woods, but the trees weren't moving.* Then I raised my eyes towards the grotto and I saw a woman dressed in white, with a sky-blue cincture and a yellow rose on each of her feet, the same color as the beads of her Rosary...[32]

---

[30] GONZAGA AYRES FONSECA, L., *Nossa Senhora de Fátima*, Petrópolis, 1939, 22; PEREIRA REIS, A. *A Senhora de Fatima*, Sao Paolo, 1991, 17.
[31] *Ib.*
[32] RAVIER, A., *Les écrits de sainte Bernadette Soubirous*, Paris, 1961, 53.

It was February 11, 1858. A sudden gust of wind, like a thunderclap, surprises Bernadette and marks the beginning of *the apparitions of Lourdes*. The same thing now happens in Garabandal.

There is another text that echoes a mysterious thunderclap marking the commencement of extraordinary events. It is to be found in the Sacred Scriptures in the *Acts of the Apostles:* at Pentecost. That day, as would happen later in Lourdes, Fatima and Garabandal, an inexplicable thunderclap marked the beginning of a series of absolutely extraordinary occcurrences:

> And suddenly there came from the sky a noise like a strong driving wind, and it filled the entire house in which they were. Then there appeared to them tongues as of fire, which parted and came to rest on each one of them... At this sound, they gathered in a large crowd, but they were confused because each one heard them speaking in his own language... They were all astounded and bewildered, and said to one another, "What does this mean?" (Acts 2:2-3,6,12).

This is a very strong parallel to draw, but it is undeniable. It is striking also that Sacred Scripture does not present any case of ecstasy, properly speaking, before *Pentecost:* only afterwards. This strengthens even further the connection with the experience of *the seers*. It is true that, historically, certain passages of the Old Testament have been read as cases of ecstasy (e.g. Moses before the *burning bush*, the *inspirations* of the prophets), but these texts are evaluated by modern-day exegesis "with clear attenuations"[33] and not as ecstasies in the strict sense. Nor has the Christian tradition systematically embraced the image of an ecstatic Jesus during the *Baptism* (Mt 3:16), the *temptations* (Mt 4), the *Transfiguration* (Mk 9:1) or the *hymn of jubilation* (Lk 10:21). The reason for this is that "in the structure of ecstasy there is a

---

[33] ÁLVAREZ, T., *"Éxtasis"* en ANCILLI, E. (dir.), *Diccionario de Espiritualidad*, Barcelona, 1987, 93.

negative factor that is difficult to render compatible with the spiritual life of Jesus."[34] Ecstasy means *to go out of oneself*, and this entails a limitation, an incapacity to harmonize the totality of one's own being—soul and body—in the extraordinary presence of God; hence this *going out*: the soul, in some way, momentarily abandons the body. And this cannot happen in Jesus. Therefore, "the neotestamentarian ecstasy appears after the resurrection of Christ, and does so as a *Pentecostal* event."[35] In fact, it is only after Pentecost that we find the word *ecstasy* in the Scriptures: three times, in experiences lived by the apostles. This is corroborated by Saint Peter, in the very discourse that follows the events of Pentecost, when he speaks of *"the last days"*:

> Then Peter stood up with the Eleven, raised his voice, and proclaimed to them, "You who are Jews, indeed all of you staying in Jerusalem. Let this be known to you, and listen to my words. These people are not drunk, as you suppose, for it is only nine o'clock in the morning. No, this is what was spoken through the prophet Joel: 'It will come to pass in the last days,' God says, 'that I will pour out a portion of my spirit upon all flesh. Your sons and your daughters shall prophesy, your young men shall see visions, your old men shall dream dreams. Indeed, upon my servants and my handmaids I will pour out a portion of my spirit in those days, and they shall prophesy. And I will work wonders in the heavens above and signs on the earth below: blood, fire, and a cloud of smoke. The sun shall be turned to darkness, and the moon to blood, before the coming of the great and splendid day of the Lord, 'and it shall be that everyone shall be saved who calls on the name of the Lord" (Acts 2:14-21).

In a certain sense, these words also shed light on the events of the above-mentioned apparitions: "Your sons and your daughters shall prophesy, your young men shall see visions, your old men

---

[34] *Ib.*

[35] *Ib.*

shall dream dreams... And I will work wonders in the heavens above and signs on the earth below..." (Acts 2:17, 19; Joel 2: 28). In fact, there are some who interpret Fatima's *miracle of the sun* as one of these signs and wonders. The resonances with *Pentecost*, the "commencement" *par excellence* of the mission of the Church, would seem to indicate that these little seers were destined for a great mission.

Poor Vessels of Clay

God Himself guides the work begun in *Pentecost*. The apostles are few and many things are unknown to them, but they are capacitated for a universal project. Certainly, on the day of *Pentecost, the twelve* were not ready for the mission they receive—Benedict XVI affirms—but "she [the Virgin] is present, before the doors are thrown open and they begin to announce the Risen Lord to all peoples, teaching them to observe all that the Lord had commanded (Mt 28:19-20)."[36]

The seers of Garabandal are not ready either; nor are they saints. Moreover, they have just finished stealing apples. In such circumstances, is it possible to experience an ecstasy? The experience of the saints indicates that it is. Saint Paul, for example, was busily killing Christians when he heard the voice of Jesus:

> On his journey, as he was nearing Damascus, a light from the sky suddenly flashed around him. He fell to the ground and heard a voice saying to him, "Saul, Saul, why are you persecuting me?" He said, "Who are you, sir?" The reply came, "I am Jesus, whom you are persecuting." (Acts 9:3-5)

---

[36] BENEDICT XVI, General Audience, March 14, 2012.

Even so, Conchita herself has never ceased to be amazed at having been chosen in a way that is, for her, incomprehensible:

It's a source of joy! You don't need to be perfect to see her. I was a little girl with many defects. The day that the Angel appeared to us, I had just been fighting with Jacinta... [But] *She comes precisely to make us good....*[37]

The recognition of one's own weakness is a constant characteristic of Garabandal; and this contains a great lesson. From the beginning, from the moment of the *thunderclap*, the children are moved to renounce their selfishness:

Lord, what have we done! Now that we've taken those apples, that weren't ours, the devil is happy, and our poor guardian angel is sad![38]

The seers are moved from the first moment to recognize that they have done wrong. And yet, that is not the end of it. When, having tired of throwing stones, they begin to play marbles with little pebbles:

A very beautiful figure suddenly appeared to me—Conchita writes—*in the midst of dazzling light that did no harm to my eyes.*[39]

These concise words in the simple language of village children contain an extraordinary significance. The figure that appeared was so far beyond everything striking and beautiful that may be contemplated here below, that Conchita is seized out of herself and the world by wonder and surprise. The other three, seeing her in rapture, became frightened and began to cry out. "Conchita, with her hands joined together, pointed towards *the apparition* and said: *"Ay!... Ay!."*[40] Filled with fear, Mari Loli jumps to her feet to run for help. But she stops for a moment to look in doubt and

[37] PESQUERA, 2004, 300.
[38] *Diario de Conchita*, 17.
[39] *Ib.*
[40] SÁNCHEZ-VENTURA Y PASCUAL, F., *El Interrogante de Garabandal*, Zaragoza, 1970, 48.

fright in the direction indicated by Conchita. Her two companions do the same and, *suddenly*, all exclaim together: *"The Angel...!."*[41] The four of them stand *in ecstasy* in the middle of *the Calleja*, alone, outside of themselves, as though withdrawn from the natural habitat they know and belong to.

"Suddenly"

"Grace has simply irrupted in their souls."[42] The unforeseenness of this situation, the absence of preparation, of a preceding ascetic phase that would lay the way for *the ecstasy*, is—according to the principles of Theology—a clear indication of authenticity.[43] To be capable of making this step by itself, the soul needs an intermediary period of time; a time, for example, of prayer. Only God can "take hold of a soul brusquely and in a violent way, elevating it to a state of high contemplation."[44] This kind of graces is called *"gratis datae."*[45] And more specifically *raptures*, not *ecstasies*, because:

> The simple ecstasy is a kind of *fainting* that occurs tranquilly... It is opposed to the impetuosity and the violence of the *rapture*, in which the soul feels itself to be suddenly *seized* by God, in the sense of being taken hold of by a superior power.[46]

The rapture typically makes the soul feel it has lost "the use of the senses."[47] In Garabandal, this is precisely what the children describe, without realizing it; and numerous witnesses will soon begin to testify to it.

---

[41] *Ib.*
[42] Cf. ALBA CERECEDA, J. M., *Informe sobre los hechos de S. Sebastián de Garabandal*, Barcelona, 1962, 3.
[43] Cf. GARRIGOU-LAGRANGE, R., *Las tres edades de la vida interior*, Madrid, 1995, vol. II, 1108.
[44] *Ib.*
[45] Cf. ALBA CERECEDA, J. M., *Informe sobre los hechos de S. Sebastián de Garabandal*, Barcelona, 1962, 3.
[46] GARRIGOU-LAGRANGE, R., *Las tres edades de la vida interior*, Madrid, 1995, vol. II, 1108-1111.
[47] *Ib.*

"The Angel!"

The four girls find themselves before *an Angel*. The supernatural has *irrupted unforeseeably* into their lives, and they cannot understand how this has happened. They hope that he will explain to them what is happening. But *the angel* does not utter a single word. And since they do not dare to speak either, *the apparition* concludes without breaking the silence. *The angel* disappears as *suddenly* as he had come. The four children find themselves again upon the steep, stoney path of *La Calleja*, alone and overwhelmed; so silent it seems they wish to hold onto the moment that just passed. The day will come when even they themselves will be unsure as to what happened. But now, when they describe the events, they will coincide without realizing it in every point of correct theology: the ecstasy has ended, as is typically the case, "in an ordinary way, by a spontaneous awakening."[48] So:

> *Returned to normality and very frightened, we ran toward the church, passing the dance function that was going on in the village. Then one of the village girls, named Pili González, said to us: "How pale and frightened you are! Where have you been?"*
>
> *Ashamed to confess the truth, we told her: "Picking apples!" And she said: "That's why you look like that?" We all answered at once: "We've seen an Angel!"*[49]

"Ashamed to confess the truth," they instantly do precisely that. They make a slight attempt not to refer to *the vision*, but immediately see that there is no point in dissimulating, and, since they do not wish to lie, they feel obliged to confess everything,

---

[48] *Ib.*
[49] *Diario de Conchita*, 18.

including *the apparition*. They are disconcerted. How can they, who have just behaved so badly, be the object of such a grace from heaven? They are ashamed of themselves; *the vision* has stirred an intense remorse in them, and repentance for the fault they have committed. Once again the experience coincides with theology. Precisely one of the principle effects of ecstatic union is "an immense sorrow for sins committed and for everything that separates from God."[50] And so they don't hesitate to provide explanations to the girl who surprises them on their way to the church: *"We've seen an Angel!"* they cry, without interrupting their march *towards the church*. They do not seek recognition or comprehension: *"a great detachment from creatures"*[51] is another of the peculiar effects of ecstasy, which is present in the children's experience. They are not remotely concerned about *"what others might say"*:

> And we continued our way in the direction of the church, while this girl remained behind telling others what we had said. As soon as we got to the door of the church, we had second thoughts and went behind it to cry.[52]

To unburden themselves of indescribable emotion they take refuge behind the walls of the church. It is a moving image. "A mysterious instinct of their Christian soul has brought them there. They are unable to explain what has just happened to them, but they sense obscurely that it is something very big... and they even sense that it could be the beginning of even greater things; where else to seek shelter and protection but in the place [the Church] where God's presence is especially kept?"[53] Thus, as the sun sets

---

[50] GARRIGOU-LAGRANGE, R., *Las tres edades de la vida interior*, Madrid, 1995, vol. II, 1111.
[51] *Ib.*
[52] *Diario de Conchita*, 18.
[53] PESQUERA, 2004, 24.

on the 18th of June 1961, something mysterious has begun to unfold in the village of Garabandal.

III

An Open Secret

It Becomes Known

Pili, the girl whom *the seers* encountered in the plaza on the way to the church, is confused. Having heard the four *seers* unanimously cry that they have seen *an angel*, without stopping to say more, she doesn't know what to think. Although not fully believing her own ears, Pili nonetheless does a good job of spreading the news swiftly among the other children in the plaza. In a matter of moments the entire village knows about it. But the first adult person to enter the scene is the school-teacher, Serafina Gómez:

> *When we had finished crying at the church door we went inside—* Conchita writes. *At that very moment the lady school-teacher arrived. She was agitated and straight away said to us: "Girls, is it true that you have seen an Angel?" "Yes, Miss!" "Are you sure you didn't imagine it?" "No, Miss, no! We saw the Angel!." Then the teacher said to us: "Well, let's pray a station to Jesus in the Blessed Sacrament in thanksgiving."*[54]

Serafina knows the little ones well and does not hesitate to listen to them with trust, in spite of the surprising nature of their story. She acts with great prudence and Christian wisdom; she

---

[54] *Diario de Conchita*, 18.

does not rush to rash conclusions, for or against. Rather, she guides the children towards prayer and the Eucharist, praying a *Station*, a typical devotion in the village at the time, prayed before the Blessed Sacrament: in visits to the Tabernacle or as a collective act of *thanksgiving* after receiving Communion.[55] The girls pray this unforgettable *station*, with tears and laughter. "*I don't know how to describe our state,*" Mari Loli tries to explain, "*but we were laughing and crying.*"[56] The school-teacher gives maternal care to her frightened pupils, who gather round her seeking refuge and stability.

A Difficult Reception at Home

Heading for home, Conchita realizes it is already late; it is nine o'clock in the evening. Sure enough, as soon as she crosses the threshold, her mother scolds her for being late:

> "*Haven't I told you to be home before nightfall?*" I was all worried about both things: having seen that figure so beautiful and now arriving home so late. I didn't have the courage to enter the kitchen and stayed standing by a wall, very sad....[57]

Conchita, who recently turned 12 years old, leans disconsolately against a wall, her only source of support. She realizes that the story seems far-fetched, but she cannot conceal it from her mother and responds nervously and without subtleties: "*I have seen the Angel!*"[58] In her *Diary*, Conchita always writes the word Angel with a capital letter at the beginning; a sign of respect towards her *vision* from the very first day. Still, she is under no

---

[55] Cf. PESQUERA, 2004, 25. «*The stations*» consist of praying six times an Our Father, Hail Mary, and Glory Be, with the invocation "*Viva Jesús Sacramentado. Viva y de todos sea amado*" "*Long live Jesus in the Blessed Sacrament. Long life and may He be loved by all.*"

[56] *Ib.*

[57] *Diario de Conchita*, 18-19.

[58] *Ib.*

illusions about how Aniceta will respond, and, sure enough, Aniceta does not believe her ears: *"What! On top of arriving home late, you come up with such nonsense?' I answered again: 'But it's true, I've seen the Angel.'"*[59]

At first Aniceta is inclined to think that her daughter is inventing an infantile and silly excuse. But in the face of her insistence, which is not at all typical of Conchita, she feels "less and less secure in her denials, [and] ends up inclined to admit that, effectively... something must have happened to her daughter."[60]

The mothers of Jacinta and Mari Loli were more benign. Jacinta's mother, Maria González, did not believe her daughter that night, when she got home. However, just a few days after seeing *the ecstasies*, she would say: *"I then began to believe her a little bit... And later on I greatly respected the apparition... although there were other times when my doubts returned."*[61] Thus Maria lived the years of *the apparitions*, between ardent fervor and bitter doubts.

But Mari Cruz suffered what was perhaps the most severe reception. Her mother Pilar testified years later: *"I scolded Mari Cruz very severely that day... I have not beaten or scolded my daughter... [but] at the beginning I did..."*[62] These brief words recall the reception that, on another day, Lucia of Fatima experienced, and later described in her *Memoirs*:

> My mother [at the beginning], *in order to oblige me to tell the truth, as she put it, made me feel more than once the weight of a stick from the pile of firewood or a brush handle... The truth is that she was right to*

59 *Ib.*
60 PESQUERA, 2004, 26.
61 GONZÁLEZ, M., *"Testigo de Garabandal"* in PÉREZ, R., 1991, 272.
62 PESQUERA, 2004, 26; PÉREZ, R., 1991, 166.

judge me unworthy of such a favor, and this led her to believe I was a liar.[63]

In Garabandal, as in Fatima, *at the beginning* more than words were used to correct those *"childish pranks."*

The First Contradictions

At sunrise on June 19, when Garabandal awakens, the kitchens and streets are flooded with one item of news. And *the seers,* now on their way to school, have to put up with all kinds of commentaries:

> *When we woke up that morning*—Conchita writes—*people were already talking: "Those four girls must have seen something because when they came down... The look on their faces!"... Everyone had their own theory.*[64]

It was to be expected. Nothing of the kind had ever occurred in San Sebastián. Even the teacher, when they arrive at the school, asks them again, in front of the whole class: *"'Are you sure, girls...?' 'Yes, Miss.' And they re-told the story to the wonder of the other girls... Classes continued, and*—Conchita concludes—*we behaved as always, without any worries."*[65] The girls do not get carried away by all the commentaries. Everyone in the village is judging them that day and asking questions, but they continue with their schoolwork *"as always, without any worries"*—a good sign.

The local parish priest, Fr. Valentín Marichalar, was visibly worried and *"nervous"* that morning, with the fuss surrounding the news. And he did not hesitate to devote all his time to investigate the matter. But the girls are in school and the priest has to wait before he can speak directly with them. As soon as the classes are

---

[63] LUCÍA DE FÁTIMA, *Memorias,* Fatima, 1999, 74.

[64] *Diario de Conchita,* 19.

[65] Cf. SÁNCHEZ-VENTURA Y PASCUAL, F., *El Interrogante de Garabandal,* Zaragoza, 1970, 51.

over, he sees two of them, Jacinta and Mari Cruz, making their way home together. He approaches them without further ado. And, "*all agitated, he said to them: 'Okay, let's see! Is it true that you saw the Angel?' Together they answered: 'Yes, Sir!' 'I'm not sure. I don't know if you are deceiving us,' he replied. Smiling, they added: 'Don't be afraid that we've seen the Angel!'*"[66] The parish priest is taken aback by the calmness and sureness of the little ones. Deep in thought, but still worried, he sets out in search of Conchita, who, being the eldest of the three, should be the most mature:

> *He found me close to my house*—she writes—*and, very agitated, he said to me: "Conchita, be sincere, what did you see last night?" I explained it all to him....*[67]

"*Very attentively*" the parish priest listens to the child's every word, asking for numerous clarifications and repetitions. In the end, finding nothing reproachable in the account, or contradictions of the other girls' story, he simply tells Conchita that, if *she were to see* this mysterious "*Angel,*" she is to ask him "*who he is and what he wants.*" Conchita assents to the priest's demand. She has never seen him so serious and worried. Fr. Valentín, seeing that the girl has nothing more to say, lets her go. Satisfied, but still deep in thought, he now heads towards the home of Loli. His intention is to find out "*if we all coincided... [And] Loli,*" Conchita writes, "*answers the same as us. So,* [Fr. Valentín] *was more and more impressed, because the four of us coincided in everything.*"[68] The priest, who had begun his investigations "*all agitated,*" has become more and more perplexed, because he understands with sincerity that he had to discard, one by one, all the arguments that he anticipated would expose and undo their story. So, after all his enquiries that morning, he concludes:

---

[66] *Diario de Conchita,* 20.
[67] *Ib.*
[68] *Ib.*

40

Alright, let's wait two or three days to see if you continue to see this figure you say is an Angel and to see what he says to you.[69]

This is all that Fr. Valentín can say at this point in time, and, although it is really quite favorable, to the children it doesn't seem much. In any case, it was one of the most positive reactions they got throughout the day. José Díez Cantero, for example, a carpenter who was working in Conchita's house during those days, thought that the story should be cut at the root. *Pepe*, as he is usually called, as soon as he hears the reports, becomes indignant, and when he crosses paths with the children he addresses them severely, openly attempting to intimidate them *to make them see sense*:

> *"If you keep this up the Civil Guard will get involved; and they will come, they will write down statements, they will interrogate you... and you may well end up in jail. What about the mess your families are going to end up in? Expenses, problems, shame..."*[70]

They hear him out, frightened and without offering reply, but they do not yield; they ask Pepe to put himself in their shoes: what can they do, if they have invented nothing? Nor do they offer assurances that they will not return to *la Calleja*, the place where they saw the *Angel*.

In the midst of it all, *the girls* do not try to escape from their daily chores. They go about their business as usual. Only in the evening, having completed their tasks, and only after great insistence, do they finally get permission in their homes to return to *la Calleja* to pray: *"and very happily we headed for that placed called the "calleja" (a little piece of heaven).*"[71] After writing this sentence, Conchita underlines the last words: *"a little piece of*

---

[69] *Ib.*
[70] PESQUERA, 2004, 32.
[71] *Diario de Conchita*, 23.

heaven." It hints at the special significance that this little corner of the village will have for *the seers* from this time on. And this is not surprising, because *the majority of the first apparitions of the Angel and of the Blessed Virgin happen precisely there.* The girls sense that they will be flooded with graces in that place; they realize that what happened the previous day will not be an isolated incident.

But, after praying in *la Calleja*, they had to return home in desolation that evening. Despite their enthusiasm, there is no *apparition*. However, that night, while laying in bed unable to sleep with the emotions of the whole day, "around ten o'clock each girl heard a voice that said: *'Do not be worried: you will see me again.'"*[72]

The following day, the third day after the *"vision of the Angel,"* the girls carry out their daily tasks as usual: *"We carried on with our normal life the same as the day before."*[73] And in the evening, the same as the day before, they ask for permission to go to *la Calleja* to pray: *"My mom,"* Conchita writes, " *and the parents and siblings of the other girls were very worried and had a very hard battle, because even though they were inclined to believe it was true, they also thought the opposite."*[74]

Aniceta, Conchita's mother, is particularly against it all. She was hoping that her daughter would forget the whole business as the days went by, and she doesn't like the shape things are taking. So, when her daughter asks for the permission to go and pray, she dryly responds: *"If you want to pray, go to the church."* At this, the other three girls, who already have permission from their parents to pray at the place of *the apparition of the angel,* insist and

---

[72] Cf. PÉREZ, R., 1991, 14; *Diario de Conchita,* 23-25.
[73] PESQUERA, 2004, 32.
[74] *Ib.*

implore so much that, in the end, they succeed in getting Aniceta to give in.

And so the four girls head off again to pray at *la Calleja*. They pray the Rosary, but nothing happens. "*The Angel wouldn't come!* [Then] *we decided to go to the church; and when we got up, having been on our knees, we saw a very bright light, which enveloped the four of us; all we saw was this light.*" It was so strong that "*we took shelter behind one another. We were completely dazzled by that light, so we started to cry out, because we were terrified; but the great light had already disappeared.*"[75]

A strange experience. An "all-embracing blinding light covers their path and isolates them from everything."[76] It seems as though the children were being prepared for something as yet unknown. By means of this phenomenon, their spirit and their eyes seem to become disposed for what will happen next; namely, the extraordinary connaturality of the marvels and transparency of an absolutely superior world. This blinding light does not blind them. Yet it covers their path, producing in them a deep sensation of anguish. They feel lost, as though floating in a mystery, in something totally unknown, in which their strength counts for nothing. Withdrawn from their familiar environment, the little ones experience helplessness and even fear.

Theology confirms that, according to the logic of visions, in the state of wakefulness it is normally required that *the vision* be accompanied by ecstasy; that is, by the suspension of the external senses. This momentary loss of contact with the world of the senses "makes it possible to distinguish *the interior apparition* from *the exterior impressions*... because the enraptured soul, united to

---

[75] *Diario de Conchita*, 24.
[76] PESQUERA, 2004, 36.

God, loses contact with external things."[77] In Garabandal, this reality is manifested in the form of *a light* which totally overwhelms the girls, and, at least initially, fills them with confusión and even fear.

But in all of this there is a careful *divine pedagogy* working in their souls. If on the first day, June 18, they had experienced—with the *thunderclap* and the *Angel*—something akin to a *tap on the shoulder*, on the 19th, when nothing actually happens, it is made known to them that "what may happen in that order of miraculous contact with the Mystery does not depend on them... but at the same time, so that they do not succumb to nervousness and discouragement, they are given [in a *locution*] the security that their experience the previous evening was very real: *"Do not be worried; you will see me again."*[78] Now, on the 20th, the children, enveloped in *"a very bright light,"* must learn something else: "They must become accustomed to an easy naturality of the wonders and transparency of a superior world."[79]

The blinding light disappears, and the children find themselves once again on *la Calleja*. This time they make a pact to avoid complications, agreeing not to tell anything to anyone. They do not wish a repetition of the previous days. The shepherd children of Fatima at the beginning did the very same. But in Garabandal there is a problem. Fr. Valentín has ordered that anything new that happens in relation to *the apparitions* be reported to him immediately. For this reason alone, wishing to obey the priest in all things, the girls decide in the end to speak to their families. And the next morning—June 21st—their parents relate everything to Fr. Valentín. They do so confidentially, *but something seems to have*

---

[77] GARRIGOU-LAGRANGE, R., *Las tres edades de la vida interior,* Madrid, 1995, vol. II, 1180.
[78] PESQUERA, 2004, 36.
[79] *Ib.*

leaked, because as the day unfolds an air of expectancy may be felt once more throughout the whole village. Up until now, there had been no other witnesses to the strange phenomena of *la Calleja*; but on this Wednesday afternoon, for the first time, there were external observers.

Conchita sums up this day, the 21st, in one line: *"In the evening, after doing what we had to do...."*[80] She herself probably did not realize it, but a major key to the entire *message* of Garabandal is contained in that line. The observation is very important, because heaven teaches always *"to fulfill,"* because all order springs from this. The saints have always spoken of this: "When one sees a person who undergoes raptures in prayer... and yet there is no ecstasy in his life—that is, he does not lead an elevated life of union with God by abnegation in worldly things and mortification of natural whims and inclinations, with inner gentleness, simplicity, humility, and, above all, with continuous charity— believe me, oh Theotime," writes Saint Francis de Sales, "such raptures are dangerous and greatly to be doubted."[81] In Garabandal, the presence of the extraordinary does not prevent the children from fulfilling their obligations. Rather, the little ones feel moved to a greater responsibility.

After their daily chores, the children make their way again to the site of *the apparition of the Angel* to pray the Rosary. In spite of everything, however, the Angel does not come. In reaction, *"the people laughed a lot and said: 'Pray a Station now.' So we did, and when we finished, the Angel appeared to us...."*[82] The candidness of *the seers* is surprising: they are not upset by the incredulity of the bystanders. Their minds and hearts are occupied with something

---

[80] *Ib.*
[81] FRANCIS DE SALES, *Treatise on the Love of God*, I. VII, c. VII.
[82] *Diario de Conchita*, 26.

else. As soon as they see the angel, they recall that the parish priest has given them an instruction: to ask him *who he is and what he wants.*" Straightaway they ask: *"But,"* Conchita writes, *"he did not answer us."*[83] So, for the moment, all are left in uncertainty about the identity of this mysterious figure and the motive for his visit, which has turned the entire village upside down in the recent days.

"Are you here in body and soul?"

In the year 2000, Cardinal Ratzinger stated that, in apparitions, the seers truly *contemplate* a real person before them. Although the vision is presented only in their interior, it is not a question of a subjective or non-existent imagining:

> Interior vision does not mean fantasy, which would be no more than an expression of the subjective imagination. It means rather that the soul is touched by something real, even if beyond the senses... seeing by means of the *"interior senses."*... It involves true *"objects"*... [belonging to] deeper [but authentically present] dimensions of reality... *"Interior vision"* is not fantasy but... a true and valid means of verification.[84]

In Garabandal, the children also asked *the Blessed Virgin* one day about the *"reality"* of their *vision.* This they do at the urging of a priest who orders them to do so to test *the apparitions.* He considers that, since the girls are so little, this question, complicated even for a theologian who is a specialist in the area, will suffice to unmask the fraud. During *the ecstasy, the seers* comply, and are heard asking *their vision: "Are you here in body and soul?"* Evidently, no one hears the answer the little ones receive.

---

[83] *Ib.*
[84] CARD. RATZINGER, J., *"Theological Commentary"* in CONGREGATION FOR THE DOCTRINE OF FAITH (CDF), *Documents on "The Message of Fatima,"* June 26, 2000.

Everyone waits attentively at the end of *the apparition* to find out the result of the test to which the children have so joyfully been submitted. When *the ecstasy* ends, they are promptly interrogated and, without delay, they repeat the response of *the apparition*: *"No, I am not here in body and soul, but it is I."*[85] This response is not situated in the academic ambit of the Cardinal's words. Nevertheless, it is very much in harmony with them. With simplicity and equilibrium, it affirms—as does the quoted text— the *real presence of the apparition*, while at the same time denying a presence *"in body and soul."* Ratzinger—in conformity with Garabandal—goes on to explain that apparitions consist of an *"intermediary point"* between our natural-physical vision and the intellectual-mystical vision (without images) proper to some saints. But it seems that *the apparition* in Garabandal does not deem it necessary to give such explanations to the little ones: it is enough for them to know that *"it is really Her."* No more is needed to disconcert the perspicacious priest who formulated the question.

The First Witnesses

The first external descriptions of *the ecstasies* of Garabandal date to June 21. The few witnesses who contemplated it are left totally confounded. They pass quickly from a distrusting incredulity to enthusiastic commitment to *the apparitions*. They are overwhelmed by a presence that underlies what their eyes behold: the little ones on their knees on the steep, stony path, their faces raised up towards something or someone enrapturing them; mouths half-opened before unseen grace, a slight smile that lends them an *aura* of beauty, the gaze of those eyes so pure. When the *ecstasy* ends and the four *seers* return to their senses,

---

[85] LÓPEZ DE SAN ROMÁN, J.L., *Letter to the author*, March 21, 2013.

they observe in amazement that people around them are weeping, others hold their hands pressed against their breast, and one in particular, Clementina González, is already running towards the village to call everyone. Clementina, deeply moved and sure that Heaven was acting there, addresses Conchita: "*Little one, ask the Virgin of Mount Carmel, ask the Sacred Heart, to protect us... to tell you what They want of us.*"[86] As of this moment, the spectators of the phenomena in Garabandal, like the very first witnesses who are filled with contrition, will always experience a strong and inexplicable call to conversion, commending themselves—as in the case of Clementina—to the prayers of four simple little girls. From very early on, the events demonstrate an enormous capacity to move hearts.

"It all seems to be from God"

The presence of witnesses on the 21st of June manifests, for the first time, the great impact that *the ecstasies* have on the spectators. The ecstasies recur throughout the following days, and news of *the apparitions* spreads like wildfire throughout the region. The crowds of people grow day-by-day, coming from farther and farther away. From these days on, the records in *Conchita's Diary* usually include the note that: "*there were lots of people.*" As early as the 25th of June 1961 (one week after the first *apparition*), there is testimony of "the presence of at least five priests and numerous known physicians"[87] amidst the crowd.

Among the *physicians*, the impulse arises very early on to scientifically investigate the inexplicable phenomena witnessed by so many people. To this end, *the seers* are constantly submitted to tests before, during and after *the ecstasies*. The medical

---

[86] PESQUERA, 38.
[87] PÉREZ, R., 1991, 16.

inexplicability of the phenomena is soon established. Already on June 25, for example, an astonishing alteration of the children's weight is discovered. Brigadier Álvarez Seco records that:

> During the ecstasy a physician attempted to lift Conchita, and, owing seemingly to the excess of weight that her body experienced while in that state, he dropped her from such a height that she hit the ground with her knees making a loud "crunch" sound. When it was over and the girls were examined, the marks of Conchita's fall were clearly able to be observed, along with scrapes, bruises and scratches from tests that some had performed on the seers, without any complaint of pain on their part or the slightest reaction while the tests were being inflicted.... They noticed nothing, nor did they experience hurt when the ecstasy was over; only the marks remained.[88]

Saint Teresa of Jesus, the *mystical Doctor*, teaches precisely that in a true *rapture*, the soul *"neither sees nor hears nor feels."*[89] Antonio Royo-Marín, a renowned author in the area of mystical theology, explains that even "the most painful incisions, the roughest shakings, even burning, etc., are useless for awakening those who are in this divine sleep... They perceive absolutely nothing in the realm of material things, as may be demonstrated by passing brusquely before their opened eyes a light or any object without producing the slightest movement in their eyelids or pupils."[90] All of this happens in Garabandal. In fact, the Dominican seems almost to have in mind the events of our story when addressing this mystical question, but his book—published in 1958—pre-dates these occurrences (1961). In fact, Pepe Díez, who often witnessed the tests performed in Garabandal, reveals in his testimony the extent to which many physicians were prepared to go in these tests:

---

[88] BRIGADA ÁLVAREZ SECO, J., *"Informe sobre Garabandal"* in PÉREZ, R., 1991, 372.
[89] TERESA OF AVILA, *Life*, ch. XX, 18.
[90] ROYO-MARÍN, A., *Teología de la perfección cristiana*, Madrid ,1958, A., 679.

[The physicians did] *stuff with very powerful flashlights and apparatuses in front of their eyes and faces by way of testing them... Another would be behind the girls while they were kneeling, sticking needles into their legs, one of which was grabbed by someone at the time* [because its great size shocked and angered the families] *but then it got lost, because there was a big row over it* [sic].[91]

In truth, the physicians get carried away in their investigative zeal and family members find themselves alone in their defense of the children. This being so, these excesses aside, everyone— family members, neighbors and visitors included—favors the performing of tests. All are united by a common desire: to test the authenticity of what is going on. They are overwhelmed by what they are seeing and cannot quite believe their eyes

The insensibility during *the ecstasies* in Garabandal, tested from the outset by numerous physicians, is—according to theology—a strong indication of authenticity.[92] In fact, seeing the results of their analyses, the physicians are compelled to consider the possibility that they are facing authentically supernatural phenemona. It is in ecstasy that *"the suspension of the external senses"*[93] occurs, and, without this explanation, medicine possesses no other answer to explain the events of Garabandal. Now, if ecstasy is proven, would this scientifically prove the presence, the existence of God? The more prudent physicians, before venturing overly premature answers, understand one thing clearly: that the phenomena are worthy of study and that the results of their examinations could perhaps scientifically establish the presence of a supernatural sign, a sign of the presence of God in the midst of the world.

91 DÍEZ CANTERO, J., *"Testigo de Garabandal,"* in PÉREZ, R., 1991, 243.
92 TERESA OF AVILA, *Life*, ch. XX, 18; Cf. ROYO-MARÍN, A., *Teología de la perfección cristiana*, Madrid, 1958, 679
93 GARRIGOU-LAGRANGE, R., *Las tres edades de la vida interior*, Madrid, 1995, vol. II, 1107; Cf. ROYO-MARÍN, A., *Teología de la perfección cristiana*, Madrid, 1958, 673.

Gradually, the tests seem to point to the extraordinary. Everyone, neighbors and visitors, is absolutely astonished. However, with the findings of the physicians comes another question that nobody knows very well how to answer: *"Where will all this end?".*

The phenomena are in the process of being examined with great expectancy when, at a very early stage, the first contradictions appear: personages with dubious motives seem to wish to take control of the events. A young teacher who arrived in the village to give summer classes to the son of a wealthy *Indian*, Eustaquio Cuenca, succeeds in getting permission from Fr. Valentín to accompany *the seers* and take note of everything that happens. After each *ecstasy* he takes the four children aside and locks himself away with them privately for extended periods of time. People begin to wonder if he is rehearsing or hypnotizing them, or giving them tablets.

The Civil Guard, with two members stationed in the village from day one, soon takes a hand in the matter:

> After an apparition—writes Commandant Álvarez Seco—a comrade Sergeant of the Civil Guard informed me that, after Conchita had emerged from an ecstasy, the teacher had taken her to the home of the Indian, and that what the people are saying may turn out to be true, that the teacher is giving them pills. I immediately went to the home of Eustaquio (the Indian) and, effectively, discovered the teacher there in a room with Conchita... with the idea of producing a kind of *Report* for Fr. Valentín for him to give, in turn, to the Lord Bishop.[94]

Nobody trusts this self-appointed investigator who sets himself up as an authority in the middle of everything, and the atmosphere begins to get tense. The Civil Guard, Conchita would later recall, did not

---

[94] BRIGADA ÁLVAREZ SECO, J., *"Informe sobre Garabandal,"* in PÉREZ, R., 1991, 384.

permit *"that the teacher take us away and we went with the parish priest to the sacristy of the church, where he asked us questions, calling us in one by one, to see if our stories coincided."*[95]

Fr. Valentín, who was inclined from the beginning more towards suspicion regarding the whole business of *the apparitions*, does have the trust of the people; who remain "deeply impressed, both the natives of the village as well as those who had come from neighboring villages;"[96] and they want to know what to believe. The parish priest interrogates the girls separately and seems to be satisfied. Emerging with them to the porch, he addresses encouraging words to the people who are impatiently waiting: *"So far IT ALL SEEMS TO BE FROM GOD."*[97] Fr. Valentín's *"so far"* expresses his preoccupation, the tension that all of this causes him. However, his honesty and solid sense of responsibility before his parishioners and before God do not allow him to deny the evidence; which, in his judgment, is strong. So, while bearing in mind the caution of the priest's words, we can imagine the joy of those good people in response to so encouraging a judgment: *"It all seems to be from God."*

Events continue along the same lines in the following days, with an ever-increasing number of spectators. Brigadier Juan Álvarez affirms that "after those days [June 26 and 27, when there was no *apparition*], *the Angel* appeared again, and each day between 500 and 3,000 pilgrims were present in Garabandal to witness it."[98] In total, from the 18th of June, the children *see the Angel* nine times. The Angel appears every day except the 26th, 27th and 29th. The absence of an apparition on those days was a great source of trial for the children, not only interiorly, since such

---

[95] *Diario de Conchita*, 27.
[96] *Ib.*
[97] PESQUERA, 2004, 41.
[98] PÉREZ, R., 1991, 370; cf. *Diario de Conchita*, 30.

enormous expectancy had been generated around them by this time:

> On Tuesday the 27th, we had no apparition; there were lots of people. That evening we went with everyone else to la Calleja to pray the Rosary and prayed it there together with the people. When we finished praying and saw nothing, we were sad because we thought we would not see anything any more. The people were very disappointed but when God wants it that way, that's how it has to be... The people of the village were sad but they did believe; the outsiders on the other hand, who had come and seen nothing, went away laughing and saying: "Of course, since there are lots of us here today and they're not used to it, they don't dare to do it in front of so many!"[99]

These two days without an *apparition*, June 26th and 27th, provoke a backlash in the crowds, who accuse the children. *The ecstasies* would resume very soon, but *the seers* cannot provide any reasons. They can only try to suffer with patience the harsh remarks that rain down upon them and make an act of humility, given that matters do not depend on them: "*When God wants it that way, that's how it has to be.*"

But *the ecstasies* immediately return, and the phenomena leave no one in a state of indifference. Those who witness them welcome the truth of *the apparitions* with faith. However, a pattern begins to develop when the people who arrive from afar are often tremendously demanding with the *little ones*. Their judgments, frequently superficial, will as of now form part of the scenario of *the apparitions*. The patience with which the girls accept this situation is another impressive factor for many:

> Conchita seems unconcerned about public opinion. She does not care whether opinion is favorable or adverse; the child remains in the

---

99 *Diario de Conchita*, 31.

objective narration of the pure truth, which she defends with an unshakeable firmness.[100]

---

[100] ANDREU, R. M., *Nota 25* en *Diario de Conchita*, 31.

IV

The Verdict of Medicine

The First Diagnosis of Garabandal

Many and varied are the opinions that circulate in the village concerning *the apparitions*. Loli's father (Loli being one of *the seers*) eventually gets tired of all the gossip and, desiring to get to the bottom of things, visits the village doctor, José Luis Gullón, to ask him to examine the girls. The doctor does not delay. He promptly makes his way up from Cosío and, after a few brief examinations, he makes a firm pronouncement on the events. His diagnosis is conclusive and negative. His arguments, however, are unconvincing:

> *The doctor says that the girls are epileptic and sickly; that everything is due to this sickness that they have. But what I see*—writes Brigadier Álvarez—*is that the seers are in the best of health and every day are more beautiful and healthy; whereas the parents and siblings look tired; their faces give the impression that they are physically exhausted, lacking rest and sleep.*[101]

Dr. Gullón offers no argument in his diagnosis, no symptom, no proof. Moreover, disregarding several facts known to all, he diagnoses an illness that fails to explain what has happened,

---

[101] BRIGADA ÁLVAREZ SECO, J., *"Informe sobre Garabandal,"* en PÉREZ, R., 1991, 371.

without identifying any recognizable symptom in the girls. Dr. Gullón himself outlined years later in a television interview the "*scientific*" method he employed to disqualify *the seers*: he sent a written document to his old professors at the Faculty of Medicine in Valladolid relating his impressions; "These, without ever studying the patients directly, dictated by letter that this was a case of *collective hysteria*."[102] During the televisión program, one of the participants confronts the doctor with the fact that this manner of proceeding cannot in any way be considered scientific. And he was not mistaken.

An Incomprehensible Freshness

Dr. Gullón will never offer proofs of his conclusions. For this reason he is distrusted from the beginning by prudent people like Brigadier Álvarez Seco who, even without profound medical knowledge, remain perplexed by his diagnosis. Moveover, Álvarez shows great objectivity in responding to this first examination of the children, and, at the same time, a sharp critical sense in expressing his reservations: "*... but I see that the seers are healthier every day; their families, on the other hand, seem exhausted.*" The Brigadier realizes that what is happening in Garabandal cannot be the work of the children, who are healthy, and less still, the fruit of collective attacks of epilepsy.

The pressure imposed upon the girls highlights a detail that does not pass unnoticed by more seasoned observers: their disconcerting freshness.

The only ones whose health seems to be suffering as a result of the events, with worry and anxiety, are their family members. The girls themselves, on the contrary, after three long months of trances and

---

[102] GARCÍA DE LA RIVA, J. R., *Memorias de un cura de aldea en Garabandal*, Santander, 2011, 100.

almost daily occurrences, with so many night hours spent in vigil, remain completely normal: playing and running about like the other girls, making long journeys through the fields (sometimes of five and more kilometers), going about their daily tasks in the home; in a word, they live just like any other girl of their age and environment.[103]

Very soon many more physicians would arrive to study in depth all of the phenomena of Garabandal. One of the first is Dr. Apostolides, Chief Doctor of Pedriatric Services of the Hospitalary Center of Troyes (Aube, France).[104] Apostolides is a specialist in Pediatrics, a relevant area of expertise when it comes to documenting a clinical diagnosis of the health and sincerity of the children. The French doctor is immediately surprised by the *inexplicable freshness* of the girls, mentioned by the Brigadier. The spirit of serene welcome with which the girls receive the growing number of often indiscreet visitors is, for Apostolides, a cause of admiration. The French doctor finds it incomprehensible that the *siege* to which the crowds submit the girls does not produce in them a sickly spirit of conceitedness "but rather one of simplicity," as he himself writes.[105] This leads him emphatically to affirm:

They were very far from all affectation, and for me it remains a cause of wonder that, after having been so surrounded, so sought after, these girls, especially Conchita, the one most exposed, have not become remotely self-regarding, self-promoting, in spite of the obvious fact that they have been the center of everyone's focus, and that some have travelled thousands of kilometers to see them. Truly, the candour of Conchita's manner of receiving people, after all she has suffered for several years now, is itself almost miraculous.[106]

---

[103] Quoted in LANÚS, S., *Madre de Dios y Madre Nuestra. Fátima, Ámsterdam y Garabandal*, Madrid, 2013, 122.
[104] *Ib.*
[105] PÉREZ, R., 1991, 187.
[106] *Ib.*

The children's inexhaustible patience is noted also by the theologians. The Jesuit Ramón María Andreu highlights it: "Spending time in the village one soon sees that the girls must have a very great patience. When people see them, they touch them—even cutting off pieces of their hair—and give them rosaries, medals, marriage rings, for them to pass to *the Blessed Virgin* to kiss, or ask them for kissed objects, for photographs... I have never seen them angry. When they become tired by the avalanche, which even confines them often to their homes, they simply remain silent and smile. I asked them once: "*How come you don't get angry?,*" and they answered me: "*The Blessed Virgin has told us to be well behaved and to respond to their questions, if we can.*" Nor have they gotten angry with those who, with their singing and dancing and drunkenness, have sometimes been an impediment to *the visions.*"[107]

It is an amazing fact: even though *the ecstasies* were as likely to occur at seven in the evening as "at three, or four, or six o'clock in the morning," as Pepe Diez relates, "nobody can say that they seem tired; so you may ask, do they sleep then during the day? No, I know they don't, because during the day, people are always arriving; one person, and then another, and another... so many people were coming to ask them questions that they were not able to sleep; I mean during the day, of course."[108]

"*Never any sign of tiredness or fatigue,*" Miguel, Jacinta's brother, testifies, "*but the very opposite; [always] so fresh.*"[109] These and many other testimonies evidence the presence of a gift which *mystical theology* denominates as *wakefulness* or *prolonged deprivation of sleep*. This gift is analogous to that of *inedia* or

[107] PESQUERA, 2004, 110.
[108] DÍEZ CANTERO, J., *"Testigo de Garabandal,"* in PÉREZ, R., 1991, 243.
[109] GONZÁLEZ, M. A., *"Testigo de Garabandal,"* en PÉREZ, R., 1991, 305.

absolute fasting proper to some saints who lived on the sole sustenance of the Eucharist, without other nourishment (e.g. St. Catherine of Siena).[110] In Garabandal, however, this gift does not take the form of *absolute wakefulness* but rather that of an *aid* to facilitate the nocturnal *ecstasies*; an *aid* which permits the children to function normally in their daily activities and duties the following day, while their family members and those who accompany them show signs of exhaustion.

"To remain silent would truly be an act of scientific cowardice"

One very early medical document (1970), jointly signed by two experts who had studied the events *in situ*, strongly supports the supernaturality of the phenomena: Dr. Alejandro Gasca Ruiz, who at the time of *the apparitions* worked in Santander and witnessed abundant phenomena in Garabandal, and Dr. Celestino Ortiz González, a Pediatrician also based in Santander, who spent *52 days*, almost two months, in the village during the time of *the apparitions*, meticulously studying the events. The conclusions of these two experts coincide with those of Dr. Apostolides:

> Two facts have drawn our attention as medical professionals: 1. The absolute psychosomatic normality of the girls, then as well as now... 2. The combination of parapsychological phenomena that have accompanied *the ecstasies* of the four, such as: instances of telepathy, premonitions, clairvoyance, rear sight, hierognosis, gliding during the marches, levitation (this latter in the case of one of the four)... [In summary] we find no convincing scientific explanation that might explain such phenomena.[111]

---

[110] Cf. ROYO-MARÍN, A., *Teología de la perfección cristiana*, Madrid, 1958, 846.
[111] SÁNCHEZ-VENTURA Y PASCUAL, F., *El Interrogante de Garabandal*, Zaragoza, 1970, 132.

Drs. Gasca and Ortiz have no doubt: *the seers* of Garabandal are, in their judgment, *"completely normal children."* Numerous studies coincide in this. Dr. Ricardo Puncernau, a neuropsychiatrist from Barcelona who also examined the four *seers* personally and thoroughly during the time of *the apparitions,* left a record of his findings in the valuable *Report on Garabandal.* This Report, signed in 1974 while its author was Vice-President of the Spanish Society of Sophrology and Psychosomatic Medicine and President of the Spanish Association of Parapsychological Investigations, demonstrates Dr. Puncernau's credentials as a specialist and authority in this very area.

Puncernau personally studies the state of health of *the seers* with interminable neurological and psychiatric tests. Furthermore, he painstakingly observes the children's behavior in their daily life and during the phenomena.[112] His diagnosis is entirely without vacillations:

> All is simple and normal. I have never even observed them feigning to be little saints... no signs of infantile piety... [In fact,] everyone—men and women, young and old, priests and lay people—seek out the company of the little girls.[113]

The Jesuit Ramón María Andreu, approaching matters from the theological point of view, comes simultaneously to identical conclusions:

> Their psychological age during the first month of the alleged apparitions would be about 8 or 9 years of age, in comparison with city and school children. Their conduct, up to the moment the events began, was good, according to the judgment of the local priest, the

---

[112] Cf. PUNCERNAU, Dr. R., *Informe médico sobre las videntes de Garabandal*, Barcelona, 1974, 5.
[113] *Ib.*, 10.

school-teacher and their own parents. Their normality is notable also before the beginning of the trances, and remains so after them.[114]

"Simple and normal girls"

Numerous experts, after studying the little children from diverse points of view, coincide in their conclusions: all four seem, without room for doubt or suspicion, to be *"simple and normal girls."* Dr. Jerónimo Domínguez affirms as much, having interviewed *the seers* personally.[115]

Dr. Puncernau pays special attention to the eldest: Conchita. He realizes, along with the majority of the visitors, that she has a peculiar role among *the seers* and should be studied more closely.[116] His description is very interesting, given that he devoted himself to this task with particular determination. His conclusion is clear: Conchita is a normal girl:

Enchanting, pretty and mischievous in the good sense of the word; with an intelligent and fine sense of humor. Good without being prudish or childish. Completely normal. Playful and charming... exquisitely correct and polite, without the remotest trace of impurity... I never observed in her the slightest hint of unhealthy craftiness... We used to have contests, for example, to see who was the taller. Both of us would cheat by standing on our tippy-toes... This was the best way to get to know the girl, better than performing examinations and tests, although I did these too. I could say the same about Jacinta, Mari-Loli and Mari-Cruz.[117]

[114] Quoted in LANÚS, S., *Madre de Dios y Madre Nuestra. Fátima, Ámsterdam y Garabandal*, Madrid, 2013, 121.
[115] DOMÍNGUEZ, J., *Entrevista con Conchita y Mons. F. Garmendia (Obispo Auxiliar de Nueva York)*, New York 1981, 23.
[116] PÉREZ, R., 1991, 187.
[117] PUNCERNAU, Dr. R., *Informe médico sobre las videntes de Garabandal*, Barcelona, 1974, 5.

Altogether, "more than 40 doctors examined the girls in different periods."[118] Among these, one study undoubtedly stands out; that of Dr. Celestino Ortiz González, the above-mentioned Pediatrician from Santander. His study is one of the most relevant from the time of *the apparitions* and even afterwards, by virtue of its dedication (two months of direct work during the phenomena), reflection, systematization, along with the experience and authority of the specialist who signs it. These are his conclusions:

1. From the pediatric and psychiatric point of view, the four girls have always been and continue to be normal.

2. The ecstasies, in which we have seen these children, may not be included in any of the categories of physiological or psychiatric pathologies currently known.

3. Given the prolonged time during which these phenomena have occurred, if they had contained a pathological nature of whatever kind, we would easily have been able to discern the signs.

4. In child psychology, be it normal or pathological, I find no explanation that might account for the phenomena, which, according to all the knowledge available to us, transcend natural realities.[119]
[Therefore,] to remain silent would be scientific cowardice. We find no convincing explanation for such phenomena.[120]

The arguments and conclusions of Dr. Ortiz effectively agree with those of many other physicians, like those we have studied, as well as others who would arrive on the scene later, like the neuro-psychiatrist and microbiologist Dr. Honorio Sanjuan Nadal from Barcelona and Dr. Serge Fournier, specialist in General Medicine in Uzerche (France), whom we will see later.[121] After a detailed study, they all coincide in positively evaluating the health of the children. They provide arguments and foundations for their

---

[118] http://www.garabandal.us/spanish/garabandal3.html (latest revision: January 25, 2014).
[119] PÉREZ, R., 1991, 185.
[120] http://www.garabandal.us/spanish/garabandal3.html (latest revision: January 25, 2014).
[121] Cf. ch. XV, "Official Pronouncement of the Church," The "Denials" in Perspective.

conclusions, aware that what they sustain cannot, by its own nature, be sustained. Their critical sense remains open to the possibility of a supernatural explanation, given that the evidence requires this precisely because, scientifically, the phenomena are incomprehensible. All of these physicians are opened to the possibility of a miracle.

Dr. Puncernau, for example, in his *Report* provides details of the enormous amount of *tests* to which he submitted Conchita during more than two hours of consultation:

> Her response to the Rorschach Test was surprising: she gave more than 70 answers, completely logical and many involving movement, at an incredible velocity. She had the most vivid imagination with a tendency toward fabulation. The Wechier-Bellevue Test showed a superior level of intelligence.[122]

Dr. Puncernau proceeds to ask if that *most vivid imagination* might not be the source of *the apparitions*. And he answers his own question with surety, offering the arguments in which he bases his conclusion:

> 1) Those states of ecstatic trance, with loss of sensibility and sensoriality;
> 2) The cessation of the photomotor reflex and of palpebral occlusion;
> 3) The pliable muscular plasticity during the trances;
> 4) The resistance to fatigue;
> 5) The exact mimicry in the emotional changes of expression of the face, in all four simultaneously (without contact of any kind) and in the same instant, etc., etc.;
> [All of this] cannot in any way be considered a childish game. [To conclude:] The medical historicity of the facts of Garabandal, of

---

[122] PUNCERNAU, Dr. R., *Informe médico sobre las videntes de Garabandal*, Barcelona, 1974, 14.

which there are abundant graphic testimonies, is incontrovertible.[123]

This last adjective employed by Dr. Puncernau was carefully chosen. *Incontrovertible*, according to the *Diccionario de la Real Academia Española*, means that which "*admits no doubt or dispute*," and shares its meaning with adjectives like *irrefutable, unquestionable, conclusive* or *proven*. As far as Dr. Puncernau and the aforementioned experts can see, *the ecstasies* of Garabandal, according to the judgment of Medicine, seem authentic.

---

[123] *Ib.*

V

The *"First Words"* of Garabandal

July 2, 1961: *"Our Mother"*

There is a strong sense of expenctancy in Garabandal among villagers and visitors alike, but during the almost fifteen days *the Angel* has not yet uttered a single word. At last, on the 1st of July, *the seers* hear a voice in *an ecstasy*. Conchita records its words in her *Diary*: *"I come to announce to you the visit of the Blessed Virgin under the advocation of Mount Carmel, who will appear to you tomorrow, Sunday."*[124] Now the reason for the repeated visits of the mysterious celestial figure is finally known: he had come *to prepare the way* (Mt 3:3). Given the fact of such a preparation, prolonged and intense, the question hanging in the air for everyone is: if this has only been an announcement, what must be still to come?

This announcement was not the only thing that the Angel said on the 1st of July: *"That day,"* Conchita writes, *"he said many things to us."*[125] This lengthy dialogue does not escape the notice of the people. When *the ecstasy* ends, the children are mobbed by

---

[124] *Diario de Conchita*, 32.
[125] *Ib.*

65

people asking what has happened. The girls explain as best they can. But the limited village lexicon of these young girls is poorly equipped to speak of such things.

Bearing this in mind, we can better evaluate the description they give of the Angel. First of all, it adds nothing to the traditional Catholic imagery:

> [The Angel] *wore a long loose blue tunic, without a belt; the wings were a bright rose color, quite large, his face was very beautiful, neither large nor round, with a very handsome nose; the eyes were dark and the face tanned, the hands were well shaped and the fingernails cut; the feet could not be seen.*[126]

One curious aspect, which the children refer to in the description of their *vision of the Angel* does stand out: *"in spite of his childlike appearance* ['*around 9 years old'*[127]], *he gave an impression of great strength."*[128] It is surprising that the children should notice such strength in him when he was visibly younger than them, who are 11 or 12 years old. This impression of *"great strength,"* however, coincides with what the Church has always believed about these celestial creatures.

"The angels are, truly, one of the highest manifestations of God's glory."[129] They are *pure spirits.* They do not have a body and, therefore, they cannot die, since death involves the separation of body and soul. They are the only purely spiritual beings in the entire work of Creation. That is why they occupy a place of preference, above all material creatures. And yet, their fundamental function, along with serving God, consists of serving men.[130]

---

[126] *Ib.*
[127] PESQUERA, 2004, 292.
[128] *Diario de Conchita,* 49.
[129] LÓPEZ DE MENESES, U., *Iniciación a la Teología de la Creación,* Madrid, 2004, 95.
[130] Cf. SAYÉS, J.A., *Teología de la creación,* Madrid, 2002, 330.

For this reason, they appear to men in a visible way. Now, when they become manifest, since they do not have a body, they do so by "*adopting the human image*: to Zachariah, to the Virgin Mary, to the shepherds and a long etcetera, in both Testaments."[131] In Fatima, for example, an angel appears prior to the visit of the Lady, to prepare the three shepherd children. This seems to be his mission also in Garabandal: to prepare the hearts of these girls for a great visit. The news of this visit, which the children immediately relate to the public—*an apparition of the Virgin*—stirs suspense in the whole village: "*the Virgin of Mount Carmel will appear to you tomorrow, Sunday.*"

The First Apparition of the Virgin

The following day, the 2nd of July, is a feast-day in Garabandal, because in those days the Liturgy celebrated the Visitation of the Blessed Virgin Mary to her cousin Saint Elizabeth on that day.[132] In San Sebastián everything revolves now around the news of another visit, the one announced by *the seers* the previous day. Everyone observes the parallels in the Mass readings. The Gospel narrates how "*Mary went in haste to the mountain*" (Lk 1:39). Coincidentally, this area of Cantabria is popularly referred to as *the Mountain*; and it had been announced that precisely on this day *Mary would visit the Mountain*. The air is filled with expectation:

On Sunday the 2nd, Mass was celebrated with great solemnity; at three in the afternoon the Rosary was prayed in the church. Then the children headed to Cosío, about seven kilometers from San Sebastián, to welcome Conchita's siblings back from a journey. They had to turn back at half way, because the people, who were flocking to the village,

---

131 *Ib.*

132 This feast-day will be transferred to May 31 in the *Missale Romanum* of Paul VI (April, 3 1969).

recognized the girls from photographs and would not let them pass: some giving them Rosary beads... others taking pictures... most of them asking questions. When they arrived back they found the streets packed with strangers, among them eleven priests and several physicians.[133]

Among the physicians may be found two from Santander who will re-appear in our story. They are members of the Committee of Studies nominated by the Bishop of the diocese to study the phenomena. All eyes are fixed on the four little girls. At around six in the evening they make their way towards *la Calleja,* the site of *the apparitions of the Angel.* An enormous crowd follows them.[134] Conchita herself tells what happened next:

> *Before we got there, the Virgin appeared to us with an Angel on either side. Two Angels came with Her. One was Saint Michael; the other, we don't know. He was clothed the same as Saint Michael: they seemed like twins.*[135]

Saint Michael

It is the first time that Conchita mentions in her *Diary* the name of the mysterious *Angel* of the numerous *ecstasies* of the fourteen preceding days. In fact, the girls did not know the identity of the *Angel* of their *apparitions "until the Virgin told them that day, the 2nd of July."*[136] They were unable to identify him as Saint Michael from the altarpiece of their parish church which they visited daily, where Michael is represented, clothed as a Roman centurion, crushing the devil.

Even then, this name probably did not mean much to the children. They do not know that, in Sacred Scriptures, the name *Michael* is associated with *"one of the chief princes"* (Dan 10:13) and

[133] BRIGADA ÁLVAREZ SECO, J., *"Informe sobre Garabandal,"* en PÉREZ, R., 1991, 372.
[134] Cf. SÁNCHEZ-VENTURA Y PASCUAL, F., *El Interrogante de Garabandal,* Zaragoza 1970, 65.
[135] *Diario de Conchita,* 35.
[136] PESQUERA, 2004, 54.

is, in *Salvation History*, God's instrument for the greater tasks: *"Then war broke out in heaven; Michael and his angels battled against the dragon..."* (Ap 12:7).

Mika'el—which means *"Who is like God?"*—is the leader of the good in the battle against the rebellious angels who, rising up against God, seek to avenge their fall by seducing man, to impede man's friendship with God. "His *altercation* with Satan (Jude v.9) constitutes an expressive episode of this open and constant war, initiated immediately after the creation of the angels."[137] By divine design, Saint Michael stands out as *protector and defender* of the new People of God, the Church, in the most difficult moments of *Salvation History* (cf. Ap 12: 1-17).

The Other Angel

We know well the identity of Saint Michael, but that of his companion, in contrast, remains concealed even from *the seers*. We can only speculate: it must have been an angel of similar dignity, given that they seemed so similar that they could have been taken for *twins*: another of "the seven angels who enter and serve before the Glory of the Lord" (Tob 12:15). We know that Saint Michael "belongs, in the angelic hierarchy, to the triad he forms together with Gabriel and Raphael."[138] All indications are that Saint Michael's *unknown companion* must be Saint Gabriel: "Who better than he to accompany Mary, to whose existence and destiny he was so closely bound [since the Annunciation]?"[139]

---

[137] ZUDAIRE, I., *"Miguel Arcángel, San"* en GER, XV, 795.
[138] ZUDAIRE, I., *"Miguel Arcángel, San"* en GER, XV, 795.
[139] PESQUERA, 2004, 54; Cf. ROMAN-BOCABEILLE, C., *El misterio de las apariciones de Garabandal*, Barcelona, 1987, 41.

A Trinitarian Symbol

"*Beside the Angel on the right, at the height of the Virgin, we saw an eye of great proportions,*" Conchita writes, "*which seemed to be the eye of God.*"[140] The image of the *eye* is classical in Christian iconography. It represents the omniscient vision of God: "*But the Lord's eyes are upon the reverent, upon those who hope for His gracious help*" (Ps 33: 18). The mysterious eye appears framed by a triangle. In iconography, the *equilateral triangle* is a symbol of the Trinity: the three equal sides united by three equal angles symbolize, with the equilibrium of geometry, the equality and unity of the three Divine Persons.

When all is said and done, nowadays we may find this image somewhat *dated*. But the children are not concerned about being *modern*. They tell what they see. However, this representation points to a biblical truth, which is always contemporary: "*No creature is concealed from Him, but everything is naked and exposed to the eyes of Him to whom we must render an account*" (Heb 4: 13).

The Lady

[In the apparation] *the Virgin comes dressed in white with a blue mantle, crowned with little golden stars. Her feet cannot be seen. The hands are outstretched with the scapular in the right. The scapular is brown. Her long hair is a dark chestnut color and wavy, the parting in the middle. The face is thin, the nose fine, the mouth very beautiful and the lips just a little full. The color of the face is tanned, but clearer than the Angel's, and different, very pretty. Her voice is very strange; I don't know how to explain it. There is no woman who resembles the Virgin, in her voice or anything else.*[141]

---

[140] *Diario de Conchita,* 35.
[141] *Diario de Conchita,* 36.

In spite of the limited vocabulary of the children, their description is quite surprising. It is interesting to compare this way of writing with others that relate mystical experiences. Affirmations alternate with negations, suggesting that what has been said does not measure up to what they have seen, since this cannot be explained with words.

Brigadier Juan Álvarez picks up another interesting detail: according to the children, *the Virgin* "seems to be about 17 years old and is quite tall, all four stating that her voice is unmistakeable and very melodious."[142] Here again there is an echo of the stories of Fatima and Lourdes. The scholar Juan Antonio Monroy points to this: in Fatima, the three shepherd children put the Virgin's age at about 18; in Lourdes the Lady, according to *Saint Bernadette*, was about 16. Monroy, however, attributes this coincidence to the fact that:

> The children see *the virgins* [in Lourdes, Fatima or Garabandal] as they have contemplated them behind the altar of the church... *Those virgins* are conceived in accordance with the original, which [previously] they have seen.[143]

Monroy, a Protestant author, is reasonably critical of Marian apparitions. However, the girls in Garabandal add a detail which contrasts with his scholarly criterion. The four girls coincide in saying that *"the Virgin wears a white dress, with a blue mantle."* Also, *"they claim to see the Virgin of Mount Carmel."*[144] But the Virgin of Mount Carmel, as they know Her, wears the Carmelite habit, which is brown. The girls "are surely unaware"[145] that Our Lady of Mount Carmel is elsewhere represented *in white and blue*. Something does not add up: the *Virgin of Carmel* that the children

[142] BRIGADA ÁLVAREZ SECO, J., *"Informe sobre Garabandal,"* in PÉREZ, R., 1991, 373.
[143] MONROY, J. A., *El mito de las apariciones*, Tánger, 1963, 107.
[144] BRIGADA ÁLVAREZ SECO, J., *"Informe sobre Garabandal,"* in PÉREZ, R., 1991, 372.
[145] Cf. ANDREU, R. M., *Nota 38* in *Diario de Conchita*, 36; cf. *Diario de Conchita*, 116.

know does not coincide with the *Virgin of Carmel* that they themselves describe. In fact, they thought at first that it was Our Lady of Perpetual Help. The surprising thing is that, unbeknown to them, they describe Our Lady of Mount Carmel just as She is represented in Mount Carmel itself. There, in the Holy Land, the Lady wears precisely a white dress and a blue mantle, as the girls describe in Garabandal. This detail, while not conclusive, throws doubt on the theory that the little ones "saw" what they already knew. Monroy needs to find another argument.

But what happened to the Mexican Father Gustavo Morelos is perhaps even more surprising. In 1967, when he showed Conchita the image painted in Mexico by the artist Octavio, she makes a gesture of delight and, taking it in her hands, she makes the following observations:

> [*The Virgin*] *had no crown, the stars around her head were interlaced forming what they called a crown. There was no belt at the waist, the face was looking slightly upwards; she held the scapular in the right hand and in the form of a maniple...*

The following day, Morelos visits Loli and Jacinta in their respective schools. Then something happens that greatly impresses the priest. Loli, seeing the image, takes it in her hands and, very slowly, remarks:

> *Father, the Virgin that we have seen had no crown, her head did not lean to the side, she had no belt and she held the scapular in the right hand like a maniple.*

These observations, made many kilometers apart and years after *the apparitions*, constitute a proof of *the apparitions* for Morelos, in 1967, when *the seers* are undergoing a time of doubts. Even then, the Image of *the Blessed Virgin* is very deeply branded in their memory. For Morelos this is beyond doubt. This fact entails for him a decisive impulse in his work to make known *the events* of Garabandal, first in Mexico and from there in Latin America.[146]

"Our Heavenly Mother!"

How the apparition acted: Conchita, in the *Diary*, devotes abundant pages to describing the impact *the apparition* had on them from the first encounter: *"That day we spoke a lot with the Virgin and She with us. We told Her everything."*[147] The girls converse, with intimate trust and familiarity, with the Queen of Heaven. But this Queen is also Mother. So, *"we told Her everything: that we went to the fields every day, that we were black from the sun, that we had the grass in heaps, etc... She laughed. How much we talked to Her!"*[148]

René Laurentin, speaking in general of the relationship of the seers with their vision, refers to a constant element that is present in Conchita's words: "The familiarity of the seers with Our Lady, the simple, even ingenuous manner with which they speak to Her, deeply moves everyone who witnesses it, and gives them a very clear vision of our relationship with Heaven, reciprocal relations, like in a family, proper to the one living body we form in Christ."[149]

The girls' expressions show that *the Lady* does not inhibit them in the slightest: they use colloquialisms with a heavy rural accent, they tell Her they are *black* from the sun and continually being outdoors, they speak of all the work they have to do; referring to the piles of cut grass that has to be gathered up for fear of the rain and scattered again to dry when the sun comes out. Along with

---

[146] *Ib.*
[147] *Diario de Conchita,* 35.
[148] *Ib.*
[149] LAURENTIN, R., *Apariciones actuales de la Virgen María*, Madrid, 1991, 212.

the charm of the rustic commentaries and words in the little narrator's unselfconscious account, we catch a glimpse of the tough working days of these village girls of *the Mountain*. The girls, in the height of harvest season, are right in the thick of the hard work of gathering, transporting and storing the hay. It is not surprising then that they tell the Mother who visits them for the first time what undoubtedly most stands out among their daily chores.

But above all, the girls capture the maternal closeness of *the Lady*. And this feeling of *the seers* on the first day sets the pattern for all that will happen afterwards. For some of the witnesses, however, these dialogues that are so simple totally discredit *the apparitions*. They do not realize that, in fact, exactly "the same happened in *Lourdes*, where *Saint Bernadette*, at the beginning, used to answer the Lady with a comical *"yes, ma'am"*."[150] The revelation of God seems to show signs of a certain predilection for the simplest people:

> *They didn't believe it*—Conchita writes—*because they said how could the Virgin talk that much, since we told Her many things. But the majority did believe because they said She was like a Mother whose daughter hasn't seen her for a time and tells Her everything. All the more reason then when we hadn't seen Her ever, and on top of that She was our Mother in Heaven!*[151]

Prayer Lessons

The Blessed Virgin does not limit herself to listening to the girls. She is, from the beginning, Mother and Teacher, and She seems set upon spiritually forming the children: *"We prayed the Rosary while seeing Her and She prayed with us to teach us how to*

---

[150] SÁNCHEZ-VENTURA Y PASCUAL, F., *El Interrogante de Garabandal*, Zaragoza, 1970, 67.
[151] *Diario de Conchita*, 35.

pray it well."[152] If they are read with attention these words do not present *the apparition* as *praying the Rosary in its own honor,* although this accusation would soon be made. The girls themselves explain it perfectly: it is *"to teach us."* Conchita herself, years later, would recall the vivid impression it left in her *to see the Virgin praying,* reciting the *Our Father* and the *Glory Be*: *"Her whole being became prayer then...* [With the Hail Mary, though,] *her praying was not an exercise of prayer, but of teaching."*[153]

Here again we find a parallel with the apparitions of *Lourdes* and *Fatima*: the Rosary. On the 11th of February 1858, in the first apparition of *Lourdes*, Saint Bernadette prays the Rosary on the bank of the Gave with the Lady: *"I began to pray the Rosary,"* Saint Bernadette writes, *"as the Lady counted off the beads, but without moving her lips. At the end of the Rosary the vision disappeared."*[154] In Fatima too, the last words of Our Lady on the day of the first apparition (May 13, 1917), attribute enormous power to this prayer, linking it to measureless fruits: *"Pray the Rosary every day to obtain peace for the world."*[155]

These prayer lessons of the Virgin recur in Garabandal. On Friday, August 18 (precisely two months after the beginning of *the apparitions*), Conchita notes in her *Diary* how the Virgin now begins a new task with them:

[That day] *She told us: "I will pray first, and you follow me."* And she prayed very slowly.[156]

The girls repeat word by word what they hear from *the apparition,* trying to assimilate her aura, her tone and even her pronunciation: *"All,"* Conchita repeats, *"very slowly... And She told*

[152] *Ib.*
[153] PESQUERA, 2004, 60.
[154] RAVIER, A., *Les écrits de sainte Bernadette Soubirous,* París, 1961,54.
[155] GONZAGA DA FONSECA,S.J. L., *Las maravillas de Fátima,* Barcelona, 1951, 30.
[156] *Diario de Conchita,* 48.

us to sing the Salve, and we sang it."[157] These *lessons* are filled with Christian wisdom. In this *"She prayed very slowly," "all very slowly,"* the children learn in a practical way that it is not by doing many things or praying just any way that we bear much fruit, but by doing the things we do as well as possible. Holiness is not about saying many prayers hastily but in immersing oneself profoundly in a personal relationship with God through prayer.

The children pray the Rosary in this manner many times in Garabandal during *the ecstasies*. Captivating audio cassette recordings still exist of the children praying like this in *ecstasy*: the *Hail Mary* is always prayed very slowly, with an intense and slightly trembling voice, and the words are pronounced with perfect distinctness. They are taught by the encouragements and corrections of *the Mother*, oriented solely to the good of her children, and with such affection and delicacy that they cause no resentment.

> *When we finished the Rosary She said She was leaving. Then we asked Her to stay a little while, that She has only been there for a very short time. She laughed and told us that She would come back on Monday. When She left, we were very sad.*
> *And so ended the 2nd, Sunday; a very happy day! We have seen the Virgin for the first time. We are all with Her, whenever we want.*[158]

"What better conclusion than this to the great chapter of a *new Visitation of Mary*."[159] *"Blessed are you who have believed,"* Mary was told on the day of her Visitation to Saint Elizabeth (Lk 1:45); how blessed these four village girls must also have felt when they went to bed on the night of the 2nd of July 1961.

---

[157] *Ib.*
[158] *Ib.*, 35-36.
[159] PESQUERA, 2004, 61.

VI

Mother of God and Our Mother

The Lady of Garabandal's Way[160]

Frequency of the Apparitions

In the first *apparition*, the children express sorrow at the Lady's departure, and their petition for Her to stay with them is not left unheard. She returned not that same day but hundreds of other times. Innumerable authors remark about this. Judith M. Albright, for example, affirms that *"the Lady appeared more than two thousand times."*[161] René Laurentin, discussing Garabandal in his book *Modern-day Apparitions of the Virgin Mary*, highlights *"the abundance of extraordinary events that took place in Garabandal from 1961 to 1965."*[162]

This multiplication of phenomena and its long duration distinguishes Garabandal from the great classical apparitions. In Guadalupe, for example, there were just 4 apparitions, in Lourdes there were 18, in Fatima 6. However, the *multiplication of occurrences* in Garabandal does not entail a problem for the

---

[160] "Way" is the word chosen to translate the Spanish word "trato," which has a richness of meaning. The sense of the word as used here is "the way of communicating with or acting towards another person."
[161] Cf. ALBRIGHT, J. M., *Our Lady at Garabandal*, Ohio, 1992, xi.
[162] LAURENTIN, R., *Apariciones actuales de la Virgen María*, Madrid, 1991, 244.

Church; its long duration (1961-1965) coincides significantly with many cases of recent apparitions among which several stand out by virtue of having already been approved in the Church: Akita in Japan (1973-1981) and Finca Betania in Venezuela (1976-1984), among others.[163] In the light of these cases, the *"long history"* of Garabandal is not a novelty; in fact, Akita and Betania *double* its extension. According to Lucas F. Mateo-Seco, professor of the University of Navarre (+2014), the *contemporary Marian apparitions* clearly converge in the area of *"an extraordinary multiplication of the signs;"* that is, in their lengthy duration.[164] From here on this *multiplication* will feature prominently in our story.

The Extraordinary Becomes a Daily Reality

On Monday July 3rd, as promised, *the Lady* appears again to the girls. *The ecstasies* in Garabandal multiply to such an extent that, if up to now we have followed the unfolding of events step by step, from now on this will no longer be possible:

> From July onwards, the visions multiply so that it becomes difficult to establish a chronological order. The seers fall into *ecstasy* several times a day. The duration varies between ten minutes and up to five or, on one occasion, seven hours.[165]

Conchita herself, having recorded the first seventeen days of *apparitions* one by one in her *Diary*, after the 3rd and 4th of July, no longer follows the calendar; her narrative goes back and forth and mixes things, developing only what she esteems most striking or what is better retained in her memory. In a somewhat more ordered fashion, we will do the same.

---

[163] *Ib.*

[164] MATEO-SECO, L. F., *Fe y visiones en la literatura espiritual del Siglo de Oro," Estudios Marianos,* 75 (2009) 133.

[165] PÉREZ, R., 1991, 21.

"Much more than a Mother"

Very soon the children would provide an expression of their experiences in a revelatory way, characteristic of Garbandal. On the 1st of August, a few weeks after the initiation of *the apparitions, the seers* are heard in *ecstasy,* very clearly and for the first time, praying the *Hail Mary* with an unknown novelty: *"Holy Mary, Mother of God 'and Our Mother,' pray for us..."* The girls, in *ecstasy, surprisingly inspired,* unanimously manifest in this way their shared experience of their relationship with *the Lady* of Garabandal.

They feel they are daughters and they see *the Lady* as *"Mother of God,"* of course, *"and Our Mother."* The Lady, in the apparitions of *Rue du Bac,* had presented herself as *"Mary conceived without sin";* in Lourdes She said: *"I am the Immaculate Conception";* in Fatima: *"I am the Virgin of the Rosary";* in Banneux: *"I am the Virgin of the poor";* in Kibeho: *"I am the Mother of the Word";* in Medjugorje: *"I am the Queen of Peace."*

On a crucial date, the 18th of June 1965, in the second and final message of the apparitions in Garabandal, *the Blessed Virgin* defines herself precisely with this title that has entered so deeply in the hearts of *the little seers: "I, your Mother."* The children, from the very beginning, had sensed this peculiar maternity of *Mary* in Garabandal. And they manifest this in their affectionate addition to the *Hail Mary: "Mother of God and Our Mother."*

The Blessed Virgin, however, does not permit *the seers* to employ this expression habitually until it be authorized by the Church; thus showing, as we will see on other occasions, an attentive deference to the ecclesial Hierarchy. And Her teaching this to the little ones is a constant feature of Garabandal, as well as being an indispensable criterion for ensuring the orthodoxy and eventual approval of the events. The children, for their part, will always be faithful to this norm given by *the apparition*. Thus, many years afterwards, when Conchita was in Fatima praying the Rosary at some distance from the Shrine of the apparitions, a well-known Spanish university professor who was accompanying her, remarked to her: "*Conchita, when praying the Hail Mary you don't say 'Mother of God, and Our Mother' like the devotees of Garabandal usually do.*" "No," she answered, "because one can only say that in private...".[166] Even at a distance, where nobody could hear her, she faithfully respects *the Lady's* command given to her as a child.

From the beginning, the intimacy of the relationship between *the seers* and *the apparition* is remarkable:

Not only does She—the Mother!—pay attention, with interest and enjoyment, to all the children's chatter, their joys and sorrows, their *"puerilities"*; She truly acts like a *mother* with the four of them. This is their experience:

She was like a Mother whose daughter hasn't seen her for a time and tells Her everything. All the more reason then when we hadn't seen Her ever, and on top of that She was our Mother in Heaven![167]

This *Mother* adapts to her daughters' level and indulges their innocent desires: "She lets them touch and study her crown of *"little golden stars*," She puts her Child in their arms, receives and returns kisses, and even sometimes plays with them."[168] Conchita relates this more than once:

The Virgin laughed and smiled a lot. She inspired no fear!

---

[166] LANÚS, S., *Madre de Dios y Madre Nuestra. Fátima, Ámsterdam y Garabandal*, Madrid, 2013, 301.
[167] PESQUERA, 2004, 64.
[168] *Ib.*

"She is so very good. Good like a mother!," she once replied to a lady who had come from France to Garabandal with her family.

"No!," the child exclaims, *"much more than a mother! She is good like someone who, as well as being a mother, is also a best friend, because we can tell Her everything that enters our mind. And She understands us. She helps us. She laughs, She even plays with us. One day She let Loli have her crown so that she could have fun putting it on her head (although Loli was nervous of burning herself with the stars that were so lit up...). With a mother you don't feel so free and as trusting as with the Blessed Virgin. No one confesses their own faults to their mother, or reveals to her their hidden defects..."*[169]

From *the Blessed Virgin's* relationship with the girls, there flows a spirituality that is typical of Garabandal and the best manifestation of the interiority of *the Lady* in *these apparitions.* To give one example narrated by Conchita: *"If you could only see how human the Virgin is! Sometimes She would jokingly repeat our verbal mistakes just to gain our trust. But we trusted her from the very beginning."* The child often erupted in expressions indicative of the relationship with *the Lady:* "*I love the Virgin as if She were my mother. You can talk to her about everything. One day She told us: 'Make sure you're always clean; I also paid attention to that when I lived on earth.'"*[170]

Loli had a particularly vivid experience that reflects this maternal aspect of Garabandal: one night—that of the 4th to the 5th of November 1962—in which:

> The wind began to blow, threatening a downpour, the child's mother told her to bring in the clothes, which were hanging outside. Loli went to obey, but was clearly fearful of leaving the house at that hour... She was heading toward the door with the lighted lantern in her hand

[169] LAFFINEUR, M. - LE PELLETIER, M.T., *La estrella en la montaña,* Tielt, 1967, 108.
[170] PESQUERA, 2004, 300, 290.

when she fell into *ecstasy*. She blessed herself repeatedly, gave the crucifix to bystanders to kiss, and went out. Shortly afterwards, while still *in ecstasy*, she returned to the house with the clothes... The Virgin had observed both her good will and her fear, and, like a Mother, had come to accompany her.[171]

The goodness of *the Blessed Virgin* is greatly reflected in these details: her affection for the little ones and firm commitment to their growth in virtue. In fact, *the apparition* in Garabandal shows the importance of the virtues in many ways; such as by repeating often to the children that they must not put themselves in the center. Conchita would always remember this:

> [During *the ecstasies*] *the Virgin would often look not exactly at us but farther away, towards the people behind us. Her expression would sometimes change, but without ceasing to smile. I asked her: "Who are you looking at?" And She told me: "I am looking at my children."*[172]

The apparitions are not only for *the seers*; they are *graces gratis datae*—as theology puts it—which they must communicate, because *much will be asked of those who have received much* (Lk 12:48). *Apparitions* are not given for the self-satisfaction of the recipients, but for the spiritual good of the Church.[173]

Materne Laffineur also mentions an interesting incident that reveals the simple *familiar spirituality* of Garabandal. In his early book, *L'Etoile dans la Montagne* (1967), he relates that one day *the seers* arrived, *in ecstasy*, at the atrium of the church, suddenly breaking into joyful laughter. Initially Laffineur was not impressed:

> We were scandalized. How could they laugh like that in the presence of the Blessed Virgin, even if their laughter was so beautiful? ... [When

---

[171] *Ib.*, 482.
[172] *Ib.*, 292.
[173] Cf. ROYO-MARÍN, A., *Teología de la perfección cristiana*, Madrid, 1958, 792.

the ecstasy ended,] we asked them why they had laughed that way, which had disconcerted us so much. Conchita explained to us:

-*The Virgin burst out laughing.*

-*At what?*

-*At how badly we were singing.*

This was certainly true, and our tape-recorders testify to it.[174]

The French priest's initial scandal dissolves in the face of the *innocence* that envelops *the apparitions.*

On another occasion, Conchita narrates, one night when the ecstasy lasted from nine at night until seven in the morning, *"that night we played 'los tíos' with the Virgin [a game similar to hide-and-seek]. Two of us hid and the other two looked for them."*[175] For the girls, this "time-wasting" by *the Lady* constitutes the clearest proof of love and intimacy from the one whom they call *their Mother from Heaven.* Naturally, *the Lady* does not come to be entertained or to entertain them. If *She* descends, it is to elevate. And so, all of those things that are *"so lacking in seriousness,"* which disconcert so much the *"wise and the learned"* (Mt 11:25), turn out to be, in her hands, the elements of a divine pedagogy that teaches, prepares and fortifies hearts for the the Lord's difficult tasks ahead. The words of *the Lady* to Conchita in the final *apparition* of Garbandal, in November 1965, are a good example of this:

> She came with the Child Jesus in her arms, dressed as always and smiling... I was chewing gum, but as I watched her, I stopped chewing, placing it behind a tooth. She noticed I had it and said to me: *"Conchita, why don't you throw away your chewing gum, offering it as a sacrifice for the glory of my Son?"* Embarrassed, I took it out and threw it away....[176]

---

[174] LAFFINEUR, M. - LE PELLETIER, M.T., *La estrella en la montaña,* Tielt, 1967, 37.

[175] *Diario de Conchita,* 61.

[176] *Ib.*

The Blessed Virgin avails of the simplest things to give lessons to form the girls' spirit, to encourage them to be fully generous. They must make known her love, but also the urgency with which Heaven asks its children to *"offer your bodies as a living sacrifice, holy and pleasing to God, your spiritual worship"* (Rm 12:1). In this self-giving, *the Blessed Virgin* will not abandon them. That is why, together with the sacrifice, She says to Conchita:

> *Have trust in us and you will offer it up gladly to our hearts, for the good of your brothers and sisters, because that way you will be more united to us... Do all that you can and we will help you.*[177]

It is true that the Mother asks all of them, but it is also true that She offers a great promise and predilection to her children.

---

[177] *Ib.*, 97

VII

Signs of Predilection

Objects "Kissed" by the Lady

From the first day of the apparations in Garabandal, the maternal delicacy shown always by *the Virgin* stands out; the girls do not remain at the level of admiration of the beauty of *the Lady* and her aura *beyond that of a Queen*. Rather, capturing above all her *maternity*, they make spontaneous gestures of familiar affection: they frequently kiss her and are kissed by her: "During *the visions the seers* may be seen kissing... Their gestures are evident and afterwards they say they have kissed *the Virgin, the Child, Saint Michael*. They are also kissed by *Them*. The movements of kissing, being kissed, receiving *the Child*, holding the crowns, are perfectly defined so that all may perceive them. [This is habitual] in the numerous trances I have witnessed."[178] It is evident that the phenomena of Garabandal are marked by *familiarity* from the first days. Conchita reflects as much in the *Diary*:

> Sometimes [the Virgin] brings the Child in Her arms, very small, like a newborn babe with a little round face the same color as the Virgin's, a tiny little mouth, the hair slightly long, fair, with small hands and wearing a blue tunic... And since we liked to make up games for the Child Jesus, we picked up pebbles. And I put them in my braids, Loli put

---

[178] *Ib.*, 94.

them in her sleeves, and Jacinta gave them to Him. But He didn't take them; He only smiled. [179]

Carlos Vidal Martínez, student of contemporary Marian apparitions, has highlighted a distinctive feature here of Garabandal: "Among the epiphanies considered, *Garabandal* is alone in presenting the Blessed Virgin with the Child-God in her arms." In his study, Vidal considers up to eighteen of these *epiphanies*. Regarding Garabandal Vidal highlights that there the vision "appeared joyful."[180] In this atmosphere of *joy*, the little ones feel authorized to approach the Child Jesus. They begin to *"make up games for the Child Jesus"*—as they put it—and to offer Him pebbles to play with. The Child smiles a lot. However, He does not take the stones. He doesn't, but the Mother does.

From the very first days, *the Lady* takes the stones from the children's hands. She kisses them and returns them to *the seers*, instructing them to deliver them to certain persons after the *ecstasy*.

At first it was little pebbles, but the spectators soon realize that this is an opportunity to *"introduce themselves"* to *the apparitions* and begin to load the four girls with religious objects to give to *the Virgin* to kiss. When there are too many objects or the girls are not to be found at home, the pilgrims place them on a table in the children's homes. But neither they nor *their apparition* seem overwhelmed by the enormous amount of objects piled up every day. Conchita notes this quite simply: *"She kissed everything."*[181]

Medals, Rosaries, crucifixes, cards and even an occasional Missal; the objects number in the hundreds every day and,

---

[179] *Diario de Conchita,* 36 and 40.
[180] VIDAL MARTÍNEZ, C., *"...Y los suyos, no la recibieron." Estudio... de las epifanías marianas,* Alcalá de Henares, 1988, 92.
[181] *Diario de Conchita,* 39.

amazingly, they are all returned precisely to their owners. No one can understand how this is possible, given the posture of *the ecstasies*: the head raised always upwards, the eyes fixed on the sky, and being mobbed by crowds of people whom the children had not even seen or known beforehand. And yet the children always return the objects correctly; they never make a mistake. Brigadier Álvarez expresses astonishment at this phenomenon:

I have witnessed many times how, while still in ecstasy, the children unerringly returned the objects kissed by the Virgin to their owners. Some people gave their medals a second time to others to pass to the seers so that the Virgin would kiss them again, but they were told that the objects were already kissed and would not be kissed a second time. Someone handed up rings that were rejected; She would only kiss marriage rings, and these were delivered [by the seers] back to their proper owners in the midst of many people; this happened many times and without confusing them with others that they carried in their hands.[182]

The owners are amazed by this inexplicable *precision* of the little ones. And many repeat in their testimonies that the children always return the objects with no mistake and without ever looking at the object that they return or at the persons to whom they return them. Absorbed in their vision, they do not focus on what they do. And yet, of the thousands of times they return thousands of objects, not once do they err:

It is very difficult—Pepe Díez remarks—because there would be more than a hundred or even two hundred [objects], for them not to get knotted together with one another, not to have them all bundled up in a ball, I mean a mess, all mixed up, chains and rosaries and rings. I mean all of that, a mess that no one could unravel; but they would pick them up and... then pick out the belonging of this gentleman or that lady... [and return them all to their owners] with enormous ease

[182] BRIGADA ÁLVAREZ SECO, J., *"Informe sobre Garabandal,"* en PÉREZ, R., 1991, 373.

and no tangles, giving back the chains and putting them all on... without looking at how they were doing it or anything [always looking upwards]... and that was very frequent; even daily.[183]

This happened, for example, with the first ring kissed in Garabandal, as the protagonist, Maximina González, narrates: "She [Jacinta] did not know that the ring was mine. She gave it [to the apparition] to kiss, and coming to where I was, without seeing me, she took my hand and, all the time in ecstasy, put the ring on my finger."[184] On another occasion, a man gave a crucifix to Jacinta to be kissed, but when she offered it to the apparition, the apparition responded: "This crucifix has already been kissed." And it was not kissed again. Then the owner said: "It's true, it has been kissed; two months ago I gave it to this girl to be kissed."[185] Whatever was kissed once was not kissed again; now, how the girls could have kept track of this on certain occasions is, to say the least, disconcerting.

Wedding Rings

Besides religious objects, wedding rings were perhaps the objects most kissed in Garabandal. There are numerous anecdotes about this. Avelina González, a villager, relates:

Loli was in ecstasy and the moment came, so familiar by then to many and so exciting for all, to distribute to each of the owners the multiple objects that had been kissed by the Virgin. As usual, the girl, without looking and without erring, began her task, taking them one by one from the pile where they were all mixed up... A wedding ring appeared. Loli picked it up and put it as usual on the right-hand finger of a lady's hand. But almost immediately, giving the impression that she was following mysterious instructions, she took the ring off that finger and

[183] DÍEZ CANTERO, J., "Testigo de Garabandal," in PÉREZ, R., 1991, 257-258.
[184] PÉREZ, R., 1991, 224.
[185] GONZÁLEZ, M., "Testigo de Garabandal" in PÉREZ, R., 1991, 276.

placed it on the corresponding finger of the left hand: the lady could not contain her emotion and broke into tears. The reason? She was from Valencia and she was moved by the Virgin's delicate touch, because in Valencia, as she declared to the bystanders, the wedding rings are worn not on the same hand and finger as in other parts of Spain, but where Loli had put hers... The matter didn't end there. Loli also said her husband's name, which she had communicated to absolutely no one.[186]

Cases like this in Garabandal are abundant. The girls always return the rings to the right person and place them on the finger according to custom. Just one further example: that of the ring of the husband of Maria Luisa Salazar, from Bilbao. Everyone knew that while the children were *in ecstasy* they would not take any more objects, but because Maria Luisa had made such a long journey, Maximina González stepped forward from the crowd to place Maria Luisa's husband's ring in Conchita's coat pocket:

*She had not seen me put something in her pocket or anything—*Maximina recounts—*and then I stood behind her and she says: "I have a ring in my pocket?" And in goes her hand. "Who put that there?... Ah, kiss it!" And then you could see it was kissed. She changed the direction she was following in ecstasy and started walking backwards, backwards, backwards... for several meters, to where the gentleman was, and took his hand and put the ring on it. And then this man says: "My God, what more do I need to believe?"*[187]

This *kissing of the rings* signifies a fundamental value, without words but very clearly: the capital importance of marriage and the family. This is very particular to Garabandal. In fact, the rings given to *the seers* by unknown strangers were occasionally returned unkissed. Why? To everyone's surprise, the interested parties *were not married*, though nobody there knew it. As the

---

[186] AVELINA GONZÁLEZ, *"Testigo de Garabandal,"* in PÉREZ, R., 1991, 324; PESQUERA, 2004, 227.
[187] PÉREZ, R., 1991, 225.

girls, filled with embarrassment, explain why their rings have not been kissed, the couples respond with deep amazement. Among the countless objects they receive, "perhaps those most kissed in Garabandal were wedding or engagement rings"; this unerring redistribution of rings provoked more than one conversion in Garabandal.[188]

In the sixties, when *the apparitions* take place, nobody suspects that the family might be in danger, at least in a country like Spain. However, precisely in these years, the hour of great crisis for the institution of the family is looming in the west. The disintegration of the family, alarmingly widespread among non-Catholics, begins to occur also among people of faith. In France, for example, between the years 1965 and 1966, one of every ten marriages ended in divorce; in Paris, one in every seven.

In Spain, this crisis is certainly less pronounced, and for the people of Garabandal it is not an issue. This circumstance shows that the apparitions are not only for the people of Garabandal or even for Spain. And if some need to be corrected for wrongs already committed, others need to be forewarned against dangers to come.

The Second Vatican Council will strongly affirm this same value (*GS*, II, ch.1). But most surprising perhaps, in relation to this singular gesture of *the kissing of the rings*, are the words of Saint John XXIII, who, entirely unaware of the events unfolding in the faraway mountain hamlet, in a beautiful allocution to Christian spouses, encourages them mutually to kiss their wedding rings, "as a deliberate sign of holding strongly to their holy and mutual commitments."[189] The Pope encourages the same gesture that is

---

[188] PESQUERA, 2004, 72; Cf. DOMÍNGUEZ, J., *Entrevista a Conchita y Mons. Garmendia,* New York 1981, 23.
[189] *Ib.*

already being made in our village, with the same intention, demonstrating the contemporary relevance of *the apparitions*. It is hard to accept that the little village girls are making all of this up. Rather, Garabandal is thus revealed as a truly interesting and timely occurrence; although, as events unfold, it is not without its difficulties. For example…

Polemic About the Powder Case Kissed by the Virgin

One day, a *powder case* appears among the many objects to be kissed. The children themselves are taken aback when they see this profane object presented to be kissed by *the Virgin*. They resist, but when *the apparition* comes, the first thing they are asked to present is precisely the powder case. Among those present, amazement is combined with doubt; it seems evident that a true apparition would not kiss such an object. "As soon as *the ecstasy* ended, they asked Conchita to explain. The girl declared that as soon as *the Virgin* came, She immediately asked for the powder case, to kiss it, saying that '*it belonged to her Son.*'"[190] And that was all she knew.

Conchita does not know. But the person who put the powder case there certainly does know. *Ramón Pifarré Segarra*, a pharmacist from Sans (in Barcelona), who had up to now remained in silence, reveals his secret before the astonished gaze of the witnesses: *during the Spanish Civil War (1936-39), in a zone where priests who did not hide were exterminated, this powder case was used to take the Eucharist clandestinely to prisoners who were about to be executed.* Now the words of *the Lady* are clear: that powder case "*belongs to her Son.*" Because the Eucharist has the capacity to make new what it touches. A beautiful lesson.[191]

---

[190] *Ib.*
[191] Cf. *Diario de Conchita,* 40; Cf. PESQUERA, 2004, 72.

"Jesus will perform wonders through the objects kissed by Her"

The *Virgin's* act of *kissing* expresses her maternal closeness: towards *the seers* and all who approach Her. However, Conchita has gone much further in explaining the value of *the Virgin's kisses*:

The Virgin [is the one who told me] that *"Jesus will perform prodigies through the objects kissed by Her... and the people who use such objects with faith will pass through purgatory in this life."*[192]

This promise recalls the one received by Saint Simon Stock in connection with the *Scapular of the Virgin of Mount Carmel*; or that of Saint Margaret Mary about *the nine first Fridays*, or that of Sister Lucia of Fatima about the *five first Saturdays*. The objects kissed by *the Virgin* have received, in continuity with a long tradition in the Church, a great healing power.

And here a question arises: are these fruits of healing truly to be found in connection with Garabandal? To this, the answer must be a puzzled yes. At least, many of the faithful around the world attribute surprising healings—physical as well as spiritual—to *the objects of Garabandal*. Many of these cases are already documented. We will return to this when we come to *the fruits* of Garabandal (PART III). Suffice to say for now what *the Virgin* promised during *the apparitions*: *"Jesus will work wonders with these objects."*

In Light of the Second Vatican Council

On the 18th of June 1965, a bystander, desiring no doubt to possess an object kissed by *the Virgin*, hands a Rosary to

---

[192] *Ib.*

Conchita... Since that day only *Saint Michael* was to come, Conchita does not wish to take it; and explains:

"The Angel doesn't kiss." "And why is that?" Conchita smiled and said: "Only the Virgin kisses! The Angel is no one as far as that goes."[193]

It's a fact: in Garabandal, the objects *are kissed only by the Virgin*; *the Angel* only kisses the children. According to *the seer*, from this it may be deduced that Mary, who is a human creature, *precedes* the angelical creatures in dignity. *The seer*, in light of the teachings of the Second Vatican Council, does not err in this affirmation. It could seem as if the *Catechism of the Catholic Church* contradicts this when it states: "As purely *spiritual* creatures angels have intelligence and will: they are personal and immortal creatures, surpassing in perfection all visible creatures, as the splendor of their glory bears witness" (no. 330). The Blessed Virgin is a visible creature. However, as the Council indicates, *She* is an exception to this rule: "The Mother of God... united to Him by a close and indissoluble tie... far surpasses all creatures, both in heaven [the angels] and on earth... having cooperated by charity" in a unique way, with the work of the redemption.[194] According to the Church's Magisterium, the most Blessed Virgin Mary is above even the angels. The clarity of the children's explanation is impressive, and they add still another nuance of profound theological significance:

"The Virgin says that Jesus will work wonders through the objects kissed by Her." This expression, *"Jesus will work wonders,"* safeguards that Jesus Christ is *"the only Redeemer,"* as the Council affirms.[195] The Blessed Virgin, however, according to Conchita, has a special place in this work of Christ: *"through"* Her Jesus will

---

[193] PESQUERA, 2004, 73
[194] VATICAN COUNCIL II, Dogmatic Constitution *Lumen Gentium*, AAS 57 (1965) 50, 53, 61, 62.
[195] *Ib.*

work wonders. Vatican II specifically proclaims Mary with the title of *"Mediatrix"* which Conchita sustains here even with the correct terminology (*LG* 62). Furthermore, the Council delineates the scope of this *"mediation,"* underlining, as Conchita does, that only *"Jesus works wonders."* In their simplicity, the village girls are in accord with the Council's reflections, even preceding conclusions as hotly debated as this Marian title. All of this is very surprising.

So, the *"wonders,"* according to the Second Vatican Council, are performed by Jesus. Conchita, in her simplicity, penetrates difficult doctrines that are the subject of the Council's reflections. Garabandal has great contemporary relevance. The fact that these *village girls* do not succumb to frequent theological errors even in such complex areas is of major importance in the matter of the approval of *the apparitions.*

The Objects Kissed by the Faithful

During *the ecstasies, the seers* always carry a crucifix which they offer to those present. They reach out their hand to whomever *the Virgin* indicates, and then the faithful can kiss it. This enables the faithful *to participate* in *the apparition.* This is a frequent occurrence from August 1961 on, very much at the beginning: "[the crucifix] during *the ecstasy,* was given to *the Virgin* to kiss; then, sometimes, the girls would kiss it, and finally they gave it to the surrounding people to kiss, although not always to everyone, and they also traced the sign of the cross over themselves or others with it."[196]

On the night of the 17th of September 1961, Conchita has *an ecstasy* in the small kitchen of her home. The child gives her crucifix to those present to kiss. All the time immersed in a trance,

---

[196] Cf. PESQUERA, 2004, 207.

her head thrown far back and eyes fixed on high, after giving it to those present to kiss, she passed her hand without the slightest awkwardness through the bars of the window, so that those outside the house could also kiss it. When it seems that all have done so, the observers note with amazement that the child keeps her arm stretched out, as if waiting for someone else to approach. Then those inside hear her saying: *"Ah! They don't want to kiss it? But why?...."*

In spite of the crowd, a dense silence descends on all, inside and outside. A man comes out of the kitchen and discovers a couple withdrawn from the only light which, being a dark night, came from the window. He approaches them, speaks with them, and they confess their fear: they consider themselves unworthy to approach. The man responds to them with simplicity. No matter how sinful they feel, God is waiting for them. It is evident, since the child is there totally absorbed, with her arm stretched out into the darkness and offering the crucifix... and they are the only ones who haven't yet kissed it! The couple ceases to resist and after those last two kisses, the child withdraws her arm from the window. Minutes later *the ecstasy* ended.[197]

---

[197] *Ib.*, 208.

VIII

For All to See

The "Wonders" of Garabandal

On one occasion, after emerging from *an ecstasy*, witnesses tell Conchita something she could not have known: "all of those to whom she had given the crucifix to kiss were priests wearing civilian clothes."[198] She doesn't know them, having never met them before. *The apparition*, however, recognizes them easily and, with special delicacy, seems to call them not to avoid wearing the exterior garb that expresses their interior consecration. In 1964, the Second Vatican Council would proclaim that the priestly ordination *"distinguishes"* the minister from the faithful *"essentially."*[199] *The apparition* in Garabandal seems to *distinguish* them too; and, delicately, seems to call them to *distinguish* *themselves* in the clothes they wear, because of their role in the Church.

What happens here is beyond the gesture of the kisses that we have seen in the last chapter. From the merely symbolic act of the kisses, we pass to a simply inexplicable terrain. Theology calls this phenomenon *hierognosis.*

---

[198] GALMÉS BELMONTE, R., *"Garabandal"* in FUNDACIÓN HM, *www.garabandal.it*, Lumezzane, 2013.
[199] Cf. CONCILIO VATICANO II, *Dogmatic Constitution Lumen Gentium*, AAS 57 (1965) 10b.

Hierognosis

Etymologically "*knowledge of the sacred*," *hierognosis* is the "faculty that some saints had, particularly those who experienced ecstasies, to recognize holy things (the sacred host, rosaries or scapulars that were blessed, relics...), promptly and unhesitatingly differentiating them from profane objects."[200] In Garabandal, this occurs many times, especially with priests and religious.

On the evening of the 16th of October 1961, for example, among the numerous spectators following *the seers*, there are two Asturian priests. However, nobody knows this, since they have come in civilian clothes. Conchita, *in ecstasy*, begins to give the crucifix to the surrounding people to kiss. Just two people remain at a distance: the priests, who, distrusting *the apparitions*, climb the exterior stairs to the landing of a house to observe the situation from above; but the child pursues them. She quickly climbs the stairs in that posture so typical of Garabandal, the head thrown dramatically backwards, which impresses everyone, because it means she cannot see the steps. Now face-to-face, alone with the two priests, she presents the crucifix to them to kiss, but both of them avoid it, turning their faces away. Without ceasing to look upwards, the child blesses the first, and again he pulls away from kissing the cross. She blesses him again twice, with such gentleness that he finally surrenders and kisses the crucifix. The same occurs with his companion.

Conchita descends the stairway. But suddenly, she turns around and offers the crucifix again to the two men to kiss, and again they reject it! The witnesses, unaware that both of them are priests, alternate between scandal and indignation. Suddenly, the child returns to normality and the more stubborn of the two

---

[200] ROYO-MARÍN, A., *Teología de la perfección cristiana*, Madrid 1958, 827

begins to shake, as if he were unwell. He is stunned: an inner thought that he has just formulated has been fulfilled:

My God, if all that is happening here is truly supernatural, make the child come back to me and put an abrupt stop to the ecstasy; then I will believe."

Since *the ecstasy* finished, Conchita has no further business there. She heads towards home, but she had not yet exited the little square and the crowd of people when she falls *into ecstasy* again. Retracing her steps, she responds to a new interior test requested by the distrusting priest:

If the girl came to me before because she supernaturally knew I am a priest, let her demonstrate that to me again by coming to give me the cross to kiss again and blessing me several times.[201]

These priests, who had come without believing anything, are astonished. Later on, after *the ecstasy*, like other pilgrims, they hand a prayer card to *the seer* to sign. In the dedication, the girl surprises them again by explicitly mentioning their priesthood. How does she know? Cases like this, numerous in Garabandal, point time and again to the same idea: the singular value of the priesthood. The children discover this value in an extraordinary way; the Christian people discovers it through faith.

The Public Participate in the Apparitions

One peculiar aspect of Garabandal is that those present during *the ecstasies* quite often intervene in some way in *the apparition*. Ramón María Andreu, the Jesuit who would make Garabandal so well known through his ample studies, was closely observing *the ecstasies* one day when an Asturian priest approached to assure him that he had proved the falsity of *the apparitions*. Taken aback,

---

[201] Pesquera, 2004, 245.

Andreu answers: ""*Wow! I've been here for four weeks and I'm still not sure about it all; and you, in ten minutes...*" To rid himself of the man, he directed him to a doctor who happened to be close by, Dr. Ortiz. Ten minutes later the man returned. Pale, trembling and disconcerted, he exclaims: "*Father Andreu: It's all true! I'm convinced.*" "*Hold on, slow down... Ten minutes ago you didn't like any of this, and now you're convinced? Don't you think you're being a bit hasty?*" "But listen to what's happened to me. I was walking alongside this Ortiz gentleman over there, when one of the girls, Jacinta, appeared *in ecstasy*, and she comes up to me and blesses me; and there was a *short little fellow* beside me whom she blessed as well, then she gave me the cross to kiss, and gave it to *the little guy* too; then she blessed me again, and blessed *the little fellow* too. Then I thought: "*If it's true that it's the Virgin who is appearing, let the ecstasy end.*" In that very moment, the girl lowered her head and stood there looking at me totally normal! My heart stopped, and I said to her: "*But, aren't you seeing the Virgin?*"

"*No, sir.*" "*Why not?*" "*Because She left me.*"

And the girl turned around and walked away. She hadn't taken four steps when she fell into *ecstasy* again, and came right back to us. She blessed me and then the little guy; she gave me the cross to kiss, and then she gave it to *the little guy* to kiss." "*Excuse me,*" Fr. Andreu interrupted, "*point out this little fellow to me, because it seems to me that the really interesting one in this case is the little fellow, not you.*"

Sure enough, "*the little fellow*" was a priest who had come to Garabandal in a state of terrible torment owing to great doubts about his priestly ordination: he worried that he had not had a clear and explicit will to be ordained and that, as a result, the sacrament had not been valid, in which case he was exercizing the priestly ministry improperly and invalidly... God alone knew how much the poor man was suffering because of those scruples.

Hearing mention of Garabandal, he thought that perhaps he could find there the way out of his dark tunnel. As soon as he could, he made his way to the village. But before arriving, he made sure to disguise himself (at that time it was very rare for a priest or religious not to wear his cassock or habit without serious motives). He disguised himself so thoroughly, says Andreu, that *"there was no way of suspecting, even remotely, that he was a priest."*

It was a first consoling response to his inner doubts when the child, soon after his arrival, repeated to him the gestures she had just performed to the priest beside him, but it wasn't enough. Pacifying scruples is no easy matter!

After an initial moment of joy, his spirit darkened again. And he thought: *"I can't leave here yet; I need more proofs."* He spent the night in a barn, waiting to see if the following day he would obtain the absolutely convincing proofs that he so needed. The new day dawned, and the poor man did not have to wait long. That morning there was *an ecstasy*. Many people turned up to witness it. The *little fellow*, naturally, was in the front row.

When *the seer* began giving the crucifix to be kissed, the people quickly formed rows along the path, so as not to miss the opportunity. The *little fellow* lined up with the others in the middle of the row and observed the grace with which *the seer* made her way along, without looking at the ground or at those around her. With much emotion the people kissed the crucifix, one by one. But he didn't just observe; his mind was working, and he formulated this precise thought: *"If I am truly a priest, instead of giving me the crucifix to kiss like everyone else, may the child come to me and bless me with it."*

Then the child stopped in front of the Brigadier of the Civil Guard (so meritorius in defending the cause of Garabandal): smiling at him, she blesses him slowly. Then she continues giving the crucifix to be kissed, arriving before him, and blessed him! The response seems crystal clear, but the little fellow was difficult and didn't take long to think: *"This is no good, because she has blessed the Brigadier too, and he's not a priest. If, instead of this, she had given the crucifix to everyone to kiss, without exception, and then she had blessed me, only me, three times, then yes, there would be no doubt."*

No sooner had he had this thought than the child interrupts her route and makes her way back to the beginning of the row, to give the crucifix again to everyone to kiss. Coming again to the Brigadier, she gives the crucifix to him to kiss like everyone else. And then she came again to the little fellow. We can imagine his emotion: the child, with great care, blesses him respectfully, three times! Furthermore, she says to him in a clear voice: "Yes."[202]

This was too much for him. The poor man tried to dissimulate his tears as the child continued along the line, and then he made his way to the church. In the sacristy he unwrapped a package he was carrying; inside was his cassock. He put it on with more feeling than ever and then knelt before the tabernacle, unable to express to the Lord and our Mother his gratitude and emotion. He came out a truly *"changed man"*; inside even more than outside.

It's Not Just for the Children

In Garabandal, cases like that of *the little fellow* are very numerous. They demonstrate that the extraordinary experiences of the children are not *for them alone. The apparitions* intimately

---

202 Cf. PESQUERA, 2004, 203-204.

touch the spectators. Everyone in Garabandal realizes that the extraordinary happenings go far beyond the little ones, surprisingly reaching all those who approach the phenomena.

The graces that the girls receive are not just for them. Their immediate object is not "the self-satisfaction of those who receive them, but the spiritual good of their neighbor."[203] Spiritual theology calls this "graces gratis datae." This is very important and is as it should be, since "it proves the legitimacy of the ecstatic procedure with two criteria: the following of Jesus and the edification of the community."[204] Both criteria are demanded by biblical revelation (cf. 1 Cor 12:3; 14:5) and both occur in Garabandal. The "following of Jesus" is testified to by the genuine graces of conversión which we are seeing and which we will see more of later; "the edification of the community" is very present in this other-oriented aspect of the ecstasies. All of this points in the best direction in the task of evaluating the phenomena.

An Inexplicable Synchronization: "The Calls"

For the spectators, there is a continual succession of extraordinary phenomena. Everything happens by surprise. The girls, however, know very well when they are going to have an apparition, thanks to what they themselves refer to as "the calls." Conchita describes these calls in her Diary:

> It is like an inner voice, but we didn't hear it with our ears, or hear our names called: it's like a joy. There are three calls: the first is a smaller joy, the second is a little greater, but when the third one happens, we get very excited and are filled with joy. That means She's coming. We started to move at the second call because if we moved after the first

203 ROYO-MARÍN, A., Teología de la perfección cristiana, Madrid, 1958, 792.
204 SUDBRACK, J., "Éxtasis" in BORRIELLO, L. et al., Diccionario de Mística, Madrid, 2002, 706.

one, we had to wait there a long time; because there was usually a long delay between the first and the second calls.[205]

These notes are dated as early as the 3rd of July 1961, the day after the *first apparition of the Virgin*. Saint Teresa of Jesus testifies to the violence of these *raptures*:

> It comes, in general, as a shock, quick and sharp, before you can collect your thoughts, or help yourself in any way, and you see and feel it as a cloud, or a strong eagle rising upwards, and carrying you away on its wings... And so trying is it, that I would very often resist, and exert all my strength, particularly at those times when the rapture was coming on me in public. I did so, too, very often when I was alone, because I was afraid of delusions... it was impossible.... We have no part in causing this pain; but very often there springs up a desire unexpectedly—I know not how it comes—and because of this desire, which pierces the soul in a moment, the soul begins to be wearied, so much so that it rises upwards above itself, and above all created things.[206]

This is what the children experiences in *their calls*. These *raptures* move the children in Garabandal towards the site of *the apparition* when it calls and creates a spectacular circumstance for the public, since they see each one coming from different places, sometimes far away, from different distances and all arriving at the same time; and they fall into *ecstasy* in the same instant, as soon as they arrive, all at once.

The public, puzzled by these impressive coincidences, immediately tries to test their authenticity. On the very first day that news breaks about these *"calls"* (July 3, 1961), *the seers* are put to the test. The parish priest arranges to separate *the seers*. And that same evening, with the whole village watching

---

[205] *Diario de Conchita,* 38.
[206] SAINT TERESA OF AVILA, *Life,* ch. XX, 3, 4, 12.

expectantly, after the girls receive *the first call*, they are separated. Placed now in different houses, Conchita herself tells what happened:

> *They separated us to see if we would coincide... and after half an hour we got the second call and the four of us coincided, arriving at the same time in the "Cuadro." The people were amazed and wondered how we could possibly coincide like that.*[207]

This test was carried out many times, always with the same result. Even when they didn't know what time it was and were in different locations, no matter what they were doing, the children reached the *Cuadro*, in the *Calleja*, together at the same time, running, with an extraordinary precision. *"Cuadro"* is the name Conchita gives to a confined space bordered with logs put there to protect them in *the ecstasies* from the enthusiasm of curious onlookers. It is one of the places that has witnessed most *extraordinary phenomena* and the site of *the first apparitions of the Virgin*.

The extraordinary synchronization of improvised sprints, the sudden simultaneous commencement of *the ecstasies*, the rhymthical movements of the four girls, deeply impresses the onlookers. We are dealing here with an exceptional experience, quite new in the history of mysticism. It must be said that in Lourdes, Saint Bernadette "felt a rather similar interior movement: *"the Virgin calls her, impels her towards Masabielle..."*.[208] But in Lourdes, with just one seer, other similarities with Garabandal could not occur. The *calls*, on a separate note, always follow a set pattern:

1) To announce the coming of *the Virgin*, not that of the *Angel* (we have already seen a clear hierarchy in Garabandal).

---

[207] *Diario de Conchita,* 39.
[208] LAURENTIN, R., *Lourdes. Relato auténtico de las apariciones,* Lethielleux, 1966, 246.

2) To produce an intense desire and great joy in the children, by pre-announcing a forthcoming ecstasy.

3) *The calls* are always three: between the first and the second the time was always ample and variable: *from one and a half to two hours.* Between the second and the third the time is shorter. The third precedes *the apparition* by just a few moments.

4) The call is not experienced as a word; it is like a great interior joy. Jacinta has tried to translate her impression into words: *"The first call is like someone saying 'come'; the second is like someone saying 'hurry'; the third is like someone saying 'hurry, hurry, hurry.' But all of this happens inside and without words."*

5) Perhaps the most relevant characteristic is that the *calls* are not preceded by any external cause; they occur at any hour of the day or night, often in clear discontinuity with the preceding activity of the children.[209]

This last circumstance immediately draws the attention of the theologians, since its verification would entail an unequivocal sign of divine operation. In other words, it would prove the authenticity of the phenomena. In fact, according to Garrigou-Lagrange, the impetuousity of the fall into ecstasy is precisely a key criterion of authenticity in apparitions.[210] But this overwhelming force of the ecstasies provokes the interest not only of the theologians. The physicians will also study this matter in great depth:

Occasionally, knowing that they had already had two *calls*, I would speak with them trying to distract them—writes Dr. Puncernau—getting them to speak about something that interested them. Sometimes they would drop suddenly to their knees in the middle of a word, in a state of trance; despite the fact that they were speaking about something that visibly interested them. This deeply impressed me. It is not the typical way of entering a trance, the more so if the person is not conditioned to

---

[209] Cf. ANDREU, R. M., *Nota 42* in *Diario de Conchita*, 38.
[210] GARRIGOU-LAGRANGE, R., *Las tres edades de la vida interior,* Madrid, 1995, vol. II, 1107.

respond to some sign or signal. Among the onlookers there was no one capable of understanding it or even of knowing what was going on.[211]

The doctors and the theologians are equally perplexed. They realize that, without a *"sign or signal,"* the synchronization and the impetus typical of *the calls* is, from the natural point of view, simply inexplicable.

"The Falls"

There is one unusual phenomenon that has few precedents in the history of mysticism but occurs repeatedly in Garabandal. The public promptly give it the popular name of *"the falls."* We know the date of the first time these *falls* occurred. It was very early on and is noted by the parish priest: on the 3rd of August 1961. The girls in *ecstasy* suddenly fall to the ground, but *with a grace and composure* that amaze everyone. A priest from Leon, Manuel Antón, present that day, affirms that:

All of us were very frightened, fearing that a serious injury might have happened. The mother of one of the children, I can't recall which [Jacinta], went to pick up her daughter, distraught with worry. I was very agitated and began to say, almost shouting: *"But is there no doctor here among so many people who can do something in such an extraordinary situation? Is there nobody?."*.. Father Valentín, the parish priest, who was there in the crowd, interrupted the general worried silence, saying with a serious voice: *"What's happening here has been extraordinary from the beginning; the problem is, we are people of little faith."* I confess that his response struck me deeply; and all these years later I remember it as if I were hearing it right now. After a while the children returned to their wits as if they had been in a marvelous dream, and stood up, fresh and normal as could be, all smiles.[212]

---

[211] PUNCERNAU, Dr. R., *Informe médico sobre las videntes de Garabandal*, Barcelona, 1974, 5.
[212] PESQUERA, 2004, 134; Cf. MARICHALAR, V., *Memoria de las apariciones de Garabandal*, Gijón, 1971, 7.

This occurs again and the public, little by little, become accustomed to it, to the extent of observing very subtle details "[these] falls and getting up without support, with modesty, when the manner of falling entailed that the skirt should have moved wrongly,"[213] manifests for many the delicacy of *the Virgin*. Thus, these strange *sculptural groupings*, disconcerting for some, beautiful for others, show the quiet beauty of God's work.

Saint Teresa of Jesus points to the possible causes of these ecstatic falls: "during the rapture itself the body is very often as if it were dead, perfectly powerless. It continues in the position it was in when the rapture came upon it—if sitting, sitting; if the hands were open, or if they were shut, they will remain open or shut... they have no power whatever to deal with outward things."[214] More concrete references to this phenomenon are not to be found among the spiritual authors, but indications are, as Saint Tereasa suggests, that this happens due to *the suspension of the external senses* proper to ecstasy. This *suspension* does not necessarily imply the levitation or elevation of the body in the air; it can manifest itself "in a more or less pronounced insensibility, delayed respiration and diminishment of body heat."[215] All of these symptoms occur in *the ecstasies* of Garabandal. So, the *falls* must surely be situated within this dynamic, just like another of the inexplicable phenomenon of Garabandal: the *weight change* of the children during *the ecstasies*.

An Inexplicable Change of Weight

The surprising change of weight in the children during *the ecstasies* of Garabandal is a phenomenon as novel and widely

---

[213] LÓPEZ DE SAN ROMÁN, *La verdad sobre Garabandal*, Valladolid, 2012, 4.
[214] SAINT TERESA OF AVILA, *Life*, ch. XX.
[215] GARRIGOU-LAGRANGE, R., *Las tres edades de la vida interior*, Madrid, 1995, vol. II, 1107.

documented as *the falls*. Pepe Díez recalls that, one day, two men who came from Santander, having heard of the apparitions, witnessed this very fact. Having heard much talk of this excess of weight in *the seers* during *the ecstasies*, the younger of the two, a big strong fellow, approaches the *ecstatic* Jacinta to find out for himself. The *seer's* father has given him permission. He tries to lift her, but even though Jacinta is just a little girl and the fellow a full grown youth, he is unable: "and with all his pulling and hauling, and huffing and puffing, he couldn't get her off the ground. Turning to Jacinta's father, he says: *"Hey... if I tell them this in Santander, they won't believe me..."* Soon afterwards *the ecstasy* ends and the child's father urges him to try again. The young man hesitates, perhaps fearing a proof of the extraordinary, but in the end he approaches. The girl waits, and Pepe Díez, present among the crowd, relates what happens next:

> He lifted her up like a doll... and he got scared, the lad was frightened, because he lifted her more that he had figured, and he says: "Wow, now I know this is all true. But I can't tell anyone because no one will believe it."[216]

The doctors discover the very same phenomenon in their tests of this change of weight. On the 25th of June 1961 (a week after *the first apparition* of *the angel*):

> During *the ecstasy* a doctor tried to lift Conchita, and, owing to the extreme weight she had when in this state, she fell from quite a height with her knees hitting the ground, producing a loud crunch. When it ended and the children were examined, the marks of Conchita's fall were clearly visible... but they don't complain of the slightest pain or make the slightest expression when the tests are being inflicted.[217]

---

[216] DÍEZ CANTERO, J., *"Testigo de Garabandal,"* in PÉREZ, R., 1991, 246.
[217] BRIGADA ÁLVAREZ SECO, J., *"Informe sobre Garabandal,"* in PÉREZ, R., 1991, 372; Cf. PÉREZ, R., 1991, 16.

Many witnesses testify to this amazing *weight change* in *the seers*.

The Ecstatic Marches

"There have been saints," Royo-Marín writes, "who, during their ecstasies, spoke of the object of their contemplative vision and even started walking [in *"ecstatic march"*]. The cases of Saint Catherine of Siena and Saint Magdalene of Pazzi are famous. However, these occurrences are exceptional; ordinarily, there is insensibility and total immobility."[218] These ecstatic marches, exceptional but not unknown to theology, will be frequent in Garabandal.

For example: Maximina González, Conchita's aunt, writes in November 1962: *"We've been snowed in, and you should see the children going up the hill to the Pines on their knees, backwards, through all the muck and snow! It was painful to see; on top of that, the hailstones, the wind, the terrible cold."*[219]

That is how it was: on the 4th of August 1961, *the seers* walk in *ecstasy* for the first time. They walk without looking at the ground, with the eyes always fixed upwards, the head raised presenting the face to the heavens, by day or by night, under sun, rain or hail... and even with a half a meter of snow on the streets, with and without witnesses, on foot or kneeling, forwards and backwards. Onlookers are amazed. The girls walk along all the streets of the village and even the surrounding slopes, especially the rough path from the village to *"the Pines,"* a scar in the side of Mount Hormazo situated above San Sebastián, overlooking the village. In their marches, the girls often stop in favored sites like the *Calleja* and the *Cuadro*—where it all began—and the small

---

[218] ROYO-MARÍN, A., *Teología de la perfección cristiana*, Madrid, 1958, 679.
[219] GONZÁLEZ, M., *Carta a la familia Pifarré*, November 25, 1962; PESQUERA, 2004, 481, nota 15.

cluster of pines. But their *visits* occur throughout the entire village.[220]

The "Visits" of the Seers

In their *ecstasies*, the children enter the houses: "they visited all the houses of the village, all of them." And "when they prayed in *ecstasy* [in the houses], it was very moving...." They give their cross to those present to kiss, make the sign of the cross over all kinds of places: "they went to the headboards [of the beds] and would trace the sign of the cross once... if just one person usually slept there. If they did it twice, two slept there, a married couple or children... [without ever making a mistake, without knowing the house. But] exactly." No one ever saw them get it wrong. Rather, they know unthinkable things: over one bed, for example, "they made the sign of the cross at the feet and again at the head." It turns out that, even though there was only one pillow, in that bed two sisters of *Casa Tiva* slept side by side, topping and tailing.[221]

The girls *in ecstasy* visit all the houses of the village, with special preference towards the houses of the sick or deceased. Simón González, a villager, recalls how the children, *in ecstasy*, "would pray a station beside the corpse in the house when someone died... They led the prayer and we responded; but idle talk? Not a word, just a prayer and then they'd leave. They went to the sick too, but didn't pray; just blessed them." The marches of the little *seers*, solely to bless, console and provide company, brought great comfort and joy to the homes. They were a consolation for the entire village. All of the witnesses refer to it

---

[220] Cf. SÁNCHEZ VENTURA. *El interrogante*, 93; DE DIOS, J. M., *El gran portento de Garabandal: Teología, opiniones críticas y puntualizaciones*, Zaragoza, 1969, 133; ROMAN-BOCABEILLE, C., *El misterio de las apariciones de Garabandal*, Barcelona, 1987, 51.
[221] GONZÁLEZ, S., *"Testigo de Garabandal,"* in PÉREZ, R., 1991, 352.

with nostalgia; including Simón González, whom we have quoted: "When they prayed *in ecstasy* it was very moving... very moving."[222]

Levitations

Brigadier Juan Álvarez in his *Report* notes an interesting detail of the children's *marches* around the village:

> As well as *the ecstasies*, I have witnessed hundreds of *ecstatic marches, running swiftly* in this state through the village streets and even sometimes backwards... Some villagers ran after them but couldn't catch up, and even *the seers* who were in a normal state could not catch up with the ones who were *in ecstasy*.[223]

All of the testimonies coincide in pointing out that "the speed of the girls was simply astonishing and there was no way of keeping up with them."[224] Pepe Díez vividly recalls the extraordinary swiftness of these *marches*:

> *I observed this closely: the pace of the girls, their velocity, was normal. With one normal step they would advance three times more than any other person... It was impossible to follow them... The movement of their legs was normal but the ground they covered was extraordinary... I was usually the first one to arrive, at my thirty-five or so years of age, and the others couldn't beat me running... but I wasn't the only one who ran [after them]... When they walked on their knees or backwards it wasn't so fast, but a normal person walking couldn't keep up with them.*[225]

Dr. Puncernau, with greater erudition, affirms the same idea:

> One had the impression that they scarcely moved, in a winged march, like a slow motion picture or a levitation, but the speed was

---

[222] *Ib.*
[223] PÉREZ, R., 1991, 373.
[224] PESQUERA, 2004, 74.
[225] DÍEZ CANTERO, J., *"Testigo de Garabandal,"* in PÉREZ, R., 1991, 244.

incredible, so much so that the boys of the village, young and strong, couldn't catch up with them no matter how hard they tried. After running *the length and breadth of the village*, they would return to a normal pace and then emerge smiling from the trance.[226]

Theology speaks of two types of *levitation*: "If the elevation is slight, it is usually called *ascensional ecstasy*. If the body is elevated to great heights, it is given the name of *estatic flight*. And if it runs speedily over the ground, without touching it, it consists of what is called an *ecstatic march*."[227] Witnesses perceive this *ecstatic march* in Garabandal.

There were other levitations in Garabandal—not many—mostly of the *ascensional* type, of slight elevation. Simón González, a villager, saw a test performed by Dr. Celestino Ortiz, a pediatrician from Santander. While Conchita was stretched on the kitchen floor of her home in *ecstasy*, the doctor notes a slight levitation. Owing to the slight margin of elevation, he has doubts. Dr. Ortiz then passes his hand under the child. It's a fact: Conchita is not touching the floor at any point. "A moment later she fell to the floor. Yes, I saw that in Conchita's house," Simón relates.[228] Brigadier Álvarez Seco, also present, singles this out as "one of the apparitions that most impressed me."[229] It is true that the angels and demons "can lift bodies in the air,"[230] but this phenomenon of levitation, when it is from God, "is an anticipated participation in the gift of agility, proper to glorified bodies."[231] Levitation anticipates on earth the qualities that risen bodies will have in eternal life.

---

[226] PUNCERNAU, Dr. R., *Informe médico sobre las videntes de Garabandal*, Barcelona, 1974, 4; Cf. DE DIOS, J. M., *El gran portento de Garabandal: Teología, opiniones críticas y puntualizaciones*, Zaragoza, 1969, 133.

[227] ROYO-MARÍN, A., *Teología de la perfección cristiana*, Madrid, 1958, 857.

[228] GONZÁLEZ, S., "Testigo de Garabandal," in PÉREZ, R., 1991, 345.

[229] BRIGADA ÁLVAREZ SECO, J., "Informe sobre Garabandal," in PÉREZ, R., 1991, 381.

[230] ROYO-MARÍN, A., *Teología de la perfección cristiana*, Madrid, 1958, 858.

[231] *Ib.*

Members of the public are amazed by *the ecstatic marches*: without ever ceasing to look upwards, head turned back (as may be seen in many photographs): "The children navigated all obstacles with great ease... better than when watching where they put their feet, and all this going backwards... looking at the skies with a smile..."[232] They don't perspire; nor does their breathing or pulse accelerate like those who attempt to follow them. Rather, as mystical theology affirms, their "vital functions, during the ecstasies, seem to be interrupted: no respiration, no appreciable noticeable of blood."[233]

Furthermore, the girls often follow their *march* without the attendance of witnesses, in the night: "with almost a half a meter of snow in the village," Loli is accompanied only by her father, Conchita only by her mother. The neighbors know about these winter nights. Simón González recalls how one of those cold nights, with nobody on the street, he discovered Conchita in *ecstasy*, alone: "there was no one with her apart from her mother... during a terrible hail storm... Hailstones were falling on her face... I was shivering; and she, not a bother, totally natural."[234]

Spiritual theology explains that sometimes in ecstasy, "the gaze remains fixed on an invisible object," and "instead of weakening the body, this state communicates *new energies* to it,"[235] capacitating the subject to carry out actions that would otherwise be impossible. In Garabandal, all of this is so frequent that neither neighbors nor strangers are able to follow phenomena that recur day and night, sometimes in very adverse conditions. What might be the meaning of this superabundance of

232 DÍEZ CANTERO, J., *"Testigo de Garabandal,"* in PÉREZ, R., 1991, 244.
233 ROYO-MARÍN, A., *Teología de la perfección cristiana*, Madrid, 1958, 679.
234 GONZÁLEZ, S., *"Testigo de Garabandal,"* in PÉREZ, R., 1991, 321.
235 GARRIGOU-LAGRANGE, R., *Las tres edades de la vida interior*, Madrid, 1995, vol. II, 1107.

phenomena? One is tempted to guess that it points to something that is hard for man to recognize, today perhaps more than ever before: the gratuity of love.

The "Mystical Question" in the 20th century
Jacques Maritain and Garabandal

In the *ecstatic marches,* it seems as though *the apparition* desired to reach all the streets, houses and byways; and in such a manifestly supernatural way, through four children who pray, walk and run, without ceasing for an instant from their heavenward gaze. It seems like a nod in the direction of what Jacques Maritain (1882-1973) would call *"contemplation in the byways."*[236] The French philosopher coins this phrase in the context of what was perhaps the sharpest theological polemic of the 20th century: the so-called *"mystical question."* Two visions of holiness confront each other in this polemic: those who affirm two ways of holiness (ascetical and mystical) against those who integrate both ways in one form of holiness: *"the universal call to mysticism."*[237]

Maritain cannot accept that only some Christians are called to the intimacy of contemplation of God and defends, together with his wife Raissa, a strong position: *a universal call to mysticism.* The Maritains reject the idea of an elite of mystics who are chosen apart from all other Christians, who are called only to *ascesis.* They integrate the contemplative life into the personal circumstances of each Christian under an evocative title: *contemplation in the byways.* They maintain that, even though not all Christians are called to an extraordinary mystical life, all are called to the highest contemplation. They argue that *mysticism and asceticism* are not two paths to holiness but rather two inseparable

236 SESÉ, J., *Historia de Espiritualidad,* Pamplona, 2005, 285.
237 Ib.

dimensions of the only holiness possible, which is at once *ascetical and mystical.*

In Garabandal, the *ecstatic marches "throughout the village,"* at any hour of the day or night, openly express, in an extraordinary way, the *"contemplation in the byways"* proposed by the Maritains in the academic sphere: that all places and all moments of daily life are favorable for the encounter with God, even the most uncomfortable and adverse (*ascesis*), since all are *"ways"* that lead to God *(mysticism)*.

Every detail of *the apparitions* in Garabanal seems to contain a spiritual richness that would be comprehended over time. However, there are shades as well as lights. The *ecstatic marches* would soon be overshadowed by the severest controversy, perhaps, of the early days: that of the *feigned marches.*

The Feigned Marches

The witnesses who were closest to *the apparitions,* namely villagers who know the girls well and assiduously verify the inexplicable events unfolding in the village, speak also without niceties about a delicate subject in the context of *the apparitions:* the *feigned ecstasies.*

Pressurized by the expectations of large groups of people come from afar who haven't seen *an ecstasy* in their sometimes overly brief visits, the children find themselves trapped in truly tense situations. In their *village-girl* simplicity, they feel they are to blame for the suspicions of these demanding visitors and occasionally try to please them. They think that, perhaps by pretending and thus undoing the tension, they are doing something good. They do this rarely, and only after the second call; that is, when they understand that they are about to have *an apparition*.

Pepe Díez, a habitual witness of the events, unwaveringly frames the question. He affirms that *at the beginning*, although rare, *feigned ecstasies* undoubtedly occurred; but, he explains, they occurred because the groups of visitors sometimes "came with demands; and this practically obligated the children to make things up. But it was very easy to see through it."[238]

Other times what happened was that, when a pre-announced *apparition* was delayed, the families sent the girls to bed because it was late. So the girls, in order not to miss out on those extraordinary graces, in the very early days, occasionally feigned *the ecstasies*: "We looked upwards as if we were already seeing *the Virgin*," Conchita confesses, "and stayed there on the streets with our parents alongside us, and then *the Virgin* would call and we were together; we always ended up seeing *the Virgin*."[239]

They are discovered very quickly. Pepe Díez, describing the *feigned ecstasies*, offers enormously interesting details that favor the supernatural nature of the *"other"* ecstasies, which he considers unequivocally authentic:

> *The true apparitions were so different that I saw through it very easily when they were faking, because they had to go by themselves along flat ground, more slowly; they covered very little ground, in a house, a stretch of a street, small stuff like that, where they could walk easily, naturally enough. Whereas in the true apparitions... they walked on all kinds of surfaces without ever tripping over obstacles of any kind, forwards and backwards, in a posture very difficult to maintain; but they maintained it, with great ease... I can say that I noted a big*

238 DÍEZ CANTERO, J., "*Testigo de Garabandal,*" in PÉREZ, R., 1991, 253.
239 DE DIOS, J. M., *El gran portento de Garabandal: Teología, opiniones críticas y puntualizaciones*, Zaragoza, 1969, 99.

difference... It didn't last long because it was impossible... because they were so closely watched... and before being found out they would declare that the ecstasy was gone... In the supernatural apparitions, as far as one could see, it was something totally extraordinary and lasted maybe an hour... or four hours long, which is the most difficult thing imaginable; that is, it's sufficient to be able to say this is something supernatural, because to hold one's head in the position that the children held their head and their body, going forward and backward, running up and down these paths to the Pines, all of this is the hardest thing to do, and they, on the contrary, did it with an enormous ease... And this explains the difference between the true ecstasies and the others.[240]

The girls are reprehended very quickly for this. Nothing justifies it; neither the good intention of *pleasing* a visitor, much less the desire to remain together so as not to miss *an ecstasy.*

Díez himself immediately spoke to the children: *"I said a thing or two to them too, apart, just to them... 'Hey, I didn't like that last night. Why did you do that?'"* And the little ones, once corrected, *"didn't do it again; they weren't seen to fake it after that."*[241] Feigning, even with good will, rather than doing good, casts doubt on everything else. They need to learn that it is God who decides the times; even though this might mean they have to suffer incomprehensions and even the disbelief of visitors who are, at times, very indiscreet. The fact is that the positive reception of *the apparitions* does not depend on them. It is not their fault if people sometimes get angry with them, besiege them or ridicule them because they haven't had a vision; they must learn to leave everything in the hands of God.

[240] DÍEZ CANTERO, J., *"Testigo de Garabandal,"* in PÉREZ, R., 1991, 254.
[241] *Ib.*

The Gift of Clairvoyance

In our narrative so far, several events have occurred that point to what theology denominates as the *gift of clairvoyance*, a faculty that permits one to know things hidden to natural possibilities.[242] In Garabandal, this entails a unique and privileged point of encounter between *the apparition* and the spectators. On occasion, visitors are overwhelmed by the slightest gestures— sometimes a mere word—of the little ones, which then leave an indelible testimony in the form of a decisive conversion attributed to such moments.

Dr. Puncernau, for example, recalls in his *Report* the case of Concepción Zorrilla, a dancer of the well-known *Cabaret Folies Bergére* of Paris. This lady "had no religious belief. She came to Garabandal out of simple curiosity." But after speaking with Dr. Puncernau in the village tavern, she accompanies him to see *the ecstasies*. On seeing *the seers*, the dancer thought to herself:

> *If it's true that the Virgin is appearing, let one of the girls come and give me a proof... No sooner had I thought this, than Conchita came running towards me to give me the crucifix to kiss. I didn't want to and I held her hand away. But with exceptional strength she put the crucifix in front of my lips and I had no choice but to kiss it. Once, twice, three times, I the unbeliever, the atheist, who didn't believe in anything. I was deeply moved by it.*[243]

Seeing Conchita come towards them, Concepción had thought she was coming to "*play-act*" in front of the doctor. But *the seer* was interested only in her. Dr. Puncernau comments: "*I know that later she [Concepción] left the Folies Bergére and returned with her*

---

242 MARCOZZI, V., "Clarividencia" in BORRIELLO et al., *Diccionario de Mística*, Madrid, 2002, 415.
243 PUNCERNAU, Dr. R., *Informe médico sobre las videntes de Garabandal*, Barcelona, 1974, 3.

family to Uruguay, because we exchanged letters several times";[244] *"and she changed her life, completely converted, became a great person and continues, I believe, to be so."*[245]

Another time, "one of *the seers* blessed all the people around her, except one... We can imagine that person's distress. Afterwards, the priest asked the girl why she hadn't blessed that person and the child replied that the Virgin had told her that that person was the only one of those present who had made the Sign of the Cross earlier that morning. Upon inquiry, it was verified that this was in fact the case."[246] It seems that *the apparition* wished to show with this gesture that no work of faith is small or hidden to the eyes of God. And it will not be left unrewarded. At the same time, *the vision* seems to hint with this gesture that each day should begin with a raising of the heart to the heavenly Father.

Plácido Ruiloba is the protagonist in another surprising case. He himself tells the story:

> I arrived in the village at night. [It was autumn and] the days were very short. When I arrived, the children were *in ecstasy.* I deliberately stayed apart, in a place where the girls' well-known *ecstatic marches* didn't usually pass, and tormented as usual by my doubts, I began to say to myself in my mind: *"Blessed Virgin, look at all the people who have come to see this! Imagine if it's all a lie... the harm it could cause! Lady: so that I may see for once and for all that all of what is happening is really from you, I ask that, even though I am separated here, one of the girls come to me, from wherever she happens to be, to give me the crucifix to kiss."* From the corner where I had slotted myself, behind the fountain, I could observe a lot of what was going on without being noticed; I saw that the girls had come out of *their ecstasy:* only

[244] *Ib.*
[245] LANÚS, S., *Concepción Zorrilla,* Buenos Aires, 2014, www.virgendegarabandal.com (last visited August 20, 2014).
[246] PESQUERA, 2004, 90.

Conchita remained *ecstatic*, and I saw her come towards her house, close to my hideout. I saw perfectly how she went in... and suffered in that moment a tremendous disappointment, realizing that my prayer had not been heard, and that as a result my doubts were confirmed... I was savoring this bitterly when, suddenly, I saw that the people who had entered the house quickly began to come back out, with the child behind them, still *in ecstasy*: my heart jumped, as I guessed what might be the motive. In effect, Conchita came straight towards me, keeping her head always unimaginably turned upwards, which impeded her from seeing anything before and around her; she came to the corner where I had hidden myself, stopped in front of me, and three times gave me the crucifix to kiss! The response was clear and my doubts vanished... at least for the time being.[247]

A final example, from Mother Nieves García, confidant of Conchita from her time in Burgos in 1966; Conchita herself told the story and the religious passes it on as she heard it: "One day *the Virgin* told me that when I finished speaking with Her, I had to turn to a couple behind me and say to them: *"You are not living well."* I did so, even though it was hard for me. I know they were deeply moved, because they cried and went to confession that same day. There were lots of things like that, where She gave me instructions."[248]

It is striking that the children were able to get things so right with people—the moment, the response, the appropriate gesture—to move so many hearts, one after another; sometimes hearts that were far from God, resistant to *the apparitions*, hostile towards the sacraments. And very often the effect is achieved with just a word, or a slight gesture. And yet, in Garabandal, cases like these, with abundant fruits in souls, are countless.

---

247 *Ib.*, 274.
248 Cited in *Ib.*, 291

Objects Found

The seers often find objects kissed by *the apparition* in circumstances so clear that the witnesses are confounded, realizing that it was impossible that the little ones could know the location by themselves: "On the 15th of August [of 1961], for example, one of the girls prayed the Rosary with beads that I had given her," narrates Ramón M. Andreu, "and when she returned it to me afterwards, we observed that the cross was missing: it had come off and gotten lost. It was useless to look for it on those streets, byways and dirt paths... Twenty days later, on the 5th of September, it occurred to me to say to the children to ask *the Virgin* for the cross of my Rosary... I heard the dialogue myself as they asked *Her*, and how they specified the exact location. When the trance concluded, we went without delay to the place indicated, and there was the little cross, under a stone, in the mud."[249]

Items were lost among the crowd, in the mud of the paths, in the rain or the night, and at the request of the pilgrims, the girls *in ecstasy* head many times straight to the exact location, without dithering, without ceasing to look upwards, to find the objects referred to. *The seers* put the hand in the mud, the grass or the stones and draw forth the objects lost by the pilgrims. People were greatly surprised on seeing how the girls so often find, so quickly, those objects that had been *kissed by the apparition*.[250]

Conclusion. René Laurentin and the Challenge of the Signs

There are other signs in Garabandal, but for lack of space we will not detain ourselves with them. They are less frequent and do

---

[249] *Ib.*, 90
[250] Cf. *Ib.*, 164

not relate so clearly to the public. Such is the case, for example, of the *supernatural perfume* that some witnesses and even doctors perceive, like Dr. Puncernau, who includes it in his *Report* with perplexity and without any doubt.[251] This supernatural sign, in any case, appears frequently in the history of mysticism, and is not therefore distinctive of Garabandal.

Now, in the conclusion of this chapter, replete with *mystical phenomena*, we must confront a serious question: what does this overwhelming display of the extraordinary mean? Isn't the proliferation of phenomena in itself a proof of inauthenticity? Why would Heaven want such a thing?

René Laurentin, in his study of *Modern-day apparitions of the Virgin Mary*, points to this proliferation of *signs* as a *constant feature* of contemporary apparitions. The response of the French theologian, an expert abundantly cited by Benedict XVI, is unavoidable in the conclusion of our brief journey through the phenomena of Garabandal:

> The apparitions shock the prudent and the wise, including many theologians. Often, they are accompanied by concrete, simple, elemental signs, which are sometimes prolific: effusions of tears, of blood, of perspiration and oil, emissions of perfume or light, etc. These sensible and expressive signs affect man in his ambiguous nature as rational animal. They speak with a language that is above words. A language of this nature may seem weak and insignificant to certain categories of intellectuals (all of those who lack the meaning of life and of poetry). But it recalls and actualizes the biblical language. It represents all the languages of love that seek their expression in the ineffable. And this is disturbing in times so given to logomania and verbosity.

---

[251] PUNCERNAU, Dr. R., *Informe médico sobre las videntes de Garabandal*, Barcelona , 1974, 8

The effusion of signs speaks to the heart and recreates the attraction that is blurred at times in the ecclesiastical mechanisms... These facts, and the apparitions themselves, recall that God is present, that He is close, through the Virgin, through the angels and the saints, who are his servants and friends.[252]

Laurentin, who does not have Garabandal concretely in mind in writing these lines but *the Marian apparitions* in general, responds penetratingly to the question concerning the purpose of the extraordinary events that form part of these Marian apparitions:

Theology rightly insists on the transcendence of God. But it does so often with a timorous and abstract language. On the basis of saying that God is the Absolute Other, it forgets a no less essential point of Revelation: He has created us in his image and likeness, with a connaturality that invites us to friendship; because we are similar to God, even though He is transcendent. He has created us that way. He is familiar and at the same time transcendent, and to forget this familiarity, this closeness, is ruinous for the Christian life, for the encounter with God and the dialogue with Him. The seers have the sense of this familiarity. Simplicity, poverty, evangelical freshness, usually accompany the messages, in reaction against the wisdom of the prudent of this world, who all too frequently twist and force and sometimes disintegrate the Gospel, reducing it to the level of the human sciences or ideologies that do not lead to anything fruitful.

The function of all these phenomena (healings, light, solar phenomena, effusions of oil and perfume [Laurentin, without expressly citing the phenomena of Garabandal, encompasses them in his reflection]) is to invite to conversion. The God whom we now see in shadows has little use for the language of the wise, in the Bible as much as in the apparitions; He ordinarily avails of a language that is disconcertingly simple (though always clear and coherent). Those who love immediately capture its unreplaceable meaning.[253]

---

[252] LAURENTIN, R., *Apariciones actuales de la Virgen María*, Madrid 1991, 212-213
[253] *Ib.*

Though perplexing, the superabundance of phenomena in Garabandal has, then, a very concrete meaning: *"The function of all these phenomena... is to invite to conversion."*[254] Conversions are a constant feature of Garabandal, constituting a new effect of the apparitions. They are overwhelming in number and quality, in their unforeseeable force and persistence. We will devote attention to them later.

---

[254] *Ib.*

IX

In the Light of Theology

Theological Assessment of the Phenomena

At this point it is necessary to re-consider what we have seen. By the light of reason, we will now evaluate the extraordinary phenomena of *the apparitions*. If thus far we have seen the verdict of the *medical studies* performed on *the seers* (ch. IV), we will now add to this a *theological judgment*. This will permit us to clarify other important questions, without which it would perhaps be confusing to continue.

"Imaginary visions are very susceptible to illusions"

Garrigou-Lagrange, one of the 20th century's best known authorities in Spiritual Theology, amply studies the key points necessary to judge the authenticity of apparitions in a comprehensive way. He affirms that "imaginary visions are very susceptible to the illusions of the imagination or of the devil."[255] For this reason it is necessary to discern attentively the divine origin of the phenomena in the light of Revelation. According to the French theologian, the criteria needed for this evaluation are just three. *Apparitions* should be welcomed if and when:

---

[255] GARRIGOU-LAGRANGE, R., *Las tres edades de la vida interior*, Madrid, 1995, vol. II, 1180.

1º. It is not possible to provoke or dissipate them with the will; when they are presented suddenly and last for a short time.

2º. They leave a great peace in the soul.

3º. They produce fruits of virtue, deeper humility and perseverance in doing good.[256]

To some extent at least we have already evaluated the phenomena according to these criteria. Now we will examine them in more detail:

1º) *The ecstasies* of Garabandal certainly occur *unforeseeably*. This is noted, for example, in Dr. Puncernau's *Report*: *"they collapsed to the ground," "sometimes in the middle of a word."*[257]

2º) *The ecstasies* in Garabandal leave peace in the children's souls and in those of the witnesses of the phenomena. The most solid medical studies point almost unanimously to this *"great peace"* in *the seers*, which Garrigou-Lagrange requires. Furthermore, according to the abundant tests performed, the children are discovered to be completely normal.[258] For them, it is evident that the phenomena bring peace:

And so ended the second day, Sunday; what a happy day!—Conchita writes—*because we have seen the Virgin for the first time. We are all with Her, whenever we want... Oh, how happy I am when I see you! Why don't you take me with you now?... Today is the happiest day of my life.*[259]

3º) There are many testimonies regarding the children's virtue, their *"perseverance in doing good."* The parish priest, Valentín Marichalar, writes of them, for example, among his notes from the second year of *the apparitions*:

256 *Ib.*
257 PUNCERNAU, Dr. R., *Informe médico sobre las videntes de Garabandal*, Barcelona, 1974, 5.
258 LAFFINEUR, M. - LE PELLETIER, M.T., *La estrella en la montaña*, Tielt, 1967, 150; Cf. ch. IV.
259 *Diario de Conchita*, 36, 98; PESQUERA, 2004, 160.

The girls lead a life of real sacrifice. Conchita's mother told me that her daughter now sleeps better in an armchair than in bed; she spends the nights seated, awaiting the apparition, like all of us. She sleeps with her head leaning against the wall. And the next day, she sets out without fail to work. The four girls work: they wash dishes, clean, go to the river to wash clothes; like all the others in everything. For that reason they are not around much on work days; but on Sundays they play in the street like the other village children. In spite of how little they sleep and rest, they look strong and healthy.[260]

Their virtues are noted by all who meet them: their *humility*, for example, "is manifested... in their way of dressing and speaking, in the little heed they pay to the public who come to see them, in the hard work they continue to do in front of everyone, in their docility to the instructions of their parents and the priests... [Furthermore,] as a result of *the apparitions*, the girls are imbued with a spirit of *obedience*, demonstrated not only with deeds but also with words: they say that *the vision* strongly recommends this to them; that *the Virgin* tells them they must obey above all their parents and the priests."[261]

Andreu, the author of these words, vigilantly studies the moral behavior of *the seers*. And in his *Report*, he includes numerous examples that he himself personally witnessed, relating events that show the great virtue of the little ones. The parish priest, for example, and Andreu himself, order the children more than once to go to bed when they are waiting for an imminent *ecstasy*, pre-announced by *their vision*. They do this to test the little ones in obedience. With the excuse that it's getting too late, they send them to bed, giving them a strict five minutes to do so, and the girls, although with much sorrow, always obey the priests. But on one occasion:

---

[260] Quoted in PESQUERA, 2004, 460.
[261] PESQUERA, 2004, 106-108.

When there was just one minute to go, I spoke again—writes Andreu—saying: *"Stay for one minute. Count to sixty, and if nothing happens before sixty, off to bed."* They began to count out loud, humming in chorus, like in school. When they got to seventeen, they weren't able to finish the word—"*seve...*"—and they were transfixed in *ecstasy*, with the head thrown back in that typical way.[262]

In Garabandal, the girls are always obedient, even at the cost of *their vision*. It is *the Lady* herself who teaches them this hierarchy, this value of obedience. And the children learn it.

"How come it sometimes lasts so many hours?"

The criteria of Garrigou-Lagrange, so far so positive for our case, do still present one difficulty. And that is that it cannot precisely be said of *the ecstasies* in Garabandal that they *"last for a short time,"* as the French theologian stipulates. Often they last *"two hours, three hours... and sometimes more than four hours. And with the position of the head, looking towards heaven, no fatigue or anything of the kind was noticeable in any of the girls."*[263] Pepe Díez, who makes this observation, mentions the duration and the amazement at the inexplicability of holding that posture for so long a time.

But Garrigou-Lagrange's principle of brevity is clear. It is shared, for example, by Saint Teresa of Jesus: "This total transformation of the soul in God *lasts a short time*." However, the Mystical Doctor expresses some perplexity in the face of her own experience. She does so in the form of an indirect question: *"How is it that rapture sometimes lasts so many hours..."* And she herself answers: *"because the Lord wishes it so."* The Saint concludes

---

[262] *Ib.*
[263] DÍEZ CANTERO, J., *"Testigo de Garabandal,"* in PÉREZ, R., 1991, 244.

saying yes, such raptures can last *"many hours"*;[264] but this case will always be exceptional. In Garabandal, therefore, the long duration of the ecstasies seems not to entail a novelty. And, as Díez suggests, the surpassing of natural limits of bodily stamina indicates that the phenomena are supernatural.

The Test of Sacred Scripture

With Garrigou-Lagrange, we have evaluated the phenomena of Garabandal from the anthropological or spiritual viewpoint: by its beginning, its development and its end. Now, with the Sacred Scriptures, we will step back more from the events to focus on the doctrine. If errors are found, *the apparitions* are beyond the bounds of orthodoxy, of faith and the possibility of approval. If, however, they pass this new examination, then the possibility of their supernatural authenticity is reinforced. With this study, we will facilitate a judgment that only the Church can definitively make (cf. LG 12).

Saint Paul, relating his own mystical experience, synthesizes with final authority the essential elements of ecstasy that would have to be present in every authentic apparition:

> I know someone in Christ who, fourteen years ago (whether in the body or out of the body I do not know, God knows), was caught up... into Paradise and heard ineffable things, which no one may utter (2 Cor 12:2,4).

These brief words express three essential elements of the mystical: *ineffability, somatic transcendence and Christ-centeredness.*[265] We will present them now in the context of Garabandal:

---

[264] SAINT TERESA OF AVILA, *Life*, ch. XX, 18-19.
[265] Cf. ÁLVAREZ, T., *"Éxtasis"* in ANCILLI, E. (dir.), *Diccionario de Espiritualidad*, Barcelona, 1987, 94.

I. *Ineffability:* Saint Paul confesses *"not knowing"* where his experience transports him to; *"paradise,"* or *"the third heaven"*... He is not very sure what happens to him: *"I do not know,"* he says. Hence, the first biblical characteristic of the mystical experience is *ineffability: "not knowing."* In Garabandal, the girls also express the feeling of being *"removed"* to a totally unknown space:

> We saw a very bright light that surrounded the four of us—Conchita writes—and we saw nothing but that light.... [The light] *hid us from one another. We were completely dazzled by that light, so we began to cry out, because we were terrified; but the great light had already disappeared.* [266]

In this "blinding, enveloping light, which blocks their way and isolates them from everything," the girls feel *"as though lost and floating in the mystery, in something totally unknown and in which they have no control."* [267] That is why they are frightened at first. This experience, recorded by Conchita in her *Diary* just three days after the first apparition of the *Angel*, on the 21st of June 1961, seems to be a preparation for the little ones, to get their spirit and their eyes accustomed, so that they come to an *easy familiarity with the wondrous* and the transparency of a superior world. The girls describe the same *ineffability* that we find in the *"paradise"* or *"third heaven"* of Saint Paul.

II. Somatic implications: *"caught up," "with or without the body," "in the body or outside the body."* Saint Paul repeatedly alludes to the double psychic and somatic dimensions of the ecstasy. The Apostle feels withdrawn from the body, elevated to beyond the body's reach, but realizes, while unable to explain how, that his body participates in this spiritual experience.

---

[266] *Diario de Conchita,* 25; PÉREZ, R., 1991, 14.
[267] PESQUERA, 2004, 35-36.

In Garabandal, the fact that the experience of *the ecstasies* surpasses the capacities of the body while also involving the body is evident not only to the girls. It is a daily occurrence with numerous witnesses:

> *I touched them many times... protecting them from the many people who wanted to lay hands on them*—Pepe Díez says—*not with bad intentions, but with the crushing and the avalanche of people... That was when I felt something very extraordinary, so extraordinary that it didn't seem like flesh, like a human person; it seemed, let's say, like a block, something rigid... I don't know... it's very difficult to explain.*[268]

Another villager, Prudencio González, who passed with his sheep among the girls *in ecstasy* in *the beginnings*, when they were still alone in the *Calleja*, tells how "*he had to lean on the shoulder of one of them, and got an enormous fright, as if he had touched the mystery. The shoulder seemed not to be of flesh, soft and warm, but so rigid and cold that he shivered.*"[269] Prudencio, who up to then had given no credit to *the apparitions*, suddenly changes opinion in the face of this *change of consistency*. Saint Teresa explains that, effectively, "in these raptures it seems the spirit does not animate the body, and hence it feels keenly the lack of natural heat. It turns cold, but with the greatest softness and delight."[270] Spiritual theology explains that "the physiognomy of the ecstatic is illumined with a heavenly beauty, which transmits the deepest wonder and most ardent love. It is a true transfiguration,"[271] which reflects externally what is happening internally: *the rapture of the soul in God.*

Neither the girls nor the witnesses in Garabandal understand very well what is happening, but they know, without doubt, that

---

[268] DÍEZ CANTERO, J., *"Testigo de Garabandal,"* in PÉREZ, R., 1991, 245.
[269] PESQUERA, 2004, 36.
[270] SAINT TERESA OF AVILA, *Life*, c. XX.
[271] ROYO-MARÍN, A., *Teología de la perfección cristiana*, Madrid, 1958, 679.

"something" is going on: "I have seen the seers look *"very ugly,"* writes Álvarez, "but when they are *in ecstasy* they have a beautiful and very angelical face."[272] Everyone notes a physical manifestation that accompanies the *spiritual rapture*. The *change of consistency* during *the ecstasies*, verified by so many witnesses, speaks precisely of this "double psychic and somatic phenomenon"[273] of the Pauline text: *"whether in the body or out of the body, I do not know, God knows."* So, there is coincidence also, in the form, between the *rapture* of Garabandal and that of Saint Paul.

III. The source: *"in Christ."* With these two words, Saint Paul points to *the root* of the ecstatic phenomenon. *Christ* is the only source and the meaning of the mystical experience. Garabandal, a *typical Marian apparition*, offer no opposition to this. The teaching that Marian apparitions are naturally Christ-centered, as in Lourdes or Fatima which have been approved by the Church, is clear also in Garabandal. We will see this in *the messages* and particularly in the *Eucharistic communions* of Garabandal, the center of which is clearly Christ. Although the girls always encounter *the Angel* or *the Lady* in their trances, these encounters are not the point of arrival but an impulse towards God. The *Lady* herself patiently inculcates this in the children:

> *"Conchita, you must visit my Son more in the Tabernacle: why do you let yourself give in to laziness and not visit Him? He is waiting for you day and night."*[274]

There was also one *apparition of Christ* in Garabandal; only one, and for only one of the seers. It was very early on, even before the

---

272 BRIGADA ÁLVAREZ SECO, J., *"Informe sobre Garabandal,"* in PÉREZ, R., 1991, 374.

273 Cf. ÁLVAREZ, T., *"Éxtasis"* in ANCILLI, E. (dir.), *Diccionario de Espiritualidad*, Barcelona, 1987, 94.

274 *Diario de Conchita*, 96.

first apparition of *the Virgin*: "On Friday, the 30th of June 1961, the last Friday of the month consecrated to the Heart of Jesus. That day, shortly before the end of the girls' *ecstasy*, Jacinta turns her eyes to the side, and there about two meters in front of her, she sees Jesus surrounded by a light that, in the form of rays, proceeds mysteriously from His body. His Heart may be seen in bright light in His chest, with beautiful white and golden rays coming from It. The way Jesus looks at her pierces Jacinta's soul to the depths of her being.[275]

He speaks no words to Jacinta, but indicates His Heart with His left hand as He invites the child to come towards Him with the right. This look, charged with love, with strength, with majesty, totally disarms Jacinta, impeding her from responding to the gesture. Jacinta can scarcely find words to express what she feels in that moment:

It was as though my soul was being seized out of my body.

The impact of this brief vision on her is so powerful that it surpasses even the splendor of the subsequent visions of *the Virgin*. Of all Jacinta's *visions, this would be the one most profoundly branded in her memory.*[276]

In the light of this, it may be said that in Garabandal, as in the *Second Letter to the Corinthians*, the mystical experience has its ultimate meaning and end *"in Christ."* So, the third of Saint Paul's requirements for evaluating *ecstasies* is fulfilled along with the previous two.

---

[275] Cf. ROMAN-BOCABEILLE, C., *El misterio de las apariciones de Garabandal,* Barcelona, 1987, 37; PÉREZ, R., 1991, 17.
[276] HANRATTY, B., *"The Heart of Christ at Garabandal,"* in NEEDLES 1977, X; PÉREZ, R., 1991, 17.

"It all seems to be from God"

The mystical experience in Garabandal may be situated in full continuity with the dynamic of biblical mysticism, as much from the *spiritual* viewpoint, as we saw with Garrigou-Lagrange, as from the *theological* viewpoint, as we have just verified following Saint Paul. *The apparitions* emerge fortified from both tests. This being said, the Congregation for the Doctrine of Faith has published up-to-date *Rules* for discerning the authenticity of possible apparitions in the Church, indicating that all of these criteria

> "are not peremptory but rather indicative, and they should be applied cumulatively or with some mutual convergence."[277]

Therefore, the fact that these requirements are favorably resolved in Garabandal does not constitute a conclusion in the evaluation of the events, but rather a call to take very seriously the pending investigation, concerning *the message and the fruits of the apparitions*. If this also produces positive signs, then Garabandal stands out as a really interesting case.

Of course, since these criteria are processed not mathematically but with faith and obedience to the Holy Spirit who dwells in the Church, it falls to the Church's Hierarchy to give a definitive response concerning the veracity of *the apparitions* (LG 12). However, from what we have seen, we are able to re-affirm what the parish priest of the village once said after interrogating *the seers*: *"So far, it all seems to be from God."*[278]

All the evidence encourages us to continue to the next question. If what we have seen really is as authentic as it seems, if

---

277 CDF, *Norms for the discernment of presumed apparitions*, 1978, I.3.
278 PESQUERA, 2004, 41.

the Virgin really has promoted these phenomena, why has She done so? *What does She want to say to us?*

PART II

"The Doctrine"

Why did Garabandal happen?

X

The Message of Garabandal

An Extraordinary "Communication"

On the 24th of June 1961, one of the first days of the apparitions, the children see for the first time *"some letters"* beside their vision. At the feet of the *Angel,* a mysterious sign appears. But the little ones cannot understand it:

"YOU MUST...-XVIII - MCMLXI."[279]

I

The First Message

Very early on, the day of the fifth *apparition* of the *Angel, the seers* receive the first hints of the message of the Garabandal apparitions, but that day they only see two roman numerals—18 and 1961—along with the first two words of the *message* they will receive later, on the 18th of October 1961. The text and the date that they see that day are incomplete. The little ones do not even know that the *series of capital letters* represent numbers. It is all

---

[279] PÉREZ, R., 1991, 15.

beyond them. And they ask the *Angel: "He smiled,"* Conchita writes, *"but he told us nothing."*[280] They will have to publicize it later, but that day *the Angel* explains nothing to them, just shows them the letters.

"It was the Virgin who explained it to us afterwards," Jacinta recalls.[281] On the 4th of July 1961, in the third apparition of *the Lady,* the children finally receive the complete *message,* the first public message of *the apparitions,* from the mouth of *the Lady* herself:

> The first thing the Virgin said to us, smiling the whole time, was: *"Do you know what the sign underneath the Angel meant?"* We all exclaimed at once: *"No, we don't know." "Well, it meant to tell a Message. I will say it now, so that on the 18th of October you can tell it to the people."* And She told us:
>
> *"You must make many sacrifices, do much penance, visit the Blessed Sacrament; but first, we must be very good. If we are not, a chastisement will come upon us. The cup is filling up, and if we do not change, a great chastisement will befall us."*[282]

The message is brief and simple, its content very evangelical. However, Conchita recognizes in her *Diary* that *"She told us this [the message] already on the first day* [the 2nd of July]; *but I understood nothing."*[283] And the others, who were smaller than she, understood even less. They need time to assimilate it. That is why *the apparition* tells them to keep it secret for the moment: "They must *know and live it* first, to be able then to make it known and lived by many others."[284] They will make it public later, on the

[280] *Diario de Conchita,* 28.
[281] PESQUERA, 2004, 42
[282] *Diario de Conchita,* 42-43
[283] *Ib.*
[284] PESQUERA, 2004, 74

18th of October. This date explains the meaning of those *Roman numerals* of *the Angel's* mysterious sign.

There is a delicate pedagogy here. Everything, from the beginning, was designed to highlight this *message*: "Heaven adapts to the children's mentally under-developed capacities."[285] That is why this pedagogy at first does not even employ words:

1) At the beginning *the apparition* is solely *visual and imaginative* through the dazzling ray of light and the figure of the *silent Angel* who was able to suggest so much to *the seers*.

2) *The Angel* is surrounded by signs that are very apt for calling attention to what needs to be said: *the light, the sign*.

3) To this are added the even more beautiful figure of *Mary*, another *Angel* and the *mysterious Eye*.

4) Then *the words* come: they are few—the *message* is extremely brief—but essential, and must be sculpted deepy in the children's spirit, even though they do not understand them.

5) Finally, extraordinary *explanations and experiences* occur, because the meaning of the most elemental notions must be explained to uncultured village girls. They did not know what was meant by *"making sacrifices,"* which *the Virgin* repeats to them so often. *The Teacher*, after smiling affectionately, turns to serious things; but with words so gracious and adapted to the little ones with such sweet love and patience, that they learn almost without noticing. Often, *the Virgin* draws new teachings from what they say. Among the lessons, the explanation of *the messages* undoubtedly stands out.

---

[285] *Ib.*

In relation to the explanations of this *message*, the girls show an attitude that greatly surprises the public. Brigadier Juan Álvarez describes it:

> The seers were in *ecstasy* in *"the cuadro"* (July 28, 1981), very serious and totally attentive to what the Virgin must have been teaching them... Some shed very large tears—the Brigadier writes—and many of those present were deeply moved. When the ecstasy ended, the girls spoke a little with Fr. Valentín [the parish priest], and he then said in the midst of the greatest silence to all of us who were there: *"The Virgin is giving the girls a message that they cannot tell for now; not to the priest, nor to their parents, nor to the Bishop himself."*[286]

It is not difficult to imagine the enormous impact that such a declaration provokes among the crowd. It is not even known if this mysterious *"message"* can ever be made known, or when. The next day—the 29th of July—*the Virgin* completes the message to the children, which they must make public on the night of the 18th of October. The message will be public, but everyone must wait. In any event, those present sense something: when *the seers wept a lot* during *the ecstasy,* "everyone understood that this was not just one more *apparition,* that *the Blessed Virgin* was explaining or showing certain very serious things."[287] Everything indicates that the day of the publication of the *message,* which has so deeply impressed *the seers,* will be a memorable one. The wait—in July it seemed an eternity— further increases the expectation. Many people will want to be present in Garabandal on that historic day.

The 18th of October 1961

On the long awaited day of the publication of the *message,* an unexpected guest becomes the protagonist of the entire day in

---

[286] BRIGADA ÁLVAREZ SECO, J., *"Informe sobre Garabandal,"* in PÉREZ, R., 1991, 374.
[287] PESQUERA, 2004, 146.

Garabandal: the rain, heavy and constant, falls unceasingly on the village, eventually turning to sleet. As if that were not enough, in the evening, the sleet becomes hailstones. This converts the six kilometers of the pathway from Cosío to Garabandal into a slippery mudslide that very few cars are able to deal with. This means that almost all who wish to witness the events must get there on foot. It would require a long three-hour hike to San Sebastián. But this does not deter the crowd. And on the 18th of October, Garabandal is packed to overflowing: "The crowd reached the figure of 5,000, a truly considerable number if one considers the isolation of this village and the great difficulty of access."[288] The mysterious announcement of the *message* in July justifies the effort for everyone.

This human avalanche absolutely excedes the village's possibilities of hospitality. And yet, throughout the whole day there is not one incident of altercation, in spite of the day's difficulties marked by the inclemencies of the weather and, for many, the lack of shelter other than a coat and umbrella:

> In spite of the atmosphere there, so propitious for the power of suggestion, given that the majority of the people had come with high hopes of a great miracle—Dr. Ortiz affirms—I was unable to discover a single case of such delusion... A very important fact, this! If one takes into account that some of my colleagues... are maintaining that it is a case of *phenomena of collective suggestion*.[289]

The doctor from Santander spent the whole day observing the crowd. Afterwards, he relates the facts as observed, which give enough light to evaluate the atmosphere of this historic day in Garabandal.

---

[288] ANDREU, R. M., *Nota 13* in *Diario de Conchita*, 22; Cf. PESQUERA, 2004, 251.
[289] LANÚS, S., *Madre de Dios y Madre Nuestra. Fátima, Ámsterdam y Garabandal*, Madrid, 2013, 129.

The Parish Priest

Valentín Marichalar, the village priest, is the only one, apart from the girls, who knows *the message* beforehand. He is visibly worried. *The seers* have shown him *the message* the previous day, and he seems unconvinced, because now, observing the tremendous crowds that flood into the village, he remarks: *"Good Lord! There is no knowing what will happen here... Look at the size of the crowd! They're not going to like the message!"*[290] He is quite shaken.

The Virgin Herself gave the girls instructions about how to make *the message* public: *"She told us we had to tell it at the entrance of the church and to pass it on the 18th of October to Fr. Valentín, so that he could repeat it at the Pines, at 10:30 that night."*[291] Fr. Valentín, however, wants nothing to do with this certain failure. Unable to bear the tension of waiting any longer, at 8.00 p.m. he intervenes; precipitating matters by changing the time of making *the message* public and the place (it will be read at *the Pines*, not in front of the church). Also, he refuses to read it personally as *the apparition* had requested. He accompanies the crowd, but stays at a distance. On reaching *the Pines*:

> Fr. Valentín read it to himself—Conchita writes—and after reading it he gave the message to us to read to everyone. The four of us read it together. But since the people couldn't hear us properly, a gentleman read it."[292]

In these hasty decisions of the priest, Pesquera—a respectable expert on Garabandal—observes not so much prudence as worry, provoked by the *"puerile"* appearance of *the message*. Fr. Valentín,

---

[290] PESQUERA, 2004, 249.
[291] *Diario de Conchita*, 43-44.
[292] *Ib.*

Pesquera claims, does not dare to make the proclamation asked of him more out of human respect, out of fear of looking ridiculous, than out of concern to safeguard the integrity of the faith, which he knows very well is not compromised by *the message*. He acts with "an excessively human prudence [which] does not allow space for trust in God and full surrender to whatever His plan might be."[293]

Pesquera's interpretation is debatable; but there is no doubt that the parish priest's attitude that day was influential. René Laurentin, speaking in general, highlights the key role of the local priests in *apparitions*, in ensuring a correct reception of apparitions in the Church: "Wherever the priests receive this grace prudently, even if matters are still unsure, their advice, the parochial environment and the grace of the sacraments provide the best conditions for matters to evolve towards the best possible outcome."[294] On the evening of the 18th of October 1961, Fr. Valentín publicly, even physically, distances himself from *the apparitions*; sending the girls away from the church building, refusing to allow *the message* to be read before the church and to read it himself.

The priest's unmistakable gesture of distrust falls upon *the message* like a jug of cold water before the attentive gaze of the crowd. However, he is not alone in taking this stance: a committee of theologians and men of science from Santander, established to assess *the apparitions*, pressurizes the priest to put an end to a long hard day for everyone. Night is falling and they fear what might happen to the crowds on those paths in the dark, in the worst weather conditions and angered by a message that, they say, is *puerile and irrelevant*.

---

[293] PESQUERA, 2004, 252-254
[294] LAURENTIN, R., *Apariciones actuales de la Virgen María*, Madrid 1991, 192

We will return to this Committee (PART III). Suffice to say for now that it fooled no one and upset many: "They [the Committee members] did not believe, and it's not surprising that they were distressed and wanting to put an end to it all as soon as possible." Pesquera investigated the reasons for this and affirms that "one of the dark or *"negative"* signs which most provoked the doubting or *"anti"* attitude of some [the Committee] towards Garabandal, was the feigned ecstasies."[295] This argument, we have seen, is not conclusive; it must be put in perspective. But the upshot is that Fr. Valentín is now besieged by doubts, which he will not overcome until the 22nd of April of the following year, 1962. That day *the Lord* will respond with another proof requested by the priest, who, from then on, will never again doubt the authenticity of the phenomena.[296]

The Crowd

Distrust has now taken root in the crowd. The girls obey the directions of the priest in everything; they read *the message*, but they can't even be heard. They read it hurriedly and with the *sing-song tone* of a schoolroom recital.[297] On top of this, even though nothing extraordinary had been pre-announced, everyone was expecting a miracle, and *the message* is totally unspectacular. The text is certainly brief, and even its form seems childlike:

> You must make many sacrifices, do much penance, visit the Blessed Sacrament; but first, we must be very good. If we are not, a chastisement will come upon us. The cup is filling up, and if we do not change, a great chastisement will befall us.[298]

---

[295] PESQUERA, 2004, 252. 276
[296] Cf. PÉREZ, R., 1991, 29.
[297] Cf. PESQUERA, 2004, 255.
[298] Diario de Conchita, 42.

The general reaction on this hard night in Garabandal is disappointment and disgust: *"All that hardship, all those hours waiting!... Just to hear that?"*[299] The crowd leaves the village puzzled and grumpy; puzzled because the background of this *"ridiculous message"* was one of absolutely extraordinary events (*ecstatic marches, levitations, conversions*); grumpy, because they expected more: a miracle, an announcement. Certainly, it was not easy that day to evaluate the dimensions of those brief words. And on that stormy night in Garabandal, it convinces nobody; it fails to fulfill the expectations invested in it. It disappoints everyone, or almost everyone.

An Abandoned Message

From the outset, many consider *the message* to be puerile and irrelevant. There is something in it, no doubt, that justifies this opinion. Its expressions are simple and innocent. However, the same may not be said of its content. The brief text possesses a profound evangelical resonance and abundant points of contact with the main modern-day Marian apparitions approved in the Church, especially *the Miraculous Medal* (1830), *La Salette* (1846), *Lourdes* (1858) and, even more so, *Fatima* (1917).[300] This affinity of content amongst the apparitions—including Garabandal—should not be read as *copying* or lack of novelty. On the contrary, it is a very positive sign, because the authentic Marian apparitions always coincide in their contents: to announce the Gospel in our times without altering it, without foreign additions.[301] The novelty, Laurentin indicates, must never be *objective* (inventing new

---

[299] LANÚS, S., *Madre de Dios y Madre Nuestra. Fátima, Ámsterdam y Garabandal*, Madrid, 2013, 129.

[300] Cf. ANDREU, R. M., *Nota 48* in *Diario de Conchita*, 42-43.

[301] BENEDICTO XVI, Apostolic Exhortation *Verbum Domini*, Rome, 2010, 14.

things), but *prophetic* (announcing the Gospel in a concrete time and place).[302]

If it is forgotten that Christ's Revelation, His sacraments, the Gospels, are what is essential, then one falls into a mutilated and impoverished religiosity of apparitions only. But the text of *the first message* of Garabandal does not fall into this reduction. Rather, it points effectively to the sacraments and conversion, to the Gospel ("*visit the Blessed Sacrament*"[303]) and it insists—even in its publication—on the authority of the Church: *the apparitions* wish to be placed under the authority of the parish priest from the very first moment. He, however, distances himself from phenomena which, as we have seen, submit to him spontaneously.

Today, unburdened by the hardships of that night (the rain, the crowds, the confusion), it is easier objectively to assess the richness of *the message* of Garabandal and its profound relevance. *The message* has four elements:

· *A call to penance.*
· *A call to faith and to the Eucharistic life.*
· *A call to purity of heart and customs, to the love of God and of neighbor.*
· *The conditional announcement of a chastisement.*[304]

All of these ideas point clearly to the same end: the personal conversion of every member of the faithful. This being said, the final point of *the message* mentions a delicate matter: "*If we do not change, a chastisement will come upon us.*" This word "*chastisement*" may seem scandalous, and yet, it is fully "in line with biblical language, which," as Laurentin affirms, "also speaks

---

[302] Cf. LAURENTIN, R., *Apariciones actuales de la Virgen María*, Madrid, 1991, 196.
[303] *Diario de Conchita*, 42.
[304] Cf. ANDREU, R. M., *Nota 48* in *Diario de Conchita*, 42-43.

of chastisements."[305] Moreover, according to Manuel Iglesias, internationally renowned exegete, to suppress the doctrine of *divine chastisement* in the sacred texts "we would have to tear out many pages from the Bible (as much from the Old as from the New Testament)."[306] In fact, this issue arises untiringly in the different approved Marian apparitions, especially in the most recent ones, like Kibeho or the *third secret* of Fatima.[307]

Today the doctrine of *the message* is amply rooted in the experience and teachings of the Church. With a simple language, *the message* is designed to awaken the Gospel values among the ordinary public. It is not addressed to the elites, it is for everyone. And yet, as we have seen, *"many left there feeling totally defrauded."*[308] This is not new. It happened in the Gospel, to Jesus Himself, in reaction to preachings as important as that of the *Bread of Life:*

> *"As result of this,"* after the announcement of the Eucharist, *"many of His disciples returned to their former way of life and no longer accompanied Him"* (Jn 6:66).

The Apparitions after the Message of the 18th of October 1961

The idea that the 18th of October meant *"the death of Garabandal"* became so widespread that two days later, on the 20th, Jacinta is heard in *ecstasy* saying: *"Nobody believes us any more, you know?... So you can do a very big miracle so that many will believe again..."* The Virgin, however, seems not remotely

305 LAURENTIN, R., *Apariciones actuales de la Virgen María*, Madrid, 1991, 205.
306 IGLESIAS, M., *La Palabra y las palabras. Pequeño vocabulario hebreo para uso espiritual*, Madrid, 2013, 15.
307 Cf. CARD. RATZINGER, J., "*Comentario Teológico*" en *Documentos sobre «El Mensaje de Fátima»*, June 26, 2000.
308 LANÚS, S., *Madre de Dios y Madre Nuestra. Fátima, Ámsterdam y Garabandal*, Madrid, 2013, 129.

surprised. And in response to the child's anxiety, She merely smiles and considers the matter settled with three brief words: *"They will believe."*[309]

Here begins a new phase for the *apparitions*, a true *winter*. There can be no doubt that the 18th of October 1961 is one of the crucial moments in the story of Garabandal: so many, who waited so long for it, feel horribly let down when the enormous expectations—which were totally unfounded, let it be said—were left unfulfilled. A message had been promised, but the flame is quenched because the people expected more. In *Lourdes*, although on a lesser scale, the spectators are also disappointed when they see *Saint Bernadette*, in one of her trances, begin to eat grass and *"wash herself"* with mud. In that moment, *"nearly everyone took her for a poor deranged wretch."*[310]

Despite the negative prognostics and the great disappointment of the 18th of October, the pilgrims continue to come to Garabandal in great numbers throughout the following months. In fact, "during 1962, the frequent apparitions continued,"[311] in the same pattern of *ecstasies and marches* as seen during the first year of *apparitions*. There would even be two great novelties after *the message*, closely related to it:

1. The Rosaries at Dawn

On the 4th of November 1961, just fifteen days after the publication of *the message*, *the Virgin* commends a new task to the children: to start getting up early to pray a Rosary at dawn in the *Calleja* every day. *"Jacinta and Mari Cruz went at six in the*

---

[309] PESQUERA, 2004, 266.
[310] *Ib.*
[311] LANÚS, S., *Madre de Dios y Madre Nuestra. Fátima, Ámsterdam y Garabandal,* Madrid, 2013, 130.

morning," Conchita writes, *"but She [the Lady] told me to go at five in the morning, and I did, because the Virgin always wants us to do penance."*[312] This, as of now, will be a constant in Garabandal. The girls, not in ecstasy, begin to lead an intense prayer life, with penance: at all hours and in all weather, unprotected from the inclemencies of a hard climate in a mountain village.

The children will faithfully persevere in their response to this desire of the *apparition*, in spite of their tender age, the winter weather descending upon the village and without the aid of mystical raptures. Jacinta testifies to the sacrifice entailed by *the Virgin's* request in a letter dated January 3, 1962:

> *We have just come back from praying the Rosary to the Virgin, Mari Cruz and I. Yesterday we had a very bad morning: there was such a stream of water coming down that we almost couldn't kneel down... Now, since it's not snowing, it's fine.*[313]

The dark awakening of the second day of the year had been accompanied by a stormy front; the rain fell so implacably over the surrounding heights that the water streamed down the *Calleja* and the early risers cannot find a stone in the current for their bended knees. *What a picture of prayer! What a Rosary, with the dismal hum of the monotonous and ubiquitous symphony of the downpour!* And this picture is repeated, in diverse forms, for many days.

The first words of *the message* of the 18th of October are very present here: *"You must make many sacrifices, do much penance."* And yet, *the apparition* does not place the accent or purpose of its visit in the penances of the girls. Conchita learns as much in an *ecstasy* in this same time period:

---

[312] *Diario de Conchita,* 63.
[313] PESQUERA, 2004, 322.

One day in an apparition of *the Virgin*, we were wearing a *cilicio*, but very loosely, and, so that She would realize we were wearing it (we had it around our waists), we touched it from time to time. [Eventually] She told us:

"Yes, I know you are wearing it, but that is not exactly what I ask of you, nor what most pleases me, but rather, fidelity in the ordinary life".[314]

The apparition, which has asked the girls for sacrifices which would not be small for a fervent adult, here gives them the key to understand their value: those penances are not the end that God awaits of them; they are a valuable means, but only a means, for carrying out God's authentic plan of love, an aid to dispose the soul to fidelity, to love and humility. And if instead of humility the sacrifices provoke vanity in the little ones, then *"they do not please God"*: they are useless. God awaits more of them. *The Virgin* will repeat this tirelessly: "She said it to us so many times: *"Fidelity in the ordinary life."*[315]

2. The Mystical Communions

The other great novelty of *the apparitions* after the 18th of October is the *mystical Communions* of *the seers* in their trances. *The Angel* had instructed the children in this matter at the beginning: *"The Archangel Saint Michael had given us unconsecrated hosts at the beginning of the apparitions... to teach us how to receive communion properly. One day he told us to go early to the Pines without having eaten."* That day, the 1st of May 1962, the little ones receive *Communion* from his hands for the first time. As of then, Conchita writes, *"He gave us Communion for a long time."*[316]

---

[314] *Ib.*, 293.
[315] *Ib.*, 298.
[316] *Diario de Conchita*, 62-63; Cf. PÉREZ, R., 1991, 29.

In Fatima, the same thing happened after 1916. An Angel, to prepare the little shepherds for the visit of the Lady, gives them Communion, saying: *"Make reparation for the offenses of ungrateful men and console your God."*[317] In Garabandal, *the Angel* also speaks to the children when he brings them Communion: *"Pray the 'I confess' and consider that you are going to receive God."*[318] Afterwards, he always invites them *to give thanks* and to recite with him a prayer that he himself had taught them: *"Soul of Christ."*

The Communions occur often, but only on days when there is no Mass in the village; so that the girls are not left without the Eucharist. This explains something that happened to Conchita one day—June 19, 1962—when she was in *the Pines* waiting for *the Angel* to receive communion. Dr. Ortiz's sister in law tells that she was waiting for *the ecstasy* with Conchita and her mother:

> *We were praying and waiting; but there was a long delay. Her mother looked down the slope and saw someone in front of her house that looked like a friar or priest... In fact, it was a Franscisan Father* [Fr. Felix Larrazábal]; *he celebrated Mass and gave us communion. Her mother remarked: "That explains the long wait above! Whenever there's a priest to give communion, she doesn't receive from the Angel."*[319]

Thus, *the Communions* indicate the central importance of the Eucharist and of the priesthood, indicated also in *the message* of October 18th, 1961 (*"You must make many sacrifices, do much penance, and visit the Blessed Sacrament"*).

> [*The Virgin*] told us once—Conchita writes—*"If you were to see an Angel and a priest together, you should first venerate the priest."*[320]

---

[317] LUCÍA DE FÁTIMA, *Memorias*, Fátima, 1999, 63.
[318] *Diario de Conchita*, 64; also 62 and 66.
[319] PESQUERA, 2004, 378.
[320] PESQUERA, 2004, 293.

The dignity of the priesthood is held very high in Garabandal. This is totally in line with the Tradition of the Church: the priest has the same dignity as Christ; He is *alter Cristus*, another Christ. Therefore his dignity surpasses even that of the angels. The girls in Garabandal, without theology, time and again express a fundamental doctrine and excellent practice, in submission to the Hierarchy of the Church and in continuity with the Council, which proposes the same doctrine (cf. *LG* 10b).

In 1965, a new message will insist in the same arguments: *sacrifices, the priesthood, the tabernacles...* pointing to Garabandal's profoundly *Eucharistic spirituality*. And we have not yet recounted one of the most extraordinary phenomena of *the apparitions*: a *"miracle,"* the protagonist of which is precisely the Eucharist.

II

The *"Miracle"* of the Visible Communion

The spectators very soon express doubts about the *ecstatic Communions* narrated by the girls. Conchita records as much in her *Diary*:

When we told this [the ecstatic Communions] *to the people, some people didn't believe it, above all the priests, because they said that the Angel cannot consecrate. When we saw the Angel again we mentioned what the people were saying and he answered us that he took the consecrated Hosts from the tabernacles of the world. We repeated this afterwards to the people, but some still doubted.*[321]

These *doubts* do not take into account something already mentioned: the approved apparitions of Fatima and an

---

[321] *Ib.*, 64.

irreproachable precedent of these *mystical Communions*: in the autumn of 1916, during the third apparition, the *"Angel of Peace"* gives Communion to *the three shepherd children;*[322] an Angel, in Fatima just as in Garabandal. This proves two things: one, the orthodoxy of the Communions of Garabandal (since the case of Fatima is approved); second, that the Cantabrian *village girls*, if they know of Fatima, it is only superficially, since they do not use it to argue with the public, when it would have been a definitive argument.[323] But in Garabandal the people distrust. And *the seers*, in the face of so much incredulity, do not know what to do. They only insist to *the Virgin* and *the Angel "that they perform a miracle."* In fact, during this time the little ones repeat this request often: *"Even if it's just a little miracle, like making us fly...*[or] *that the night turn to day...* "[But] *the Virgin*—Conchita writes—*becomes serious when we ask her for a miracle."* The Lady will always respond to these petitions the same way: *"They will believe, they will believe."* The Angel, however, eventually yields to the children's insistence, since on the 22nd of June 1962, he makes this announcement to Conchita: *"I am going to perform a miracle, not I, but God through my intercession and yours."*[324]

Conchita incorrectly employs the word *"intercession"* in her *Diary* entry—not the only time she will misuse this word—but from the sentence itself it is clear that she does not mean that with her intercession *"they will obtain a miracle,"* but that the *miracle* will be realized *"through them."* It is an error of redaction (like others that we have seen, of which the girl has many, owing to her lack of learning) but still, it is expressly underlined that the subject of the action is God: *"I will perform... not I, but God."*

---

[322] Cf. BARTHAS, C., *Las Apariciones de Fátima*, Barcelona, 1955, 23.

[323] Cf. SOUSA E SILVA, M. F., *Los pastorcitos de Fátima*, Madrid, 2008, 153.

[324] *Diario de Conchita*, 62-63. 125; PESQUERA, 2004, 76, 385.

Here we find a novelty: the destinatory of this *new proof* seems directly to be the public itself; it is no longer *the seers* who will witness a new extraordinary experience but the onlookers. Once again, we see the prominence of the *interaction of the public with the apparition* that is so typical of Garabandal. We saw this in *the vision's* kissing the religious objects of the faithful. Now, the public will receive a new grace: a confirmation of the apparitions, which will also be a call to pay attention to the *message*. *The apparition* seems to wish to remedy the widespread confusion since the day of the publication of the *message*. Everyone will be able to see this miracle.

Conchita relates the words of the *Angel,* explaining what it will consist of: "*When I [Saint Michael] give you the Holy Communion, the Sacred Host will be seen on the tongue.*"[325] Nobody, then, will feel deceived or surprised by the event. However, Conchita responds with concern to the *Angel's* grand announcement: "*So then it's just a mini-miracle!*" He smiles at the child's candor, but says no more.[326] And *the little village-girl* was left unanswered; she will always refer to this *Eucharistic miracle* with a name that was destined to become popular: "*el milagruco*" or, even more colloquially, "*el milagrucu.*" She was hoping for a "*bigger*" miracle.

The following day, Saturday, *the Virgin herself* confirms the *Angel's* announcement to Conchita and on the 29th of June, *the seers* learn the date: the 18th of July.[327] The girls receive permission from the apparition to announce the "*milagruco.*" So from that day on, they write all the letters they can; very simple, brief letters to announce the miracle and its date. Some of these letters conclude

---

325 *Ib.*
326 *Ib.*
327 Cf. PESQUERA, 2004, 386.

with a poignant petition: *"Will you believe it then?"*[328] This is the hope of the little ones.

Dr. Ortiz, after receiving one of these letters, quickly journeys to the village from Santander to find out more. He speaks alone with Conchita, and frankly tells her: "Conchita, I don't know if you realize the importance of all this. A miracle pre-announced with a set date is an enormous miracle (and added to the miracle is another value certainly of equal importance: that of the *'prophecy'*)."[329] But Conchita remains unimpressed: *"Well, to me it seems like a mini-miracle."*[330] She does comprehend, however, that *the Virgin* wants her to work to make it known. And so she writes the letters.

There is no shortage of opposition: faced with the possibility of another great crowd flocking to the village like the day of the *first message*, many hold the opinion that the girls should not be allowed to promote anything; that like the last time, it will be a resounding failure and will provoke a calamity. Fr. Valentín, for example, when he finds out that Conchita is advertizing it, orders her not to send any more letters. To him and others who insist likewise, *"I told them,"* she writes, *"that the Virgin and the Angel told me to announce the miracle; but the people of the village didn't believe it."*[331] The atmosphere around *the seers* at this point is tense.

Expectant Incredulity

In the village *"they didn't believe it"*: they are simple people who concede more authority to the voices that come from outside,

---

[328] ANDREU, R. M., *Nota 79* in *Diario de Conchita*, 65.
[329] PESQUERA, 2004, 395.
[330] *Ib.*
[331] *Diario de Conchita*, 65.

who often speak without knowledge, than to the inexplicable events that they themselves have witnessed. The result is a climate of great confusion. María González, Jacinta's mother, gives proof of this in a letter addressed to Fr. Laffineur in September of 1963: "*I do believe when I see an ecstasy; when the ecstasy ends, I don't believe any more.*"[332] Many others find themselves in this state of confusión.

In spite of everything, and yet unsurprisingly, the crowds begin to flock to Garabandal days before the 18th of July, which in 1962 fell on a Wednesday. The previous 18th of October had also fallen on a Wednesday, but this had not impeded *more than five thousand people* from getting there. This time the numbers may be even higher. The calculations vary "from five to six thousand." Pepe Díez affirms: "I was present on both occasions, and I would say there were even more than that."[333] Díez himself was hoping on the 18th of July to see something even more convincing, although two circumstances suggest that there won't be a *miracle*: one, the party atmosphere that reigns in the vilage; another, the presence of priests, because on several previous occasions when there were priests or an improper atmosphere, the girls had lost *the vision and reception of Communion from the Angel*. This day, however, was going to be an exception. Conchita's mother, who fears the worst from the enormous crowd, worriedly asks the young laborer to accompany her daughter:

"*Won't you accompany my daughter?*—Aniceta says—*She's in danger of being killed, crushed or trampled upon.*" "*Oh! How hard that is to do!*—responds Pepe Díez—*How can I accompany her with all the people? ... [But] trust me; I'll be there from seven in the morning until the hour it happens.*"[334]

---

332 PESQUERA, 2004, 396.
333 DÍEZ CANTERO, J., "*Testigo de Garabandal,*" in PÉREZ, R., 1991, 247.
334 *Ib.*

In fact, nobody, not even *the seers*, knows what time or where *the miracle* will happen, but everyone wants to be in the front row when it does. The wait is prolonged because nothing happens all day. Only at around twenty minutes before two o'clock in the morning, in her own home, does the child fall into *ecstasy*. She makes her way out onto the street and begins to walk among the huge crowd of people packing the village. Pepe Díez takes up the story:

> [The child] *began to give the crucifix to one person after another. I was sticking close to Conchita, okay. There were people in front, beside, behind, some falling over, others shouting, others walking over them trying to avoid something happening, all very difficult... because people were bunching together and falling over; everyone wanted to see... I was left, well... without clothes, without my belt... Things were taken off me, people grabbed onto me to get closer to the child, trying to take the place I was heading towards; without bad intentions. But I stiffened up as much as I could, until it got to the point where* [I thought]... *"Man, they're going to kill me!"*[335]

In the midst of the "*avalanche*" of people, however, Díez is not alone in his task; he has the support of other family members of the child and villagers, although no one is as close as he: "*Some were falling, others pulling away, others... It was war! A war in peace.*"[336] At last, the child falls to her knees on the street. And Díez is right beside her:

> *I was carrying a flashlight, a very powerful one, ready for whatever might happen and they hadn't taken it from me; I was holding on tight to it with great difficulty. The moment when the child fell to her knees there were all kinds of people there, they all remained still on the ground... Everyone is gathered around in a very difficult place, but with*

---

335 *Ib.*, 248.
336 *Ib.*

a lot of humility. Then you noticed that the people weren't pushing, no. That's why I say that people behaved quite well there.[337]

Conchita, kneeling in the middle of the crowd, says something to *the vision*; but her whisper is almost inaudible in the murmur of the still agitated crowd. Little by little silence descends; finally, *the seer* puts out her tongue. Under the powerful light that Díez focuses on her, the child is perfectly illumined in the midst of a crowd of people in the dark. All who are watching observe her tongue, which appears clean, with nothing on it, in the posture of receiving communion:

> Far from looking ridiculous or vulgar, [her gesture of receiving] was strikingly mystical and moving. Suddenly, without knowing how, without realizing it—another witness writes—without Conchita remotely changing her position, the Sacred Host appeared on her tongue. It was totally unexpected. It didn't give the impression of being deposited there; rather, one could say that it sprang up at a speed superior to the perception of human sight.[338]

The crowd is stunned, immersed in absolute silence. The pre-announced miracle has happened before the eyes of all. *The seer* doesn't move; the host is visible and remains there for some minutes; although for those present it seems only an instant. One of them, a non-believer, Alejandro Damians, come from Barcelona just to accompany his family, has an 8 mm video camera. His cousin, who owned it, asked him to take it and he did so to please him. He had followed the child in the crowd at a certain distance, with many people in the way; in that darkness, he would not have been able to record anything. But when the child fell to her knees:

[337] *Ib.*

[338] DAMIANS, A., *Testigo de Garabandal* en FUNDACIÓN HM, *Garabandal*, Lumezzane, 2013, www.garabandal.it (latest revision: July 18, 2013).

Her fall was so unexpected—he himself narrates—that the mob of people, by its own movement, went right past her; this stroke of luck freed me up from the people in front of me who were separating me from Conchita, and I unexpectedly found myself to her right and half a meter from her face... The pushing decreased, so that in the end there was relative calm.[339]

Although he has never used a camera in his life, he succeeds in recording the event. When the film was revealed, almost seventy 8 mm photograms in black and white appear, technically defective, but sufficiently clear to perceive the event. The presence of a host on the child's tongue may be discerned, and Damians' recording constitutes a visible record of the miracle. The Bishop of Santander, His Excellency Eugenio Beitia Aldazábal, promptly expresses interest in this film and writes to Damians soliciting a copy, given that *"it could be of great interest and service to the Church."*[340] Damians presented it to the Bishop along with a written report relating the details of what occurred.[341]

Another witness, Miguel González, Conchita's brother, was situated right beside her. His account coincides with that of Damians.[342]

Another, Benjamín Gómez, from the neighboring locality of Potes, states:

I was a little over a hand's reach from the child. I saw that there was nothing, nothing, on the tongue. The girl didn't make the slightest movement. Suddenly I was looking at the Host: white and shining... I can assure that she didn't move her hands, or her tongue, nothing... We

---

[339] *Ib.*
[340] *Ib.*
[341] Cf. LANÚS, S., *Madre de Dios y Madre Nuestra. Fátima, Ámsterdam y Garabandal*, Madrid, 2013, 135.
[342] Cf. PESQUERA, 2004, 415.

still had time to contemplate the phenomenon without haste, and there were lots of us. I didn't believe until that day.[343]

There are many testimonies, all alike: in the child's opened mouth, on her tongue, a white host was seen to appear. Even though it was a cloudy night, the scene and the protagonist appear clearly lit up for a prolonged period of time—we know by whom—and that's not all: among those present, this fact produced not so much the joy of having seen something extraordinary, as the t*remendous impression* of an encounter *"with the true and living God."*[344] That is how Damians describes it, having come to the event with no faith:

> It is imposible to describe the impression I felt in that moment and that I feel to this day when I recall it. Surprise, amazement, confusion... [A] wonderful impression... Tears of joy, of satisfaction, of happiness, of love...[345]

Another exceptional witness, a non-believing doctor from France, Dr. Jean Caux, converted in that same moment, in front of the *miracle*: *"*[From that night on] *I have known what God is and what He wants of me."*[346] Benjamín Gómez and many other witnesses express themselves in similar terms.

When describing their experience, all coincide in mentioning *"something"* that goes beyond the simple fact of *"seeing the Host."* The *milagruco* is accompanied by a grace that transcends the expectations of the witnesses. These abundant graces of conversion that come with *the miracle* re-ignite the amazed admiration of many in Garabandal. And thus the *ill-fated message*

---

[343] Testimony quoted in LANÚS, S., *Madre de Dios y Madre Nuestra. Fátima, Ámsterdam y Garabandal,* Madrid, 2013, 135.

[344] DAMIANS, A., *Testigo de Garabandal* en FUNDACIÓN HM, *Garabandal,* Lumezzane, 2013, www.garabandal.it (latest revision: July 18, 2013).

[345] *Ib.*

[346] *Ib.*

of the previous October is also recovered; a *message* which, together with love for the Eucharist, had requested what is now achieved, extraordinarily, by *the miracle* of the *visible Communion*: the *conversion* of the heart.

Santiago Lanús, an Argentinian scholar whose recent work (2013) contains abundant direct testimonies, including from *the* seers themselves, after telling the story of the *"milagruco,"* concludes: "There can be no doubt that this event was very important for the credibility of all that was happening in Garabandal."[347] For many, however, this did not seem so clear. And after the 18th of June, some would take a more distant position towards Garabandal.

The Repercussions of the "Milagruco"

After the communion, while still *in ecstasy, the Virgin,* according to Conchita, confirmed her worst fears: *"Not all will believe!"* So it was:

A Franciscan Father, Fr. Justo, saw the miracle but didn't believe it— Conchita writes—*and he said that he hadn't seen it and it was a lie. That it was I who did it all. After two or three days I received a letter from that same Father asking my forgiveness for having thought that way. He said it was the devil who tempted him. A few days after that letter, three Fathers came on Fr. Justo's behalf... They told me that this Franciscan Father had spent many days and nights unable to sleep, thinking about the Sacred Host, but in the end he had reacted well and accepted what happened, believing everything.*[348]

However, as soon as *"people began to doubt (since everyone was saying that it was I who had put the Host on my tongue),"* there was

---

347 LANÚS, S., *Madre de Dios y Madre Nuestra. Fátima, Ámsterdam y Garabandal*, Madrid, 2013, 135.
348 *Diario de Conchita*, 66, 68.

no going back. The notable absence of the *Official Committee of Experts* was also unhelpful. So, "from these events on," García de la Riva affirms, "the idea began to take root [among the people] that it had all been a fraud."[349] So the 18th of July 1962, which could have been a definitive clarification of the mystery of Garabandal, ended up confusing matters even more. What for some was a reliable proof, for others was the unmasking of a fraud. Some returned to God filled with stupor, others saw no more than collective hysteria. And it is in these waters that the children will have to learn to navigate from this moment on.

Nearing the End of the Apparitions

Between the distrust of some and the enthusiasm of others, *the apparitions* continue. The year 1962 had been a *peak* period in the process of Garabandal. And after the *"milagruco"* of July 18, the following months unfold with countless *apparitions* of *the Virgin* and numerous *"mystical Communions."* The abundance of *Communions* during this time accentuates even more the Eucharistic character of the phenomena. Even so, the following month of September will be seen by history as the month of a great *prophetic announcement*.

Effectively, in September 1962, Conchita reveals that a very particular kind of *"miracle"* will take place in Garabandal. In the following months *the seer* gives more details, indicating the enormous proportions of this *"miracle,"* similar to those of the *miracle of the sun* in Fatima, which was seen by more than 70,000 people, many of them non-believers.[350] In Garabandal, *the seer* knows the date when this *miracle* must occur and will announce it

---

[349] GARCÍA DE LA RIVA, J. R., *Memorias de un cura de aldea en Garabandal*, Santander, 2011, 111; PESQUERA, 2004, 425.
[350] Cf. PESQUERA, 2004, 572.

when it is near. And, as we will see later, today that date cannot be very far away.

If the sense of expectation is very much alive today—on the internet there are hundreds of pages dedicated to the *miracle foretold* in Garabandal—it was also alive in 1962. But all eyes were not fixed solely on this: the whole matter of the *"miracle"* began to appear to all as a clear indication of the end of the long process of many exceptional phenomena. With the *"miracle"* in sight, the end of *the apparitions* also became thinkable, because surely nobody was under the illusion that all that could continue indefinitely.

In fact, almost at the same time as news of the *"miracle"* comes—in September 1962—the *seers* begin to experience a decrease in the frequency of *the ecstasies*. First the littlest of them, Mari Cruz, ceases to see *the Virgin* that same month of September; then Jacinta and Mari Loli in the first weeks of January 1963, and a few days later, on the 20th of January, feast of Saint Sebastian, Conchita ceases to see *the Blessed Virgin*.

The Locutions: A Voice that Speaks without Words

The apparitions, suspended from January 1963, will be "substituted by *inner locutions*, from Jesus and from Mary."[351] This change does not occur without difficulties. It arises out of a real *crisis*. When *the seers* stop having *the visions* in 1963, they also lose for the first time their habitual certainty about *the apparitions*. Thus commences the phase known as that of "the *denials*." Each and all deny partially, contradicting each other for the first time since the beginning. *The Virgin*, Conchita mentions, had foretold these *denials* at the outset.[352]

---

351 LANÚS, S., *Madre de Dios y Madre Nuestra. Fátima, Ámsterdam y Garabandal,* Madrid, 2013, 138.
352 Cf. *Diario de Conchita,* 70, 72.

The locutions begin for Conchita in March 1963, when she most doubts *the apparitions*: *"One day,"* she writes, *"in my bedroom, doubting if the miracle would happen, I heard a voice say to me: 'Conchita, do not doubt that my Son will perform a Miracle.'"*[353] The discernment of this experience reflected in her *Diary* shows the spiritual maturity gained in just over a year of *apparitions*:

> *I felt this voice in my interior, but as clearly as if it were with my ears, even better than if it had been with words; it left me with such a deep peace and joy, more even than when I saw the Virgin.*[354]

Conchita will always manifest this preference for the *locutions*. In March 1963, for example, after two years of *locutions* without any *apparition*, she says: *"I like seeing the Virgin very much; but I like it more when She speaks to me interiorly, because She seems to be inside me."*[355]

This fully coincides with the teachings of *mystical theology*, which supports this preference: in the genuine ecstasy the great intensity of the mystical union renders the poor human body incapable of resisting the experience and it is left in a state of suspension.[356] This suspension, which seems spectacular, is, however, no more than *a corporal flaccidity*. This flaccidity, according to Royo-Marín, "disappears in the high summits of transformative union, when the soul is accustomed to receiving these strong divine communications without the body falling into the ecstatic faint."[357] Thus, in the mystical life, the soul passes to *inner locutions*, which "are distinct from the visions insofar as the locutions are formulas which express statements or desires,"[358]

---

353 *Ib.*
354 *Ib.*
355 PESQUERA, 2004, 542.
356 Cf. ROYO-MARÍN, A., *Teología de la perfección cristiana*, Madrid, 1958, 673.
357 *Ib.*
358 *Ib.*, 819.

not realized through *images* of any kind; hence *the locutions* can be captured in three ways: by hearing, by the imagination or the intelligence.[359]

In the light of the description in Conchita's *Diary*, the Garabandal *locutions* seem to be of the *intellectual* kind, since words are not used (the voice is heard, she says, "*even better than with words*"), ruling out the theological categories of auricular or imaginary locutions. They are *intellectual locutions*, "directly perceived by the intelligence, without mediation of the senses or the imagination, similar to how the angels communicate thoughts."[360] As Saint Teresa says, "*It is speech without words, the language of the homeland.*"[361]

Then, within these *intellectual locutions*, there are three sub-types: those of Garabandal do not seem to belong to the first type, *successive locutions*, given that they occur surprisingly, and not while the children are in prayer. Nor do they appear to be *formal locutions*, since these, although they occur without prior recollection, "Do not remove repugnance and difficulty from the soul, but rather increase it."[362] This is not the case in Garabandal, in which the little ones receive so much peace from *the locutions*. Those of Garabandal "substantially imprint in the soul that which they signify."[363] This happens to Conchita, who feels interiorly strengthened after receiving the *locution*:

> "*Conchita, do not doubt that my Son will perform a Miracle*"... *It left me with such a deep peace and joy, more even than when I saw the Virgin.*[364]

---

[359] *Ib.*
[360] Cf. GARRIGOU-LAGRANGE, R., *Las tres edades de la vida interior*, Madrid, 1995, vol. II, 1183.
[361] SAINT TERESA OF AVILA, *Life*, ch. XXVII.
[362] GARRIGOU-LAGRANGE, R., *Las tres edades de la vida interior*, Madrid, 1995, vol. II, 1185.
[363] *Ib.*
[364] *Diario de Conchita*, 72.

So, following Saint John of the Cross, those of Garabandal must be categorized within the third and highest type of the locutions, as *substantial locutions*, given that in them:

> The soul does or desires nothing... in doing what they say, because God never says these substantial words for the soul to perform them, but for them to work in it.[365]

In this type of locutions, the Carmelite saint and Doctor explains, the soul "neither suffers nor fears any deception; because neither the intelligence nor the devil can interfere in this... And so, these substantial words greatly aid the soul's union with God. Blessed is the soul to whom God speaks."[366] Therefore, the step to *the locutions* of Garabandal points to spiritual growth in *the seers*, although only Conchita and Loli experience them. And they will be less frequent than *the ecstasies*, with up to a month elapsing from one to another.

Among *the locutions* there are truly beautiful dialogues; such as that of the 20th of July 1963, when Conchita (then 13 years old), in thanksgiving after the Mass, asks the Lord for the *Cross*:

> And Jesus, when I asked this of Him, answered me: "Yes, I will give you the Cross." And with much emotion I asked Him for more...[367]

Little by little, *the locutions* point towards the end of *the extraordinary events*. However, this does not affect the traffic of people. The news of *the apparitions* "spread throughout the world and new visitors unceasingly arrive in the isolated village."[368] The influx of strangers was not reduced by the cessation of *the*

---

[365] SAINT JOHN OF THE CROSS, *Ascent to Mount Carmel*, 1. II, ch. XXXI, 2; Cf. –, *Living flame of love*, cant. I, v. 1.

[366] *Ib.*

[367] *Diario de Conchita*, 81.

[368] PESQUERA, 2004, 541.

ecstasies or by *the denials* of the children. Further novelties would soon occur.

III

The Second Message

On the 8th of December 1964, when the Immaculate Conception is celebrated from which her own name is derived, Conchita has an *ecstasy*. It is the first one since the 20th of January 1963, almost two years before. This new *ecstasy* is not a one-time event: there will soon be more. On the 1st of January, *the Lady* makes an important announcement to Conchita: on the 18th of June she will receive *a new message*. A new stage begins for *the apparitions* with the same expectancy, confusion and contradictions as before.

Strangers have continued to arrive throughout this time. In fact, they never stopped coming in spite of the cessation of *apparitions*. However, there is a negative atmosphere in the village and many express open distrust towards the whole business of *the apparitions*. Now, with this new announcement, it becomes clear that, effectively, there was *"in everyone a badly dissimulated desire that, at last, something would happen."*[369]

No one knows quite what to think. And this situation will be reflected in the text of the coming *message*, *"the last"* of Garabandal. *The last one, the apparition* affirms, because *"scarcely any heed has been paid to the other one* [the message of October 1961]."[370] The imminent end of the *apparitions* is now announced.

---

[369] LAFFINEUR, M. - LE PELLETIER, M.T., *La estrella en la montaña*, Tielt, 1967, 64.
[370] CONCHITA GONZÁLEZ, *Carta al P. Laffineur*, Garabandal, February 2, 1965; PESQUERA, 2004, 536.

This end is tied expressly to the irresponsible reaction given to *the apparitions*, especially to the *first message*, of which it is explicitly said: *"scarcely any heed has been paid"* to it. This recalls the conclusion of Matthew's account of Jesus' visit to Nazareth: *"He did not work many mighty deeds there because of their lack of faith"* (Mt 13:58).

The announcement of something extraordinary regenerates, as one might expect, an air of anticipation around Garabandal, with the result that, when the date arrives, the 18th of June, fourth anniversary of the beginning of *the apparitions*, the village is packed full. Compared to the previous occasions, this time, indisputably, *"strangers abundantly predominate."*[371] The presence of two large vehicles of technical equipment owned by NO-DO (a State news agency) is also noteworthy. They were there to provide an audiovisual report about *the apparitions*.

Conchita—now seventeen years old—spends the whole day at the door of her house. She finds herself unable to stay inside knowing that there are so many people so uncomfortable out on the street. So, she spends endless hours responding to the thousand questions and requests of the grateful crowd milling about in front of the house in the constant coming and going of people. The day evolves in this way until nightfall: "and we don't know," Laffineur speculates, "if she [Conchita, throughout the day] had time to eat much more than a piece of bread." *The seer* is surely thinking of the counsels of *the Lady* in the early days: *"Be well-mannered and, if you can, try to respond to the people's questions"*.[372]

---

371 PESQUERA, 2004, 546; Cf. LAFFINEUR, M. - LE PELLETIER, M.T., *La estrella en la montaña*, Tielt, 1967, 67.
372 PESQUERA, 2004, 110.

Only at around fifteen minutes before midnight does Conchita head out through the crowd. It had been announced that *the ecstasy* would take place in *the Calleja*. In a completely normal state she advances through the crowd packing the streets. She is accompanied by some priests and six Civil Guards. Reaching the place indicated, she falls to her knees on the jagged stones of the path. *The ecstasy* has begun. It is an emotional moment. Conchita's eyes are fixed upwards. She laughs and pronounces words in a very soft voice; but immediately her expression totally changes and tears roll down her cheeks to the ground. Her voice, faltering and breathless, can scarcely be heard; with the result that few words can be understood. However, all agree on these:

"Priests?... Bishops?... The 2nd of July?..."[373]

Finally, Conchita makes the Sign of the Cross with slow majesty and then quickly raises her hands to her face, protecting her dazzled eyes from the powerful spotlights. *The ecstasy* had ended. It has lasted some twelve or thirteen minutes, like so many other times. Now, "the six Civil Guards struggle to protect her from the crowd."[374] Everyone wants to see her up close, to ask her about *the message*. But she remains silent. *The message* will not be made public until the following morning. They will have to wait.

The following morning, at around mid-day, at the door of *the seer's* house, a priest reads aloud a note handed to him by Conchita, written in her own handwriting. This priest, Luis Jesús Luna, from Zaragoza, had come to the village with doubts; now, after what he has seen the previous night, he feels privileged. He holds the note-paper, with its little spelling mistakes and even smudges. He reads it forcefully, and such is the impression it

373 LAFFINEUR, M. - LE PELLETIER, M.T., *La estrella en la montaña*, Tielt, 1967, 70-71.
374 PESQUERA, 2004, 553.

makes on him that he will keep it forever *"as a precious relic,"* to use his own words.[375]

After reading the original text, it is read again in French, in English and, very probably, also in Italian.[376] This time the promulgation leaves nothing to desire. The publication is invested with great solemnity. In fact, *the message* itself invites that it be taken seriously:

> As my message of October 18 has not been complied with and has not been made known to the world, I am advising you that this is the last one. Before, the cup was filling up. Now it is flowing over. Many priests are on the road to perdition and are taking many souls with them. Less and less importance is being given to the Eucharist. You should turn the wrath of God away from yourselves by your efforts. I, your mother, through the intercession of Saint Michael the Archangel, ask you to amend your lives. You are now receiving the last warnings. I love you very much and do not want your condemnation. Pray to us with sincerity and we will grant your requests. You should make more sacrifices. Think about the Passion of Jesus.[377]

A Chilling Message

The message is not given by *the Virgin*. It is clearly *She* who is speaking in it (*"I, your Mother"*), but *the Angel* brings it. *The Lady* herself will reveal the reason for this later to Conchita, in the last of *the apparitions* of Garabandal:

> Do you know, Conchita, why I did not come personally on the 18th of June to give you the message for the world? Because it pained me to tell you these things. But you had to know them, for your good, and, if you comply with the message, for God's glory. I love you very much and I desire your salvation: to gather you together here in heaven around the

---

375 LUNA, L. J., *Garabandal*, Zaragoza, 1972, 15.
376 PESQUERA, 2004, 556.
377 *Diario de Conchita*, 86

Father and the Son and the Holy Spirit! ... You, Conchita, will you respond to us?[378]

That *the Virgin* does not directly give *the message* is in itself a sign of its seriousness. The content of the message reflects this reality in its three parts:

I. Denunciation of the World's Lamentable Moral Situation

The message points to the progressive loss of spiritual life and the scandalous marginalization of Christ, even within the Church. It is striking to note that Pope Paul VI, in the same years, expresses this same preoccupation:

> There are some who spread certain opinions on Eucharistic worship that perturb the souls of the faithful, engendering no small confusion about truths of faith.[379]

Those who commit this offense cannot be the agnostics or the atheists, who have never believed in the Eucharist. Garabandal, like Blessed Paul VI, is directed to believers; it does not present external challenges for the Church to combat (as in Fatima with *Communism*) but rather a *crisis* in the very heart of the Church: *"The Eucharist is being given less and less importance."*

This *"inner crisis"* has a clear precedent in the *Modernist crisis* of the early 20th century. Its main promoters had all been clerics: Alfred Firmin Loisy, George Tyrrel, Herman Schell, Ernesto Buonaiuti; according to whom the Church, in order *to progress*, needed internal dissent, as a tension and counter to pull forward a *"weighed down institution"* tending towards *traditionalism*. Saint Pius X checks Modernism in 1907; but from 1968 onward the resurgence of the crisis is almost uncontainable. When Paul VI

---

[378] PESQUERA, 2004, 583
[379] PAUL VI, Encyclical Letter *Mysterium Fidei*, AAS 57 (1965) 755, *Sollicitudinis pastoralis et anxietatis causae.*

published the Encyclical *Humane Vitae,* diverse sectors within the Church claim the right for everyone to decide what is right and wrong *for himself,* despite what the entire Catholic Magisterium and moral teaching say. The following crisis spreads in overwhelming proportions and velocity to all ambits of faith and morals, marking the beginning of an *internal* disorder in the Church, which makes it all the more terrible. Dramatically, this disorder tends towards persecution, because, as Javier Paredes, Chair of the History Department in the University of Alcalá, affirms, "the coherence of Catholics who have made holiness the objective of their lives exposes not the atheists or the people without faith, or *the reds,* or the freemasons, but all of those lukewarm and schizophrenic Catholics who prefer the judgment of men to that of God."[380]

"And if we do not change, a great chastisement will come upon us"

Garabandal had already spoken of a *chastisement* in *the message* of 1961: *"The cup is already filling up, and if we do not change, a very great chastisement will come upon us."* Back then, this *warning* had almost passed unnoticed. People's attention was more focused on novelties and emotions than on performing *"many sacrifices, much penance, visiting the Blessed Sacrament."* Perhaps that is why the figure of the *"cup"* now reappears.

"The cup" symbolizes the tolerable measure of our sins. If in 1961 it was said that *the cup "was filling up,"* now—in 1965—the cup *"is overflowing";* that is, the measure has been reached. Garabandal denounces what Javier Sesé, Professor of the University of Navarre, denominates *"the strong advance of*

---

[380] Cf. PAREDES, J., *"Prologo"* in LANÚS, S., *Madre de Dios y Madre Nuestra,* Madrid, 2013, 10.

secularization"[381] in the Church, which will increase after the Council in unsuspected proportions. Sin is spreading... *and the cup is overflowing.* That is why *a chastisement* is announced; a phenomenon in profound continuity with Sacred Scriptures, where sin—in the Old as much as in the New Testament—is always joined to *a chastisement,* medicinal and temporal or eternal.[382]

"Priests, Bishops, and Cardinals"

The *message* makes a chilling statement: *"Many priests are on the way of perdition, bringing many souls with them."* Certainly at that time such a statement, even referring only to priests, is for many inadmissible. Aniceta, Conchita's mother, when the child gives this message, thinks: *"That bit about the priests is false; that's from the devil."* But she adds: *"In 1962 we thought that all priests are saints, and to say such a thing was tremendous. Afterwards how true it has turned out to be. How right the child was!."*[383]

But *the message* goes even further: it speaks also of Bishops and Cardinals. To be factual, on the day of publication of *the message*, only the word *priests* was read: *"Many priests are on the way of perdition."* That is how Conchita had transcribed it. However, there are many testimonies to prove that Conchita herself, overwhelmed, censored *the message* that day. The aforementioned Fr. Luna, who was about two meters away from Conchita during *the ecstasy*, clearly heard her ask *the vision* with an air of disbelief: *"Bishops! Bishops too?"*[384] Others also heard it.

[381] SESÉ, J., *Historia de la espiritualidad,* Pamplona, 2005, 300.
[382] Cf. IGLESIAS, M., *La Palabra y las palabras. Pequeño vocabulario hebreo para uso espiritual,* Madrid, 2013, 15, 38.
[383] ROJAS, A. M., *Letter to the author,* December 23, 2013.
[384] *Ib.,* 558; Cf. LUNA, L. J., *Garabandal,* Zaragoza, 1972, 15.

And *the seer* herself will later say it, for example, in a letter to the Jesuit Lucio Rodrigo of the University of Comillas:

> *On Thursday* [Conchita]... *confirmed to me in writing that in the message of the 18th of June the Angel explicitly included "Bishops and Cardinals." But afterwards came the inclination of the child's truly supernatural and inspired prudence, to silence these words (in the text of the message) because "this was a matter for the priests."*[385]

So it is: what then seemed inverosimile would soon be made known to the entire world through two channels *less* discreet than those of Garabandal. On the 5th of January 1971, the Pope himself, Blessed Paul VI, must raise his voice:

> Countless members of the faithful feel perturbed in their faith by an accumulation of ambiguities, uncertainties and doubts in essential matters... Men of perverse doctrine arise from among us to drag disciples after them.[386]

"From among us." The Pope thus refers discreetly to the sacred ministers: *Priests, Bishops and Cardinals.* His words echo *the message* of Garabandal.

II. Warning Concerning the Consequences of Sin

"You are already in the last warnings. This message is the last." The end of *the apparitions* seems to have been *"brought forward."* The *message* itself reveals the reason for this change of plans:

> As my message of October 18 has not been complied with and has not been made known to the world, I am advising you that this is the last one. Before, the cup was filling up. Now it is flowing over.

The apparitions end because of the disinterest in and sparse diffusion of *the message* of 1961. It is true that the Garabandal

---

[385] *Ib.*, 551.
[386] PAUL VI, Apostolic Exhortation *Quinque iam anni,* December 8, 1970, AAS 63 (1971) 98.

phenomenon "has become internationalized."[387] This will be recognized even by those most contrary to *the apparitions*. However, it is still clear that *the messages* of Garabandal were not given, early on or afterwards, an ample and open diffusion. Accusations immediately rain down upon it: of fanaticism, fraud, alarmism, millenarianism, panchristianity... all without any solid foundation, but they would impede the transmission of *the apparitions* from the beginning.[388]

"I love you very much and I do not want your condemnation." The whole message is focused on awakening souls to seek salvation, to come out of the superficial indifference that quashes God's voice and leads to *condemnation*.

III. Urgent Exhortation to Remedy the Situation

Simply and clearly, the new *message* reaffirms the content of *the first*: *"You must make many sacrifices, do much penance, and visit the Blessed Sacrament."*[389] Prayer and sacrifice are encouraged. The Eucharist is highlighted: in *the apparitions* this has already been the case, with *the daily mystical Communions of the seers*, the *"milagruco"* and the *first public message*. Now, the *second message* urges greater attention to the Eucharist in the Church, because *"less and less importance is being given to the Eucharist."*[390] The recent Magisterium similarly insists on this importance: *"The Church draws her life from the Eucharist,"* declares Saint John Paul II in the opening lines of his Encyclical

---

[387] LABARGA GARCÍA, F., *"La tradición mariofánica española,"* Estudios Marianos 72 (2009) 53.

[388] Marginal groups of unsound doctrine spring up around Garabandal after *the apparitions*. To reject Garabandal because of these groups would be wrong, not unlike rejecting the Gospel because of Christian sects; the existence of sects requires that the faithful be well-formed and prudent; it would be wrong to discard the Word of God because of the errors of some followers. Likewise, in Garabandal one must distinguish the *private revelation* from certain followers.

[389] *Ib.*, 42.

[390] *Ib.*, 86.

Letter *Ecclesia de Eucharistia.*[391] The Congregation for Divine Worship also points out the importance of giving all due reverence to the Blessed Sacrament:

> In an altogether particular manner, let everyone do all that is in their power to ensure that the Most Holy Sacrament of the Eucharist will be protected from any and every irreverence or distortion and that all abuses be thoroughly corrected. This is a *"most serious duty"* incumbent upon each and every one.[392]

So, *the message* anticipates the *"most serious"* concern later expressed by the Magisterium. It shares many other points with recent documents of the Church. Together with the Eucharist, *the message* indicates:

· the need for *penance*: *"You should make more sacrifices"*;
· *meditation*, especially of the Gospel: *"Think about the Passion of Jesus"*;
· *repentance* and the gravity of sin: *"Pray to us with sincerity and we will respond"*;
· the importance of the prayer of petition: *"Ask with constant prayer."*

Owing to the clear orthodoxy of these points, there is no need for further explanation. *The message* is an authentic exhortation to *conversion*: *"I, your mother, through the intercession of Saint Michael the Archangel, ask you to amend your lives."*[393] *The Lady* appears, once again, as Mother. And *Her message* is one of penance and conversion.

---

391 JOHN PAUL II, Encyclical Letter *Ecclesia de Eucharistia*, Rome, April 17, 2003, 1.
392 CONGREGATION FOR DIVINE WORSHIP AND THE DISCIPLINE OF THE SACRAMENTS, Instruction *Redemptionis sacramentum*, Rome, March 25, 2004, 183.
393 *Diario de Conchita*, 86. As in so many other occasions Conchita writes "intercession" instead of "mediation," mistaking the expression. Evidently, the idea that she is trying to transmit is: "through the Angel Saint Michael." The error has no theological connotation; it proceeds undoubtedly from her limited formation.

IV

The Last Apparition of the Virgin

The second message is more positively received by the public than the first, at least in part. After its publication, "the multitude that came to Garabandal from afar, left the village, generally speaking, quite consoled and encouraged."[394] Many felt they had witnessed a proof of God's concern for His children. In the following days, Conchita still had some *locutions*, just a few (on the 2nd and 18th of July, anniversaries of important events in the history of Garabandal). Some believe that things will continue as before, but it will soon become clear that the 18th of June signified the end of *the apparitions*.

As September comes to an end, the children are separated: Jacinta and Loli leave the village. They are sent to a boarding school in Zaragoza. A month later, on the 30th of October, while Conchita is finalizing similar arrangements, in one of her habitual visits to the Blessed Sacrament in the church, she has a *locution* in which *the Blessed Virgin* makes another appointment:

On Saturday, the 13th of November, come to the Pines and you will see me there. Bring me many religious objects and I will kiss them all for you to distribute: my Son, through them, will work wonders.[395]

This time Conchita does not publicly share the news. And on the morning of the 13th of November, a dramatic accident involving a truck distracts attention from her. Furthermore, heavy rain falls unceasingly on the village throughout the whole evening. Conchita leaves her house and heads towards *the Pines*. She is not

---

394 PESQUERA, 2004, 563.
395 CONCHITA GONZÁLEZ, *Letter to Fr. Gustavo Morelos*, November 8, 1965; PESQUERA, 2004, 577, 582.

observed; no one accompanies her to her appointment.[396] That evening, when the rain is heaviest, *the seer* sets out with memories of the past years: "*I was saying to myself, very sorry for my faults, that I wouldn't fall into them any more, because I felt bad presenting myself like that before the Mother of God, whom my defects hurt so much; and I think that in me they are greater, because I have seen Her.*"[397]

With these sentiments in her heart, Conchita makes her way up the steep slope of *the Calleja*: "When I got to *the Pines* I began to take out the Rosaries I was carrying and while doing so, I heard a very sweet voice, *the Blessed Virgin's*, which is distinct from all others, calling me by my name... And in that moment I saw Her, *with the Child Jesus in Her arms*. She was dressed like always and smiling. [Then] I said to her:

> 'I have brought you the Rosaries to kiss.' 'I see that'—the Lady responds, and adds: '*Conchita... do you remember when I said to you on your name day: that you would suffer much on earth? Well, I say that to you again. Have trust in us and you will offer it gladly to our hearts, for the good of your brothers and sisters, because that way you will be more united to us.*'
>
> '*How unworthy I am of so many graces*—Conchita replies—*and still You come today to me to help me bear the little cross I have now.*'"[398]

The Blessed Virgin gently relieves Conchita of this burden: "*Conchita, I do not come for you alone, but for all my children, with the desire to bring them closer to our hearts.*" The apparitions are not for Conchita alone; they are a call from *the Mother* to "*all her children.*" So She adds: "*Let me see what you have brought, to kiss them all.*" After kissing all the objects, She says: "*My Son, through this kiss that I have*

---

[396] Dr. ORTIZ, C., *Letter to Fr. Andreu*, December 13, 1965; PESQUERA, 2004, 582.
[397] *Diario de Conchita*, 96.
[398] *Ib.*

given here, will perform wonders. Hand them out to others." Conchita assents: *"Of course, I will do that."*

Then *the Lady* asks about the prayer requests that people had commended to the girl. *The seer* repeats all the intentions. Finally, *the Blessed Virgin* gives free rein to her heart: *"Tell me, Conchita, talk to me about my children; I carry them all under my mantle."* Conchita misunderstands this language of love; and responds with simplicity: *"It's too small for all of us to fit."* To this, *the Lady* responds with a smile.

Then She speaks directly to her young interlocutor: *"Do you know, Conchita, why I did not come on June 18 to give you the message for the world? It was because it pained me to say it to you, but I must say it to you for your good and for God's glory if you comply with it. I love you very much and I desire your salvation, to gather you all around the Father, the Son and the Holy Spirit. Won't you respond to me, Conchita?"*

The seer, feeling overwhelmed by *the Mother's* tenderness, sincerely responds: *"If I could always see you, yes, but otherwise I don't know, because I am very bad."* *"Just do all that you can,"* the apparition answers; *"We will help you; and my daughters Loli, Jacinta and Maricruz too."* She adds a word of advice, the last of Garabandal: *"Conchita, why don't you go often to visit my Son in the Blessed Sacrament? Why do you let yourself give in to laziness, not going to visit Him when He is waiting for you day and night?"*

The Eucharist is a central theme of Garabandal.

The ecstasy does not last much longer; in total, about twelve minutes. The farewell begins, this time for good: *"Conchita, [this] will be the last time that you see me here, but I will always be with you and with all my children."* The girl, realizing that with these words *the apparitions* are coming to an end, responds with a petition that sums up all these years: *"Oh, how happy I am when I see you! Why don't you take me with you now?"* *The Blessed Virgin*, educating her till the end, invites

her to be generous: *"Remember what I told you on your saint's day...*
When you present yourself before God you must show Him your hands
filled with works you have done for your brothers and sisters and for
God's glory; now they are empty."[399]

"And that was it," Conchita concludes; *"That happy time I spent with*
my Heavenly Mama and best Friend, and with the Child Jesus, has
passed. I have stopped seeing them but not feeling them. Again they
have sown peace and joy in my spirit and great desires to overcome my
defects so that I can love, with all my strengths, the Hearts of Jesus and
Mary, who love us so much."[400]

A story that had begun four years earlier with thunderclaps on
a bright June day, now ends noiselessly in the rain of a grey
November evening. "The girl, for sure, did not hurry down from
the Pines after *the vision* ended. The state of her spirit wouldn't
have permitted that. She must stay there a while, alone with her
emotions... Lovingly she arranges and wraps up all those Rosaries,
now distinguished by the Mother's kiss; then she steps slowly,
emotionally, towards the brim of the slight hollow where the nine
solitary trees are rooted... and at that edge she pauses. There
before her eyes, a little blurred by the sheets of rain, is the
unforgettable scene: the peaks, the slopes, the narrow valleys
and, closer, at her feet, the village, her village, San Sebastián de
Garabandal. After that farewell in the rain, *"that whole business"*
begins to be history. And yet, something remains forever,
something ineffably fresh and unfading, to be found by all who
come with faith, who will draw strength from it to remain in the
highest hope and the best love."[401] Undoubtedly, in the words of
this final *ecstasy* are concealed something of that *delicacy* that
characterizes the things of God:

---

[399] *Ib.*
[400] *Ib.*, 95-97.
[401] PESQUERA, 2004, 585.

"You will not see me here again,
but I will always be with you,
and with all my children."

It is the last and best word of all those spoken in Garabandal and a compendium of its whole *"message."*

V

Conclusion: The Value of *the Messages*

We have now seen *the message of Garabandal.* Two *messages* that summarize the story of four years of apparitions, communions, the *milagruco* and a farewell rich in content, constitute the teachings of Garabandal.

Of all this, Conchita will incessantly repeat, always, that *the messages* are the most important thing, *"the center"* of *the apparitions.* In fact, she expresses deep concern when she sees the public pay more attention to her than to *the words of the Virgin*:

I fear that what I said in a personal message to some Americans in 1971, with the sole intention of leading people to think more about the message ... might somehow obscure the authentic message of the Blessed Virgin. It must be understood always that those words are mine and not the Blessed Virgin's. That's why they are without value. It has come to my notice that for a time people gave them an importance that they do not have. I tell you this to express my desire that those words not be made public. I continually receive declarations to sign, which I would rather tear up. [402]

In this letter of 1971, six years after the end of *the apparitions,* Conchita distinguishes what she calls *"the words of the Virgin"*

---

[402] CONCHITA GONZÁLEZ, *Letter to J. Lomangino,* September 8, 1971 in PÉREZ, R., 1991, 63, note 71.

from her own limited personal contribution to explaining those words. She would prefer not to speak so as not to distract, with her evident authority, from the content and meaning of *the messages*.

The seers never try to appropriate *the messages*. Rather, they call again and again for a doctrinal study to be made independently of their own personal interpretations. They believe that *the messages* must be taken very seriously: they are the center of *the apparitions*. The *vision* itself has said so: when the parish priest was overwhelmed by the multiplicity of extraordinary events, on the 6th of September 1961, he orders the girls to ask *the Virgin* what was *the meaning of so many phenomena*. The *apparition* responds with brevity: "*This will be seen on the 18th of October.*"[403] As he knew, that was the date of the publication of the *first message*: therefore, this *message*, according to *the apparition* itself, contains the meaning of everything else.

Conchita, like her companions, repeats this often: "*The message above all else.*"[404] The purpose of all the extraordinary phenomena that we saw in PART I of our story, is to highlight *the two public messages of the apparitions*.

"The apparitions are useless for us if we do not fulfill the Message"

The messages of Garabandal are transmitted by *the seers* always with clear and attentive reference to the authority of the Church:

> It is useless for us to believe in *the apparitions* if we don't fulfill the message; better still—Conchita writes—if we don't comply with what

---

403 PESQUERA, 2004, 233.
404 *Diario de Conchita*, 42.

Holy Mother Church says... fulfilling the message, we might as well not believe in *the apparitions*.[405]

To believe in *the apparitions*—according to Conchita's words—is not indispensable. Theologically, this statement is impeccable and sheds light on a delicate equilibrium: the relation between *"mysticism and asceticism," "charism and hierarchy"* (LG 12). Garabandal is very clear: for *the seers* the one important thing at the end of *the apparitions* is to obey Holy Mother Church; that is precisely the objective of *the messages* and *everything* in Garabandal.

Furthermore, *the seers* indicate that the Church has total authority to discern what they have proposed. They will always seek fidelity and obedience, which, indeed, are totally necessary for the approval of the phenomena. Without this awareness they would not be credit-worthy, no matter how *"incontrovertible"* the medical studies might find *"the facts"* to be. However, *the seers* time after time demonstrate that they are solidly grounded in the faith and in docility to the Church.

Thus, *the messages* of Garabandal are marked by a clear orthodoxy and vibrant contemporary relevance and interest for today's Church. This has been successively repeated by bishops. Just one point remains for us to examine: its scope. We will see this in PART III. But first, we will look at the most delicate point of *the apparitions*: *their prophetic warning.*

---

[405] CONCHITA GONZÁLEZ, *Letter to Fr. Alba de Barcelona, December 10, 1965* in *Diario de Conchita,* 42, note 47.

XI

The "Warning" of Garabandal

The Prophecy and its Status of Approval in the Church

Introduction: Prophecy in the Christian Message

In the year 2000, *the third secret* of Fatima is published. Some 83 years have passed since it was delivered to the shepherd children in 1917. The force of its expressions is difficult to assimilate. It is a fact that prophetic language is always difficult to interpret; in Sacred Scripture too, where prophetic language abounds, with all its contrasts, predictions and urgent demands of conversion. Jesus Christ Himself employs this genre with full rigor:

> "There will be signs in the sun, the moon, and the stars, and on earth nations will be in dismay, perplexed by the roaring of the sea and the waves. People will die of fright in anticipation of what is coming upon the world, for the powers of the heavens will be shaken. And then they will see the Son of Man coming in a cloud with power and great glory. But when these signs begin to happen, stand erect and raise your heads because your redemption is at hand" (Lk 21:25-28).

Some fundamental characteristics of *Christian prophecy* may be deduced from these verses:

1) *Prophecy* is an integral part of Christian revelation and it cannot be discounted without harming the Deposit of Faith.

2) The role of this genre, however, is secondary. In Salvation History, passages like this one from Luke 21 clearly occupy a subordinated place in relation to the Passion, Death and Resurrection of Jesus—the indisputable center towards which all of Revelation points.

3) In the divine plan, prophecy occupies a place desired by Providence; God Himself credited it with this value; therefore, *it cannot be discarded.*

4) The interpretation of the prophetic genre is *not evident to the reader* but must be discerned in communion with the Church.

5) Christian prophecy never tries *to decide the times* of the coming events. Not even public Revelation tries to predict the future, although it gives indications about it, as in Luke 21. Biblical prophecy, therefore, does not mean *prediction* so much as *conversion, holiness*: it reveals the will of God for the present more than for the future. Prediction regarding the future is secondary. The prophecy, above all, is a sign that the revelation profoundly affects its interlocutor.[406] Benedict XVI says as much in *Verbum Domini* (2010): the ultimate objective of private revelation is to help *"understanding and living the Gospel at a certain time."*[407]

Clearly, authentic private revelations, like public Revelation, will always maintain an audacious balance between *the future and the present*; but the way their elements develop is free, as is the will of their Author. Our task is not to annul this relation but to comprehend it, to accept it. In this chapter, we will see the way these elements develop in the *prophecy* of Garabandal.

---

[406] Cf. BASTERO, J. L., *"Constantes teológicas en los mensajes de las apariciones marianas,"* Estudios Marianos 75 (2009). 458; Cf. BOUFLET, J., *"Portée et signification de l'apparition unique dans l'historie des mariophanies"* in AA.VV. La Salette. Apocalyse, pèlerinage et littérature (1846-1996), Grenoble, 2000, 40.

[407] BENEDICT XVI, Apostolic Exhortation *Verbum Domini*, Rome, 2010, 14.

I

1962: A Disconcerting Announcement

After the climactic day of the *"milagruco"* in July 1962, *the apparitions* return to their normal course in Garabandal. As of now, they will have perhaps an even more Eucharistic character, accentuated by "the repeated *mystical communions of the seers.*" This being so, "the following month of September will enter history as the month of a *great prophetic announcement.*"[408] The said *announcement* will be closely connected with *the message of the 18th of October* 1961, concretely to its final point: *"the chastisement."* The visitors had not given much attention to the fact that *the message* already included an announcement: *"If we do not change, a very great chastisement will come upon us."*[409] Now, *the apparition* calls Conchita's attention to this:

> The Blessed Virgin has announced to me a miracle that God our Lord will perform through her intercession. Since the chastisement is very, very great, as we deserve, the miracle is also immensely great as the world needs it to be.[410]

"The Miracle"

After September 1962, the *chastisement* is connected to *a "very big" miracle.* Aniceta, Conchita's mother, remarks on it with perplexity: *"The other time (the 18th of July) she said to me: "Mama, there's going to be a little miracle"; and now she tells me: "There's going to be a very big miracle!""*[411] *The seer* has insisted on this point of the magnitude of the *miracle:*

---

[408] PESQUERA, 2004, 455.
[409] *Diario de Conchita,* 42, 69.
[410] *Ib.*
[411] PESQUERA, 2004, 457, 572.

It will be much bigger, much stronger than the one in Fatima [the miracle of the sun]... *It will cause such an impression that no one who sees it will be able to leave there with doubts. It would be great if everyone could be present, because then there surely wouldn't be a chastisement, because everyone would believe.*[412]

In Fatima, an *extraordinary phenomenon* occurred, witnessed by thousands of people, which constituted a great proof of the authenticity of those apparitions: the 70,000 people present on the 13th of October 1917 in *Cova de Iria* were able to look directly at the sun for ten minutes and to contemplate an unprecedented phenomenon: the sun turned, changed color several times and provoked the terror stricken clamor of the public when in one instant it seemed to fall precipitously toward the ground. Everyone, believers and non-believers alike, testified to the event, which was reported throughout the following days in the main national newspapers. After that *miracle*, Fatima would become one of the most important centers of pilgrimage of our time; even the popes would travel there.[413]

The event that Conchita speaks of after 1962 has, therefore, a direct precedent in the *miracle* of Fatima. Conchita heard news of the *"miracle"* for the first time in October 1961, but only in September 1962 does she receive permission to make it public. *The seers* never saw it; but two other people, both of them priests, did see it: Luis María Andreu and Saint Pio of Pietrelcina, privileged witnesses of Garabandal (cf. PART III). However, neither these nor the children provide sufficient details to form any idea of the announced *miracle*.[414] Even so, the girls have declared the place where it will happen: in Garabandal, at *the Pines*. The

---

[412] *Ib.*

[413] Cf. VISCONDE DE MONTELO (NUNES FORMIGÃO, M.), *Os episodios maravilhosos de Fatima*, Guarda, 1921, 25-27.

[414] Cf. PESQUERA, 2004, 526; LANÚS, S., *Madre de Dios y Madre Nuestra*, Madrid, 2013, 200.

apparition also confirmed to *the seers* that, during *"the Miracle"*—which would last some fifteen minutes—the sick there would be healed, sinners would convert and the incredulous would believe.[415]

Regarding the date, it is known by Conchita, and she has instructions to announce it eight days beforehand: *"so that the people will come."*[416] A little more may be gleaned from witnesses of the *ecstasies* in which the *apparition* spoke of this date to *the seer*. The *seer*, in dialogue with the *apparition*, says: *"And when [will that miracle happen]?... That long?...."*[417] This *"that long"* seems to point towards a long wait; a *wait* that ever since then has been a motive of great expectation among those who believe the events are true.

"The Warning"

Before the *"miracle,"* the *seers* affirm that there will be a supernatural *"warning"* pre-announcing it: everyone will see in his own interior, in his conscience, the good and the evil he has done as seen by God: each person will see the state of his soul before God. This *"warning"* will come directly from God and will be experienced by everyone in the world, regardless of his or her condition and knowledge of God, and all in exactly the same moment:

> *It will happen everywhere and will be seen and felt by everyone; it is like a chastisement. We will see what we have caused with our sins.*[418]

A mystical *vision* is being described here, interior but universal, in which *"everyone on earth will see the state of their own soul, just*

---

[415] Cf. *Diario de Conchita,* 69.
[416] *Ib.,* 70.
[417] PESQUERA, 2004, 456.
[418] *Diario de Conchita,* 99.

as God sees it."[419] The enormous proportions of this "*Warning*" are disconcerting. However, its content is not unknown to mystical theology. The children's description of the "*Warning*" sounds a lot like a personal experience of Saint Teresa of Jesus told in her autobiography:

> [While in prayer,] *I understood that it was our Lord's will I should see the place which the devils kept in readiness for me, and which I had deserved by my sins... I was so terrified by that vision,—and that terror is on me even now while I am writing,—that, though it took place nearly six years ago, the natural warmth of my body is chilled by fear even now when I think of it... I repeat it, this vision was one of the grandest mercies of our Lord. It has been to me of the greatest service.*[420]

In the biography of Saint John Maria Vianney (1786-1859), we also find a clear precedent of the "*Warning*" of Garabandal. The Holy Curé of Ars had asked God in the first years of his priesthood for "*full clarity about his own wretchedness;*" that is, the same grace spoken of in relation to the "*Warning.*" The saintly priest may have been inspired to make this request by the prayer of Saint Augustine: "*May I know You, Lord. May I know myself.*"[421] Not until years later would the Saint make any reference to his petition, testifying that he had received that extraordinary grace. He tells it in a letter to Baroness Alix de Belvey, to whom he gives spiritual direction:

> My daughter, never ask God for total knowledge of your wretchedness. I asked for it once and obtained it. If God had not then sustained me I would have despaired in that same instant.[422]

---

[419] LANÚS, S., *Madre de Dios y Madre Nuestra. Fátima, Ámsterdam y Garabandal,* Madrid, 2013, 201.

[420] SAINT TERESA OF AVILA, *Life,* ch. XXXII.

[421] SAINT AUGUSTINE, *Confessions,* X, 1.

[422] PERO-SANZ, J. M., *Aguardando el Cielo: en torno a la Esperanza,* Madrid, 2013, 52.

And to Catherine Lasagne, an intimate confidant, Saint John Maria would laconically say: "*I was unable to bear it.*"[423] He even adds that he had to wait months for the intolerable *vision* to soften; less than Saint Teresa, who remained shaken for *years* after this experience. It seems as though hell itself had opened up before these saints through this extraordinary grace.

Another saint, Saint Josemaría Escrivá de Balaguer, testifies to have experienced the grace described by Conchita in the "*warning.*" On the 27th of April 1954, the Founder of Opus Dei finds himself on the brink of death: he suffers an *anaphylactic* shock. Reactions like this are almost always unavoidably fatal. Blessed Álvaro del Portillo, who was with the Saint during that entire day, gives him absolution *in articulo mortis*. A moment later the Founder of Opus Dei was dead. Fr. Álvaro testifies to this. But hours later Saint Josemaría recovers and says:

"*Álvaro, my son, I now know how it will be when I'm dead.*"[424]

Effectively, on that day the Lord permitted Saint Josemaría "to see his whole life, with great rapidity, as if it were a movie."[425] For Saint Josemaría this was an anticipation of God's judgment, like the description of the "*Warning*" of Garabandal. Mysteriously, after this episode, Escrivá was found to be totally cured of diabetes, never suffering any relapse or experiencing the need for insulin. It was an instantaneous and scientifically inexplicable healing; things of the saints.

The stories of Saint John Maria Vianney and of Saint Teresa contain the same elements as the "*Warning*" of Garabandal: first, the experience was for them something "*terrifying,*" unforgettable even with the passing of the years; and yet, both coincide in

---

[423] GUTIÉRREZ SOLANA, M., *El Cura de Ars*, Vitoria 1998, 15.
[424] VÁZQUEZ DE PRADA, A., *El fundador del Opus Dei*, Madrid, 2009, 197.
[425] *Ib.*, 198.

considering it an extraordinary grace of conversion. The case of Saint Josemaría, additionally, reveals the *healing* power of God.

Similarly, in Garabandal, as Conchita would say, although the *"Warning"* will be *"like a chastisement,"*[426] its purpose is not to produce fear: God *"sends this to us to purify us, to see the miracle that clearly shows us His love for us and because of this the desire that we comply with the message."*[427] The *"Warning"* is thus presented as an exceptional grace of conversion in full continuity with the experience of the saints: a very *strong experience,* but for the good of souls. *"It will be very good for those who don't despair because it will be for our sanctification."*[345] Towards the end of *the apparitions,* on the 1st of January 1965, Conchita reiterates this whole explanation, speaking with security: "[The *Warning*] will certainly come *before the miracle;* but on a day and hour that nobody knows. Its hour will probably be one of mysterious darkness. In that hour there will be no refuge and consolation apart from *prayer."*[428]

"The Chastisement"

If, after the *Miracle,* the world does not change, a *chastisement* will come:

> The chastisement—Conchita says—*if we don't change, will be horrible; but I cannot say what it will consist of, because I don't have the Virgin's permission. When I saw it, I felt an immense terror, and that was while I was still seeing the Virgin at the same time in all her beauty and indescribable goodness!... The Virgin has told me that Jesus would not send the chastisement just to make us suffer but to reprehend us for not listening to Him and to help us.*[429]

---

[426] *Diario de Conchita,* 99.
[427] *Ib.*
[428] PESQUERA, 2004, 541.
[429] *Diario de Conchita,* 99.

The children have seen *the chastisement* but do not know the date and do not have permission to describe it. However, they insist with urgency that the purpose of this triple announcement is conversion, return to God.

The word *"chastisement"* has sometimes stirred suspicions among the pilgrims. However, this expression is totally "in line with biblical language, which also speaks of *chastisements*; this word appears 62 times in the Jerusalem Bible (and *'to chastise'* 90 times)."[430] According to Manuel Iglesias, the entire Bible presents God's *chastisement*: a "medicinal penalty, not vindictive; [this penalty or chastisement] is decreed by an offended infinite love in order to save us: we repair the offense by restoring what has been stolen; we are purified, we return to God."[431] *Chastisement*, therefore, is a proven biblical and theological category (cf. Job 5:17; 1 Cor 11:29-30; Heb 12:5-11). And, in Garabandal, it highlights an essential truth: that sin crucifies Christ; sin, as lovelessness, as voluntary offense against God, demands a penalty.[432] But this penalty, *this chastisement*, is not incompatible with love:

> True love—Joseph Ratzinger explains—does not consist of always giving in, being soft, mere sweetness. In this sense, a sweetened God who says yes to everything... is no more than a caricature of true love. Because He loves us, God must oppose us when we are getting ourselves lost.[433]

This is the content of the *chastisement* in Garabandal; by following the Bible, God's love is not caricatured; rather, with

430 LAURENTIN, R., *Apariciones actuales de la Virgen María*, Madrid, 1991, 205.
431 IGLESIAS, M., *La Palabra y las palabras. Pequeño vocabulario hebreo para uso espiritual*, Madrid, 2013, 16.
432 *Ib.*
433 RATZINGER, J., *Gott und die Welt*, München 2000, 180 (translated from BENEDICT XVI, *Dios y el mundo*, Barcelona, 2005, 173); IGLESIAS, M., *La Palabra y las palabras. Pequeño vocabulario hebreo para uso espiritual*, Madrid, 2013, 16.

great simplicity, the truths of the faith are recalled: the need of conversion for salvation.

Also, in *the message* of Garabandal, the *chastisement* is *"conditional"*: *"and if we do not, a chastisement will come upon us. The cup is already filling up, and if we do not change, a chastisement will befall us."*[434] Twice in the brief text of *the message*, its *provisional nature* is insisted upon. And the condition imposed is absolutely *true to the Gospel: conversion.*

Many of the recent Marian apparitions speak of *chastisement.*[435] Among them, Garabandal stands out due to the universal nature of its prophecy: "According to *the seers*, Our Lady asked God if She could come to Garabandal as a final remedy to avoid or attenuate the Chastisement."[436] If the world changes after *the Warning* and *the Miracle*, *the Chastisement* will not come; if the world does not change, then it will come. So, the words of *the Virgin* seem to suggest that *the Chastisement* will, in fact, come: *"We don't expect the chastisement, but whether we do or not it will come, if we don't cease offending God."*[437]

Fatima also includes the prophecy of a *conditional* chastisement, which depends on receptiveness and conversion: *"If my requests are heeded, Russia will be converted and there will be peace; if not [Russia] will spread her errors throughout the world."*[438] In Garabandal, as in Fatima this biblical hierarchy is maintained, this subordination or service of prophecy to what is essential: salvation.[439]

---

[434] *Diario de Conchita,* 42.
[435] LAURENTIN, R., *Apariciones actuales de la Virgen María,* Madrid, 1991, 204.
[436] LANÚS, S., *Madre de Dios y Madre Nuestra. Fátima, Ámsterdam y Garabandal,* Madrid, 2013, 210.
[437] *Ib.*
[438] RATZINGER, "Theological Commentary" in CDF, *Documents on "The Message of Fatima,"* June 26, 2000.
[439] Cf. LAURENTIN, R., *Apariciones actuales de la Virgen María,* Madrid 1991, 209

The Sacred Scriptures also present a *conditional chastisement* in several places: Jonah is sent to Niniveh to announce its imminent destruction; but the city does penance and the prophecy is canceled (cf. Jon 3:5, 10).[440] Jesus Christ also makes a conditional prophecy, offering Garabandal the most solid biblical foundation:

> *"If you do not repent, you will all perish as they did!"* (Lk 13:3).

> *"If we do not change—Garabandal repeats—a chastisement will come."*

The Gospel and *the apparitions* urge conversion in the face of an imminent chastisement demanded by the gravity of sin: an infinite offense against God.

The Night of the Screams

"An hour of darkness" is how *the apparition* describes the circumstances in which the triple announcement of Garabandal will be fulfilled; concretely, the situation that will precede the *"Warning."*[441] Mari Loli sheds light on this enigmatic *"hour"* when she explains what she saw the night of the 19th of June 1962, known together with that of the 23rd as *the night of the screams*. On both of those nights, *the seers* receive instructions about the *"Warning"* and the *"chastisement."* Their reaction is one of genuine terror. The parish priest, Fr. Valentín, notes that on that night (June 19, 1962) *"the girls are heard crying a lot."*[442] And a woman who was present, Eloísa de la Roza Velarde, recalls:

> *The girls' screams were unforgettable... and they said: "Wait! Wait!... Let them all confess!... ¡Ay!... ¡Ay!..." People began to pray and beg each other for forgiveness publicly...*[443]

---

[440] "...when the people of Niniveh believed God; they proclaimed a fast and all of them, great and small, put on sackcloth... When God saw by their actions how they turned from their evil way, he repented of the evil that he had threatened to do to them; he did not carry it out." (Jonah 3:5,10).
[441] Pesquera, 2004, 541.
[442] *Ib.*
[443] *Ib.*

Fr. Valentín's notes say that the dramatic *apparition ended at around 2.oo in the morning*. The girls then said that they would stay there the whole night in prayer. And many decided to stay there with them. Among them was Eloísa:

> *I don't think anyone left; we were praying with them until six in the morning* [Fr. Valentín says that *quite a few rosaries* were prayed]. *At that hour (with the first light of day), Fr. Larrazábal—a Franciscan friar—left for the church, with all the people following him. And the confession line began... The whole village went to confession; and seemingly the confessions were of a truly extraordinary sincerity and repentance.*[444]

Conchita also refers to this: "*When the Chastisement was announced*—she is referring to these same events—*the whole village confessed.*"[445] This positive outcome was doubtlessly favored by the tremendous experience of the previous night. Bearing in mind the norms of the Congregation for the Doctrine of Faith for discerning the authenticity of possible apparitions, we find ourselves before an important fact, given that one of the three fundamental *positive criteria* given for the approval of apparitions consists of "healthy devotion and abundant and constant spiritual fruits (for example, spirit of prayer, conversion, etc.)."[446] The multitude of confessions prompted by the phenomena of Garabandal since the years of *the apparitions* fulfills very well this condition of *abundant spiritual fruits* required by the Church for their approval. The events do not provoke self-exaltation, separating the faithful from the Church and the sacraments; on the contrary, they promote the faith of the Church. And they do so with abundant fruits.

---

444 *Ib.*
445 *Ib.*
446 CDF, *Norms for the discernment of presumed apparitions*, 1978, I.3.

II

What Does Communism Mean?

What *the Blessed Virgin* showed the children on *the nights of the screams* (19ᵗʰ and 23ʳᵈ of June 1962) is unknown to us. All we know is that, on both of those nights, *the Virgin* speaks to them of *the Chastisement*, among other things. It seems that *the seers* are also told about the circumstances surrounding *the Warning* that will precede everything. In fact, as of this moment, the girls will speak of *"a great tribulation"* that awaits the Church and that precedes both *the Chastisement* and *the Miracle*.[447] Loli will later explain:

> *A great tribulation—which is not yet "the Chastisement"—will come because a moment will arrive in which the Church would give the impression of being on the point of perishing... due to a terrible trial. We asked the Virgin what would this trial be called, and She told us that it would be "Communism."* [448]

"A great tribulation which is not yet the Chastisement"

It seems that what the children see in the first *night of the screams* is the political, social and religious scenario of the world and the Church at the time of *the Warning*. Social upheaval, Communism again aggressively on the rise and the Church *very persecuted*: *"it will seem as though the Church is about to perish."*[449] In summary, a great purification is foretold. In the midst of this situation, *the Warning*—Santiago Lanús explains—comes to the aid of the Church and humanity. Facing such a desolate panorama, Garabandal shines like a light, a message of hope in

---

[447] LANÚS, S., *Madre de Dios y Madre Nuestra. Fátima, Ámsterdam y Garabandal*, Madrid 2013, 200-201; Cf. LANÚS, S., *Letter to the author*, June 4, 2014.
[448] LANÚS, S., *Letter to the author*, June 4, 2014.
[449] *Ib.*

the midst of great difficulties. As in Fatima, the promise is ultimately one of *triumph*. Conchita states as much:

> *In a locution from Jesus—almost at the end of the apparitions, in 1965—He told me that Russia would convert.*[450]

This mention of *Russia*, together with Loli's mention of *Communism* that we have seen, is the only known reference to political realities in Garabandal. It is clear that the children do not realize the scope of what they are transmitting; they don't even understand the word *"Communism."* Conchita will prove as much with a question that surprises the Headmistress of the College of the Conceptionists in Burgos, Mother Nieves García, in 1966:

> *Mother, what does Communism mean?*[451]

This question is asked in the intimacy of spiritual direction, when Conchita attempts to organize her thoughts and feelings regarding the years of *the apparitions*, which have concluded the previous year. Unwittingly, she enables the religious Sister to understand that it was *the apparition* that had used the term; demonstrating also, of course, her total ignorance of the subject. This is reminiscent of Lourdes, where, with another expression, *"Immaculate Conception,"* Saint Bernadette totally disconcerts the priest who interrogates her. Her parish priest, Domènec Peyramale, on learning of the seer's words, realizes that the events that are taking place are quite beyond the capacities of this uncultured girl. And what happens in Garabandal happened also in Fatima, where *Russia* is also mentioned:

> When they [the shepherd children of Fatima], after one of the apparitions in which they spoke with the Lady, were discussing what the Virgin had told them, that *"Russia would spread her errors*

[450] PESQUERA, 2004, 574.
[451] MADRE MARÍA DE LAS NIEVES GARCÍA, *Letter to the author*, January 3, 2014.

throughout the world," Francisco declared that the Virgin must have been referring to uncle Joachim's donkey, named *"Rusa."* Lucia, the eldest of the three, responded that Russia was more likely to be the name of a very bad woman.

If the Virgin had wished to clarify to them what Russia was, She would have done so. The intention was to give a maternal advance warning about something unimaginable at that time, given that Russia was then a decrepit nation, governed by the corrupt administration of the *tzars,* with little international influence, where the *Communist Revolution* had not yet triumphed. It was comprehensible, therefore, that the word Russia did not even sound familiar to the three children. The errors of Russia that the Virgin of Fatima wished to warn us about were those of communism, of course; the greatest tyranny of the 20th century, second only to the abortion laws of that century and this one in the number of lives it has taken.[452]

Effectively, the victims of Communism in the world (Russia, China, Vietnam, Korea, Cambodia, Cuba, Afghanistan...) exceed a hundred million people. Stèphane Courtois affirms as much in a study published by the University of Harvard in the United States.[453]

However—Paredes continues—despite the grave consequences of that totalitarian regime, such as the lack of freedom and absence of law in human relations, all of these are only the outcome of one fundamental cause: *atheism.* In effect, atheism is the driving force that sustains and gives life to Marxism. And this is exactly what the Marxist doctrine affirms in its Philosophy of Law, borrowing one of its theses from Feuerbach: *"The goal of the critique of religion is the doctrine that for man, man himself is the supreme being."*[454] And this is the error upon which the greater part of our culture and political

---

452 PAREDES, J., *"De Fátima a Garabandal"* in DIARIO YA, Madrid, October 19, 2013, www.diarioya.es (latest revision: October 28, 2013).
453 Cf. COURTOIS, S. (Ed.), *Le Livre noir du communisme: Crimes, terreur, répression,* Paris, 2000.
454 *"Homo homini Deus,"* FEUERBACH, L., *Erläuterungen und Ergänzungen zum Wesen des Christentums,* in SA, VII, 325.

systems has been constructed, a lethal error against which the Virgin of Fatima forewarned us...

The ultimate aim of Marxism was not so much to put an end to social injustices as to implant the heavenly Paradise in this earth, to open the eyes of the alienated people so that they would see that everything must be resolved in the here and now, because according to Marxism, *"religion is the opium of the people."*[455]

Paredes thus sheds light on Loli's words in Garabandal. He looks beyond the errors of *Communism* to discover the implications of the warning of Fatima (*"Russia will spread her errors..."*) in the context of contemporary ideologies. Today, according to Paredes, there is an attempt "that is fundamentally the same as that of Marxism, although the method differs. If Marxism proposes that progress and historical advancement is produced in a dialectical way, by means of the confrontation and war of the classes, the liberal-progressive ideology [of today] attempts to implant a radical materialism in peace and harmony."[456] Paredes seems to describe the circumstances of persecution in which the *"Warning"* of Garabandal is to occur, given that, according to his reading, the reigning ideology is not likely to be a *"traditional Communism,"* but rather a development, a historical re-elaboration of its principles.

Surprisingly, Cardinal Joseph Ratzinger thinks along similar lines: he does not share the general opinion that *Communism* is *"today"* a *dated* ideology. It is true that since the fall of the Berlin Wall (1989), the defeat of Marxism is a fact; because "when politics wishes to provide redemption, it promises too much.

---

455 MARX, K., *"Zur Kritik der hegelschen Rechtsphilosophie. Einleitung,"* in MARX, K. - ENGELS WERKE, F., *Dietz*, Berlin, 1957-1969, II, 378; PAREDES, J., *"De Fátima a Garabandal"* in DIARIO YA, Madrid October 19, 2013, www.diarioya.es (latest revision: October 28, 2013).
456 LANÚS, S., *Letter to the author*, June 4, 2014.

When it seeks to do the work of God, instead of becoming divine, it becomes demoniacal."[457] However, the Cardinal goes on to say:

> The non-fulfillment of this hope [with the fall of the Berlin Wall] brought a great disillusionment with it which is still far from being assimilated. Therefore, *it seems probable to me that new forms of the Marxist conception of the world will appear in the future.* For the moment, we cannot be but perplexed: The failure of the only scientifically based system for solving human problems could only justify *nihilism* or, in any case, *total relativism.*[458]

According to the Cardinal, new re-editions of the Marxist ideology on the international stage in the present times are not only possible but *"probable."* And yet, if the idea cannot be rejected *a priori* as *"improbable,"* as Ratzinger believes, it still remains difficult to foresee what shape it might take.

Returning to Garabandal, it is helpful to recall that the visions, as the same Cardinal Ratzinger has said regarding Fatima, "can be deciphered only in retrospect."[459] This principle may certainly be applied to Garabandal, because, if the predictions prove to be true, it will be to the great surprise of many.

III

A Universal Announcement

Apparitions like Lourdes and Fatima, which have a universal impact, are rare. Most apparitions are directed to more localized

---

[457] CARD. RATZINGER, J., *Address to the presidents of the Doctrinal Commissions of the Bishops' Conferences of Latin America, held in Guadalajara, Mexico, in May 1996;* http://www.ewtn.com/library/CURIA/RATZRELA.HTM (January 26, 2015).

[458] *Ib.*

[459] CARD. RATZINGER, J., CDF, *"Theological Commentary"* in *Documents on the "Message of Fatima,"* June 26, 2000.

groups of people. The apparition of the Pillar of Zaragoza, for example, does not announce worldwide consequences like Fatima. Its focus is solely to encourage the evangelizing mission of the Church in a particular region or nation:

> Mary, surrounded by angels, presents herself to James the apostle, consoling him with the promise of the future success of his preaching in Spain, and, as a proof or sign of her presence, leaves him the testimony that guarantees the truth of the event until the end of time: a column or pillar.[460]

The announcement of Garabandal contains very different dimensions. Jesus once spoke of this to Conchita in a locution:

> *"What is the Miracle for? —*she asks- *Is it to convert many people?"*
> He answered me: *"To convert the entire world."*[461]

Conchita will always thereafter feel overwhelmed by the universality of the prophecy that she is asked to announce. She is sustained time after time, however, in this mission: her message is *"for the entire world."* These universal proportions resonate strongly with the prophecy of Fatima, which also presents a *conditional chastisement* of universal scope: *"...if you do not [convert, Russia] will spread her errors throughout the world."* It may almost be said that Garabandal is *only* about specifying these postulates.

Such prophecies require serious discernment but, as may be seen in the case of Fatima, they can perfectly be approved by the Church. And, in Fatima, the apparitions were approved without waiting for the fulfillment of the announcement (the *third secret*) because the apparitions may be judged with certainty without having to wait to see the prophecy fulfilled.

---

[460] LABARGA GARCÍA, F., "*La tradición mariofánica española,*" *Estudios Marianos* 72 (2009), 19.
[461] *Diario de Conchita,* 81.

In Fatima, the prophecy was judged according to two fundamental points: *"the credibility of the witness and the testimony."*[462] These two points were sufficient to approve the prophecy of apparitions that, like that of *public Revelation*, was still unfulfilled and in the future, without this being a deterrent. When the Gospel tells us, *"you will see the son of man come upon the clouds of heaven"* (Mt 26:64), we cannot prove its prophecy, but we can trust in it by virtue of those two points: the credibility of the Author (*Jesus*) and of its content (His *second coming*). Applied to Fatima, those criteria sufficed for approval of the apparitions. Let us apply them now to our case.

"The Testimony"

A North-American theologian, Colin B. Donovan, responds, with substance, to the question of the enormous magnitude of the prophecy of Garabandal. Donovan, having painstakingly studied the apparitions, presents a clear and condensed assessment of the judgments reached regarding their content, or *"testimony"*:

> His Excellency Del Val [Bishop of Santander between 1972 and 1991], in retirement, stated in an interview that the message of Garabandal was *"important"* and *"theologically correct."* In fact, some of the prophetic elements of the message may be found in approved private revelations... after Garabandal, in the seventies. For example, the concept of a *Warning of worldwide scope* may be found in Saint Faustina's Diary (no. 83); likewise, in another message of the [Saint's] Diary (no. 1588) and in Akita (recent Marian apparitions approved by the local bishop), a Chastisement of the human race is spoken of, if definitive repentance does not occur. Similar prophetic content may be found in the writings of Elizabeth Canori Mora and Mary of the

---

462 IZQUIERDO, C., *Teología fundamental*, Barañain, 2009, 374.

Crucified Jesus (both beatified by John Paul II), and in God's prophecies to Blessed Ana María Taigi and Saint Gaspar of Buffalo.[463]

These arguments show that the *prophetic announcement* of Garabandal is undeniably in close continuity with the doctrine of canonized saints and with apparitions approved by the Church. The *testimony*, as successive bishops will repeat, is irreprehensible: in Garabandal "there is nothing contrary to dogma and morality."[464]

"The Witness"

Concerning the credibility of the subjects, the seers, it may be said that those of Garabandal present an exemplary Christian coherency. Numerous studies, medical and theological, which follow the girls closely for a prolonged duration without finding in them a hint of deceit, support this:

> From the pediatric and psychiatric point of view, the four children have always been and continue to be normal.[465]

The reports on Conchita are especially detailed: the child is "good without being prudish or childish. Completely normal. Playful and charming... exquisitely correct and polite, without the remotest trace of impurity... I never observed in her the slightest hint of unhealthy craftiness."[466] The headmistress of the school in Burgos that she attends after the apparitions affirms: "[Conchita is] simple, ingenuous, candid, and intelligent. So normal and balanced that I would certify that in my profession as an educator I have known no other like her." The religious, who is also her

---

[463] DONOVAN, M. B., *"Garabandal"* in EWTN,
http://www.ewtn.com/expert/answers/garabandal.htm (September 8, 2013).
[464] OBISPADO DE SANTANDER, *Declaraciones oficiales de la Jerarquía sobre Garabandal,* Santander, 1970, 15.
[465] ORTIZ, C., *Informe médico sobre las videntes de Garabandal* en PÉREZ, R., 1991, 185.
[466] PUNCERNAU, Dr. R., *Informe médico sobre las videntes de Garabandal,* Barcelona, 1974, 5.

spiritual director, concludes that she is *incapable of perpetrating the sinister deception that some seek to impute to her.*[467]

The moral, spiritual and psychological calibre of the witnesses of the apparitions—the seers—is, according to numerous authoritative testimonies, beyond reproach.

This being said, there are some who reject the medical testimonies and persist in distrusting the seers. René Laurentin, without referring concretely to Garabandal, remarks that, in effect, even though the seers may behave very coherently, sowing in their families and all around them the call to holiness, their experiences are often defamed as *"hysterical"* or *"hallucinations"* in attempts to discredit and dismiss them.[468]

This happens in Garabandal. In spite of their exemplary comportment, in spite of the medical and theological studies and the close spiritual attention given to the girls by persons of proven virtue, their *announcement* is rejected *a priori*, without arguments: due to their discomfiting magnitude. It is hard to recognize this, but it is a recurrent feature of the history of Christianity: the same thing happened first to Jesus (cf. Mk 3:21; 6, 3; Jn 7:20).

IV

"The End of the Times"

The message and prophecy of Garabandal are consistent with Christian Revelation: "they simply repeat the current doctrine of the Church."[469] With this, Bishop Beitia, and three other bishops of

---

[467] PESQUERA, 2004, 304.

[468] Cf. LAURENTIN, R., *Apariciones actuales de la Virgen María*, Madrid, 1991, 218.

[469] OBISPADO DE SANTANDER, *Boletín Oficial de la Diócesis de Santander*, Santander, 1962, XI, 181; In PART III, we will focus on the Official Notes of the Ordinaries of Santander.

Santander, have highlighted the correctness of the doctrine of Garabandal in successive statements (Beitia in 1965, Cirarda in 1970, Del Val in 1991, Osoro in 2007). Nevertheless, one statement by Conchita stirred up a great polemic during the time of the apparitions and even afterwards: concerning *"the coming of the end of times."*

The seer employs this disconcerting expression for the first time on the 3rd of June 1963, during the time of the locutions (1963-64). Having learned of the death of Pope Saint John XXIII, she heads to the church with her mother to pray for the eternal repose of the Pontiff. On the way she hears a clear announcement which she will later transmit always with the same words:

> *It was the Virgin who said it to me: "After this Pope* [Saint John XXIII], *only three remain; and then* [will come] *the end of the times."*[470]

Taking the words at face value, the third Pope would be Saint John Paul II. But the Virgin immediately explains that *"She wasn't counting one of them."*[471] Strange; one of the forthcoming Popes does not count in the list. When Aniceta, the child's mother, questions her about this unusual announcement, Conchita explains that one doesn't count because *"he would govern the Church for a very short time."*[472] John Paul I, with his 33-day pontíficate, fulfills this exceptional prediction. It seems therefore that, after Blessed Paul VI and Saint John Paul II, it must be Benedict XVI who completes the list of *"the three popes."* If this is so, with the resignation of Benedict and the arrival of Francis, the

---

[470] PESQUERA, 2004, 517.

[471] "[Die Hl. Jungfrau] eigentlich, sagte sie, sind es noch vier [Päpste], aber einen zählt sie nicht mit" WEBER, A., *Garabandal. Der Zeigefinger Gottes*, Meersburg, 2000, 149.

[472] "...Dass einer nur kurze Zeit regieren wird." WEBER, A., *Garabandal. Der Zeigefinger Gottes*, Meersburg, 2000, 149. Another witness, Plácido Ruiloba, "one of the witnesses who has seen most things in Garabandal" (Pesquera, 2004, 517), also records this detail in his notes of June 1963, after speaking with Conchita. Cf. PÉREZ, R., 1991, 131.

present Pope, it seems that the *"then"* of the *third Pope* (*"then will come the end of the times"*) has already begun its course.

"Then" does not mean "immediately"

It seems that the fulfillment of this announcement is not far away. Clearly, if the announcement is true, then with Pope Francis *"something"* should *"already"* be happening. In fact, more than one observer has interpreted the pontificate of Francis as *"a 'kairos' in a special moment of grace."*[473]

Conchita's attitude of continued expectation of the Warning and the Miracle seems to confirm this interpretation. Lanús has confirmed in 2013 that this is effectively the seer's position: "[Everything] that Mr. Albrecht Weber (witness and friend of Conchita) affirms... has recently been confirmed by Conchita in private."[474]

What does this announcement mean? The most solid authors— Pesquera, Lanús, Paredes, among others—indicate that *"the end of the times"* *"cannot mean* *"the end of the world"*.*[475] Conchita exclaims that *"there cannot be a Church without a Pope!"*[476] She does not mean, then, that there will be no more Popes: *"the Virgin never said that there would be no more Popes."*[477] So, the Popes and the Church will go on: there is no question of an *absolute end*.

---

473 MONS. MUNILLA, J. I., "La comunicación en Francisco..." en AGENCIA SIC (Comisión Episcopal Española de Medios de Comunicación), November 9, 2013, www.agenciasic.com (October 1, 2014).
474 LANÚS, S., *Letter to the author*, June 8, 2013; Cf. LANÚS, S., *Madre de Dios y Madre Nuestra. Fátima, Ámsterdam y Garabandal*, Madrid, 2013, 258; Cf. LÓPEZ DE SAN ROMÁN, *Letter to the author*, February 14, 2013.
475 LANÚS, S., *Madre de Dios y Madre Nuestra. Fátima, Ámsterdam y Garabandal*, Madrid, 2013, 261.
476 *Ib.*, 260.
477 LANÚS, S., *Letter to the author*, June 8, 2013.

It seems clear that the *"End of the Times"* is not the same as the *"end of the world."* Conchita, when questioned about the difference between these two *"ends"*, always responds with a shrug of the shoulders and an: *"I don't know."*[478] In fact, she herself will ask her vision if after these three Popes the *"end of the world"* should be expected:

She [the Virgin] answered me: "No, the end of the times."[479]

The apparition distinguishes between both *"ends."* But when asked about the difference between the *"two ends,"* Conchita, who possesses no further details on the matter, does not conceal her perplexity: *"I don't know."*[480]

This perplexity of the seer recalls the confusion of Saint Bernadette, when she admitted to the parish priest of Lourdes, Domènec Peyramale, that she *"didn't know"* what was meant by *"I am the Immaculate Conception."* Lucia of Fatima also claimed *"not to know"* how to explain the prophecy commended to her: when the Third Secret of Fatima was published in the year 2000, the Holy See added an interpretive text redacted by Cardinal Angelo Sodano. But before publication it was presented to Sister Lucia, to learn her opinion and to see if she agreed. Sister Lucia, Cardinal Ratzinger explains, responded that *"she had received the vision but not its interpretation. The interpretation, she said, belonged not to the visionary but to the Church."*[481]

Conchita in Garabandal, the same as Sister Lucia, comprehends that the interpretation *"is not within her competence but the Church's."* She does not hesitate, therefore, to manifest her

---

[478] LANÚS, S., *Madre de Dios y Madre Nuestra. Fátima, Ámsterdam y Garabandal,* Madrid, 2013, 259.
[479] PESQUERA, 2004, 293.
[480] *Ib.,* 517.
[481] CARD. RATZINGER, J., *"Theological Commentary"* in CDF, *Documents on "The Message of Fatima",* June 26, 2000.

ignorance: "*I don't know.*" Furthermore, Conchita carefully avoids all commentary and protagonism. She leaves the judgment of the matter totally in the hands of the Church.

Now then, if the "*End of the Times*" is not the same as the "*end of the world,*" what *does* it mean? It is true that an *absolute end* is not announced, and yet something big is undoubtedly indicated:

> If the expression "*End of the Times*" does not mean the same as "*end of the world,*" then it has to point to something prior to it and of exceptional magnitude. What might that be? This is the question.[482]

René Laurentin believes that the Marian apparitions are fulfilling an exceptional mission which "correspond to a certain urgency; perhaps not the end of the world, but at least a serious historical turning-point at the threshold of the third millenium."[483] Lucas F. Mateo-Seco coincides to a great extent with Laurentin: the University of Navarre professor observes that the recent apparitions are not circumscribed within the sphere of *spirituality*, as in other epochs; they possess a singular *transcendence*, a strong "*public dimension*" within *Salvation History*.[484] In fact, a significant number of authors affirm that the novelty announced in contemporary apparitions is already being fulfilled, as well as the *situation of persecution* announced in Garabandal. Javier Paredes, quoting Saint John Paul II, calls it the "*martyrdom of coherency.*" This being so, the prophecy would already be "*under way.*"[485] Perhaps without realizing it, we are already in some way witnessing the beginning of what was foretold in Garabandal. However, this is not enough. The *verification* of Conchita's announcement must be clear; as clear as the description of the

---

[482] PESQUERA, 2004, 523

[483] LAURENTIN, R., *Apariciones actuales de la Virgen María*, Madrid 1991, 21

[484] MATEO-SECO, L. F., *Fe y visiones en la literatura espiritual del Siglo de Oro español*," *Estudios Marianos* 75 (2009) 133

[485] PAREDES, J., "*Prólogo*" in LANÚS, S., *Madre de Dios y Madre Nuestra*, Madrid 2013, 11

Warning, Miracle and conditional Chastisement that she gave. The outcome, be it negative or positive, cannot be far away now.

"Por fim, o meu Imaculado Coração triunfará"

A short, strong expression from Fatima lights up the dark announcement of the "End of the Times": "In the end, my Immaculate Heart will triumph."[486] This "in the end" of Fatima alludes in some way to a phase in which the faith will be re-established. Fatima contains this note of hope. Since it has been approved, it is clear that there is no question here of a millenarist or pan-Christian heresy. Even so, the darkness of the announcement, in Fatima as much as in Garabandal, demands prudence when it comes to interpretation. Such prophecies will only be clarified in the light of history.[487]

The expression "End of the Times" is not unknown to the Magisterium of the Church. In the 20th century it has been used implicitly or explicitly by all the Popes.[488] The same is true of Sacred Scripture. The Bible provides a basis to affirm that "perhaps after a great trial, a general conversion ("my Heart will triumph") might occur, and, in the view of reliable authors, such a conversion will occur through a direct intercession of the Immaculate Heart of Mary."[489] Saint John Paul II goes so far as to affirm that he feels the fulfillment of the message of Fatima is "close." These messages, "with the end of the century, seem to be nearing their fulfillment."[490] It is superfluous to insist that this

---

[486] CARD. RATZINGER, J., "Theological Commentary" in CDF, Documents on "The Message of Fatima", June 26, 2000.
[487] Cf. CARD. SODANO, A., "Announcement made by Cardinal Angelo Sodano, Secretary of State of His Holiness" in CDF, Documents on "The Message of Fatima", June 26, 2000.
[488] Cf. ANSÓN, F., "El secreto de Fátima y el fin de los tiempos" in HÜNERMANN, W., Fátima. Su historia maravillosa, Madrid, 1998, 301.
[489] Ib.
[490] Ib.

interpretation of the Message of Fatima by John Paul II coincides impressively with the *urgency* that characterizes the *announcement* of Garabandal.

Garabandal in Fatima. Fatima in Garabandal

A close bond unites Fatima and Garabandal. Saint John Paul II observed a "certain *continuity*" between apparitions.[491] This should not be understood in terms of a serial coded message of futuristic predictions, like a "*mariophanic suite*" in which each apparition "is a continuation of an earlier one and the one message progresses linearly in time *like a Marian Apocalypsis.*"[492]

But the evidence cannot be denied. Mateo-Seco in this matter underlines an authentic *contemporary novelty*: among the recent Marian apparitions, there is a remarkable "convergence of messages and the evident purpose of moving hearts to prompt conversion in the face of the complex and dramatic nature of contemporary history."[493] For Mateo-Seco, there is, in certain cases, an undoubtable "concordance of content."[494] The question that all of this raises is: "*What does She wish to say to us?*"

The relation between Fatima and Garabandal is clearly very strong; it is not an artificial link, the fruit of wishful thinking. Javier Paredes affirms that the apparitions of Garabandal are in a relation of "consonance and continuation [with Fatima]."[495] This is also the opinion of the Bishop of Fatima during the period of the

---

491 JOHN PAUL II, *Cruzando el umbral de la Esperanza*, Barcelona, 1995, 215.

492 BASTERO, J. L., "*Constantes teológicas en los mensajes de las apariciones marianas,*" *Estudios Marianos* 75 (2009) 458; SAVART, C., "*Cent ans après: Les apparitions mariales en France au XIX siècle, un ensemble,*" Rev. Hist. Spir. 48 (1972) 205-220; Cf. BOUFLET, J., "*Portée et signification de l'apparition unique dans l'historie des mariophanies*" in AA.VV. *La Salette. Apocalyse, pèlerinage et littérature* (1846-1996), Grenoble, 2000, 40.

493 MATEO-SECO, L. F., *Fe y visiones en la literatura espiritual del Siglo de Oro español,*" *Estudios Marianos* 75 (2009), 132.

494 *Ib.*

495 PAREDES, J., "*Prólogo*" in LANÚS, S., *Madre de Dios y Madre Nuestra*, Madrid, 2013, 16.

events of Garabandal, His Excellency João Pereira Venâncio (1958-1972):

> The message given by the Blessed Virgin in Garabandal is the same as the one She gave in Fatima, but actualized for our time.[496]

Bishop Venâncio shows consistent interest in Garabandal, to the point of traveling to New York to visit Conchita on two occasions.

North-American theologian Richard Gilsdorf affirms that "in Fatima, Mary warned that Russia would spread her errors throughout the whole world. By definition, the errors of Russia are atheistic materialism. I believe that the western Church has succumbed, unwittingly, to these errors of Russia."[497]

Santiago Lanús shares this opinion, because "*the end of the times,*" which would commence with the Warning of Garabandal, "*would last until the triumph of the Immaculate Heart announced in Fatima.*"[498] A close bond seems strongly to unite the apparitions of Fatima and Garabandal.

A Prophecy with a "Fixed Timeframe"

Garabandal presents one novelty with respect to Fatima: "*a timeframe.*" In Fatima a way of measuring the remaining time until the announced "*triumph*" is not given. This makes the wait more open, indeterminable. In Garbandal, on the other hand, there is a timeframe:

> It was the Virgin who said to me: "After this Pope [Saint John XXIII], only three remain; and then [will come] the end of the times."

---

[496] LANÚS, S., *El Mensaje de Garabandal,* Buenos Aires 2014, www.virgendegarabandal.com (October 7, 2014).

[497] GILSDORF, R., "*Testimonio sobre Garabandal,*" *El cielo a Garabandal* (2), Buenos Aires, (2014), 27.

[498] LANÚS, S., *Madre de Dios y Madre Nuestra,* Madrid, 2013, 266.

All of this is very big: a miracle announced with a fixed date is enormous; added to the miracle in itself there is another factor of equal value: that of the *"prophecy."*[499] However, the existence of a timeframe in Garabandal is firmly rejected by many people. Yet it must be said that *timeframes* are not alien to Christian revelation. Jesus Himself and the whole Bible presents numerous declarations with timeframes that in no way fall short of that of Garabandal:

> *"Such things must happen first"* (Lk 21:9); *"This night all of you will have your faith in me shaken"* (Mt 26:31); *"This very night before the cock crows, you will deny me three times"* (Mt 26:34).[500]

Timeframes have a proven biblical tradition. They admittedly require a particular prudence and study, in anticipation of a definitive public verdict by the Church, which—perhaps owing precisely to this issue—is still pending in Garabandal.

V

Conclusion

Although we cannot resolve all the questions that arise from the prophecy of Garabandal (like those of the the Gospel), we can, without fear of error, draw some conclusions:

· The expression *"End of the Times"* designates a change of circumstances leading to the strengthening of faith throughout the world.

· This entails the realization of the *"Triumph of the Immaculate Heart of Mary"* announced in Fatima. This change seems to coincide or begin with the extraordinary grace of the Warning.

---

499 PESQUERA, 2004, 395.
500 Cf. Gen 17:21; 7:4; Ex 11:4-5; Jonah 3:4; Dan 9:24; Lk 12:20.

· This Warning, which according to the children of Garabandal will occur in a time of persecution for the Church, will dispose souls for the change and the great Miracle by which God makes known His love to humanity.[501]

· If this grace is not welcomed, then *"A very great Chastisement will come."*[502]

· In the end, with or without a Chastisement (since it is conditional), after the Miracle *the world will be granted*—as stated in Fatima—*"a period of peace"*:[503] the time of the *"Triumph"* of the Immaculate Heart.

That is how the announcement of Garabandal is presented, as a most special grace which would specify the *Triumph* announced in Fatima: by this grace, God would renew humanity in His Mercy and His Love.

Belief in apparitions before the fulfillment of their message?

Benedicto XVI stated with crystal clarity in a homily on the esplanade of Fatima in 2010 that the message of Fatima does not refer only to past events:

"It is a mistake to think that the prophetic mission of Fatima is ended."[504]

In fact, the Hierarchy of the Church did not wait to see the prophecy fulfilled before approving the apparitions of Fatima, demonstrating with this gesture that the predictions do not occupy the center of ecclesiastic discernment. The events and messages transmitted by the three shepherd children were

---

501 Cf. LANÚS, S., *Madre de Dios y Madre Nuestra. Fátima, Ámsterdam y Garabandal*, Madrid, 2013, 201; Cf. *Diario de Conchita*, 81.

502 *Diario de Conchita*, 42.

503 CARD. RATZINGER, J., *"Theological Commentary"* in CDF, *Documents on "The Message of Fatima"*, June 26, 2000.

504 BENEDICT XVI, *Homily on the esplanade of the Shrine of Fatima*, May 13, 2010.

considered capable of justifying the approval of the apparitions without the need to wait to see their prophecy fulfilled. And how much good would have been left undone if the desire to await the fulfillment of the same secrets, still today unverified, had prevailed!

Garabandal, in this point, is not very different. It is not necessary to wait to see its prophecy fulfilled, since *its message and the events* on which it is based "contain an exhortation to prayer and to sacrifice... in praiseworthy traditional forms."[505] This has been affirmed not only by expert medics, theologians and witnesses but, above all, by those in the Church who possess the authority to approve the events: its successive bishops.

When all is said and done, the predictions, which must be verified in Conchita's lifetime (she must announce them eight days beforehand[506] and she was born on the 7th of February 1949), cannot be delayed indefinitely. All the evidence indicates that today, the wait for Garabandal is nearing its short or medium-term end.

This *"waiting dimension,"* particularly vivid in Garabandal, has not disorientated the faithful; rather, it has helped many souls in their conversion. Archbishop Carlos Osoro affirmed as much in 2007:

> *I have known authentic conversions* [in Garabandal]. *Faced with these occurrences, how can we fail to feel the need to open our hearts always to our Mother Mary.*[507]

---

[505] MONS. BEITIA ALDAZÁBAL, E., *"Nota sobre los sucesos de San Sebastián de Garabandal* (July 8, 1965)" in OBISPADO DE SANTANDER, *Boletín Oficial de la Diócesis de Santander,* Santander, 1962, XI, 181.

[506] Cf. *Diario de Conchita,* 69.

[507] OSORO SIERRA, C., *"Letter to Edward Kelly* (May 7, 2007)" in GARABANDAL JOURNAL, Minnesota 2007, V—VI, 5; LANÚS, S., *Madre de Dios y Madre Nuestra. Fátima, Ámsterdam y Garabandal,* Madrid, 2013, 174.

These conversions constitute the true motive of the apparitions of Garabandal; and this is precisely what we are going to see next: the fruits of the apparitions. Familiarity with the impact of the phenomena among the faithful will provide us with the necessary vision of the matter to enable us to weigh the value and opportuneness of the prophetic message we have seen.

Reproduction of the most recent published episcopal statement on the
phenomena of Garabandal.

Carlos Osoro Sierra
Arzobispo de Oviedo

Oviedo, 7 de mayo de 2007

Estimado D. Eduardo:

Acuso recibo de su amable carta, presentándome su visión del
fenómeno de Garabandal. Quiero que sepa que estoy abierto a toda
información, a toda consideración sobre Garabandal, y en este sentido
quiero continuar, durante el tiempo que el Santo Padre estime oportuno
como Administrador Apostólico, lo que hicieron mis hermanos en el
episcopado, en lo referente al tema en cuestión; lo que he hecho ahora es
autorizar a los Sacerdotes para que suban a Garabandal y celebren allí la
Eucaristía en la parroquia a la hora que lo deseen, y puedan administrar el
sacramento de la reconciliación a cuantas personas lo deseen allí.

Estoy seguro que el próximo obispo promoverá los estudios para que
se examinen con mayor profundidad los sucesos de Garabandal y enviarlos a
la Congregación para la doctrina de la Fe, en Roma.

Respeto las apariciones y he conocido conversiones auténticas. Ante
éstos sucesos ¡Cómo no sentir siempre la necesidad de abrir el corazón a
nuestra Madre María para decirle que necesitamos de su protección, de su
ayuda, de su ánimo, de su ilusión, de su fe, de su esperanza y de su amor!.
Les animo a seguir manteniendo esa devoción hacia nuestra Madre.

Si tiene interés de hablar conmigo, no dude en pedir una audiencia en
el obispado de Santander a través de la Vicaria General. Allí tomarán sus
datos y le fijarán hora y fecha para la visita.

Esperando poder seguir contando con su oración y colaboración,
reciba mi más cordial saludo y bendición.

+ Carlos, Arzobispo de Oviedo y
Administrad_____nder

Carlos Osoro Sierra
Archbishop of Oviedo

Oviedo, 7 May 2007

Dear Edward:

I have received your kind letter, presenting to me your perspective of the
phenomena of Garabandal. I wish you to know that I am open to all information, to
every consideration, concerning Garabandal, and I wish to remain in this disposition
throughout the time the Holy Father may deem it opportune that I act as Apostolic
Administrator, as did my brothers in the episcopate, in relation to the matter in
question; what I have now done is to authorize priests who visit Garabandal to
celebrate the Eucharist there in the parish church whenever they wish, and to
administer the sacrament of reconciliation to any persons there who may desire it.

I am sure that the next bishop will promote studies so that the events of Garabandal may be examined in greater depth, to be sent to the Congregation for the
Doctrine of Faith in Rome.

I respect the apparitions and I know of authentic conversions. Faced with such
facts, how can one fail to feel always the necessity to open one's heart to Mary our
Mother, to tell Her we need her protection, her help, her encouragement, her
enthusiasm, her faith, her hopefulness and her love! I encourage you to maintain this
devotion to our Mother.

If you are interested in speaking with me, do not hesitate to seek an audience in
the bishopric of Santander through the Vicar General. There, they will take your
details and schedule a date and hour for the visit.

Hoping to keep counting on your prayers and collaboration, I send my most
cordial greeting and blessing.

+ Carlos, Archbishop of Oviedo and
Apostolic Administrator of Santander.

Letter published in: MONS. OSORO SIERRA, C., Letter to Edward Kelly, Santander 7 May 2007,
in GARABANDAL JOURNAL, Minnesota 2007, V-VI; Cf. LANÚS, S., Madre de Dios y Madre Nuestra. Fátima, Ámsterdam y Garabandal, Madrid 2013, 174.

Reproduction of the complete text of the letter signed by Joseph Cardinal Ratzinger concerning the phenomena of Garabandal.

Addressed to the Bishop of Santander, Mons. José Vilaplana, it is the most recent letter of the Congregation for the Doctrine of Faith concerning these apparitions.

Rome, 28 November 1992

Your Excellency:

In a letter dated 12 November 1991, you transmitted to this dicastery ample documentation referring to the results of the studies concerning the supposed apparitions of Garabandal, carried out by a Commission expressly nominated by your predecessor, Mons. Juan Antonio del Val Gallo.

In the said letter—and, subsequently, on the occasion of your recent visit to this Congregation—Your Excellency expressed the wish to rely on the support of the Holy See in the matter of an eventual pronouncement concerning the above-mentioned occurrences.

The Congregation for the Doctrine of Faith, having attentively examined the cited documentation, does not consider it opportune to intervene directly, withdrawing from Your Excellency's ordinary jurisdiction a matter that corresponds to you by law. Therefore, this dicastery suggests to you that, if you deem it necessary, you publish a declaration in which you reaffirm the non constat of the supernatural nature of the apparitions in question, adopting as your own the unanimous positions of the preceding Ordinaries of that diocese and, in particular, the opinion expressed on 26 April 1991 by the commission presided over by His Excellency Mons. Del Val Gallo.

I avail of this circumstance to express to you my sentiments of esteem and to confirm that I remain sincerely yours in Christ.

Joseph Cardinal Ratzinger.
Prefect of the Congregation for the Doctrine of Faith.

CARD. RATZINGER, J., Letter of the Congregation for the Doctrine of Faith to Mons. Vilaplana, 28.XI.1992, cited by OCHAYTA PIÑEIRO, F., Estudio sobre Garabandal, Sigüenza 2004, I. 34.

The Bishop of Santander

Oviedo, 7 May 2007

Several persons have recently addressed this Bishopric of Santander to ask about the alleged apparitions of Garabandal and, above all, about the response of the hierarchy of to the Church to these events. I must communicate to you that:

1. All of the bishops of the Diocese, from 1961 to 2015, stated that the supernatural nature of said apparitions, which occurred in the 1960s, is not established.

2. In the month of December of 1977, Mons. Del Val, Bishop of Santander, manifested his accord with his predecessors, and that in his then six years as Bishop of Santander, no new phenomenon had occurred.

3. Nevertheless, Mons. Del Val himself, once the first years of passion and confusion had passed, promoted an inter-disciplinary study to examine the alleged phenomena in greater depth. The conclusion of the study coincides with the previous verdict given by the Bishops, which is that the supernatural nature of said apparitions is not established.

4. This study was concluded in 1991. Mons. Vilaplana Blasco, then Bishop of Santander, presented the cited study to the Congregation for the Doctrine of Faith, seeking orientation for pastoral action in relation to the case.

5. On the 28th of November 1992, Cardinal Joseph Ratzinger, Prefect of the Congregation, sent a response in which he observes that, having attentively examined the aforementioned documentation, he did not consider it opportune to intervene directly, removing from the ordinary jurisdiction of the Bishop of Santander this matter which corresponds to him by law. Previous declarations of the Holy See coincide with this statement (Card. Ottaviani 1967. Card. Seper 1969 and 1970).

In the same letter it is suggested that, if it is deemed opportune, a declaration be published in which *it is reaffirmed that the supernatural nature of the said apparitions is not established*, adopting the unanimous positions of the Bishops of Santander.

6. Given that the declarations of my predecessors, who studied the case, have been clear and unanimous, I have not considered it opportune to make a new public declaration, in order to avoid lending notoriety to events that are now too remote in time. However, I do consider it opportune to redact this statement as a direct response to those persons who seek orientation in the matter, accepting the decisions of my predecessors, and the orientations of the Holy See, which I adopt as my own.

7. Insofar as concerns the celebrations of the Eucharist in Garabandal, following the dispositions of my predecessors, I allow only that they be celebrated in the parish church, without reference to the supposed apparitions and with the authorization of the present parish priest, who enjoys my confidence.

Hoping that this information will be of help in the orientation of the faithful, I send my fraternal greeting in Christ, commending myself to His Mother the Virgin,

Santander, 24 June 2015
Manuel Sánchez Monge.
Bishop of Santander.

Letter published in: MONS. SÁNCHEZ MONGE, M., *Report on Phenomena of Garabandal*, Santander, 24.V.2015, in ROVIRA, J.M., *Garabandal Archive*, San Sebastián de Garabandal 2015.

R. F. Gustavo Morelos
P R E S E N T.

Esteemed Father:

Bearing in mind the indications of the Holy See and of His Excellency the Ordinary of Santander (Spain), in conjunction with the prescriptions of the Code of Canon Law, we approve and bless the publication of the Message of the Most Blessed Virgin in San Sebastian de Garabandal in our Archdiocese, in the knowledge that, in the light of Divine Revelation, it exhorts us concerning the necessity of prayer and sacrifice, devotion to the Holy Eucharist and to the Blessed Virgin, obedience, love and filial adherence to the Vicar of Christ and the Holy Church.

Therefore, we find nothing in this Message, attributed to the Most Holy Virgin, that is contrary to Faith and customs. It contains opportune, useful and salutary counsels for the obtainment of eternal salvation.

A prompt and filial obedience in the manner of receiving the dispositions of the Church has characterized the persons favored in these apparitions, and therefore, there is a sure sign for all that God is present here.

The prudence of the Holy Church in relation to this important matter has been manifested by attentive study and pastoral vigilance, and never by prohibition and rejection of same.

One of the Officials of the Sacred Congregation for the Defense of the Faith, Mons. Philiippi, declared to the Most Reverend Fr. Elías, Superior of the Carmel in the City of Puebla, who consulted him in Rome regarding the apparitions of the Blessed Virgin in Garabandal, that the fact that Padre Pío, recognized for his virtue, knowledge and adhesion to the Holy See, approved these apparitions and encouraged the four girls who received the visions to propagate the Message of the Blessed Virgin, is a great proof of their veracity.

Written in Jalapa of the Immaculate, 8 July 1966
Manuel Pío López, Archbishop of Jalapa

MONS. LÓPEZ, M. P., Letter to Father Gustavo Morelos, Jalapa 8.VII.1966 in Conchita's Diary, 14.

Graphic testimony of the openness of the hierarchy and theologians towards the phenomena of Garabandal

1. From left to right: Conchita, Lucio Rodrigo S.J., and the Servant of God, Manuel G. Nieto.

2. Mons. Del Val with Michael Tubberty, producer of *"Garabandal: The Eyewitnesses"*, video in which the prelate affirms that the message of Garabandal is *"important"* and *"theologically correct."*

3. From left to right: Mari Loli, Garabandal seer, Mons. Juan Antonio Del Val, bishop of Santander (1971-1991), and María Saraco, editor of The Vigil, a publication dedicated to spreading the message of Garabandal, an issue of which Mons. Del Val is holding in the photograph.

4. Mons. Joâo Pereira Venâncio, bishop of Leiría-Fatima (1958-1972), beside Conchita in the United States, during one of his visits to the seer when she resided in New York; a trip that indicates the prelate's interest in the phenomena of Garabandal.

5. Mons. José Vilaplana Blasco, bishop of Santander (1991-2006), receives Jacinta, seer of Garabandal, accompanied by her husband and their daughter, in 1993.

1

Missionaries of Charity
54-A, Lower Circular Road,
CALCUTA-X8016,
10/5/88.

Dear Fr. Benac,
Thank you very much for your kind letter. Thank God for people like Conchita and her family for their lives speak so loudly of the love of God in them and through them to all they meet. Please pray for me and our Society - that we may continue God's work with great love and not spoil it.

God bless you
M. Teresa mc

Missionaries of Charity
54·A, Lower Circular Road
CALCUTA-700 016

5 October 1987

Dear Fr. F. Benac,

Thank you very much for your kind letter.

Thank God for people like Conchita and her family for their lives speak so loudly of the love of God in them and through them to all they meet.

Please pray for me and our Society - that we may continue God's work with great love and not spoil it.

God bless you
M. Teresa m.c.

2

1. Conchita holding a photograph signed and personally dedicated by Blessed Teresa of Calcutta.
2. Reproduction of a handwritten note from M. Teresa. In it, she responds to a letter from the Jesuit missionary Francisco Benac, a committed promotor of the Garabandal apparitions in India. The note, as well as providing testimony of the closeness between M. Teresa and Conchita, reflects the inestimable judgment of the religious concerning the seer's virtues, in her judgment, years after the apparitions, which "speak so loudly of the love of God."

Photographs of Blessed Teresa of Calcutta: her interaction with the seers

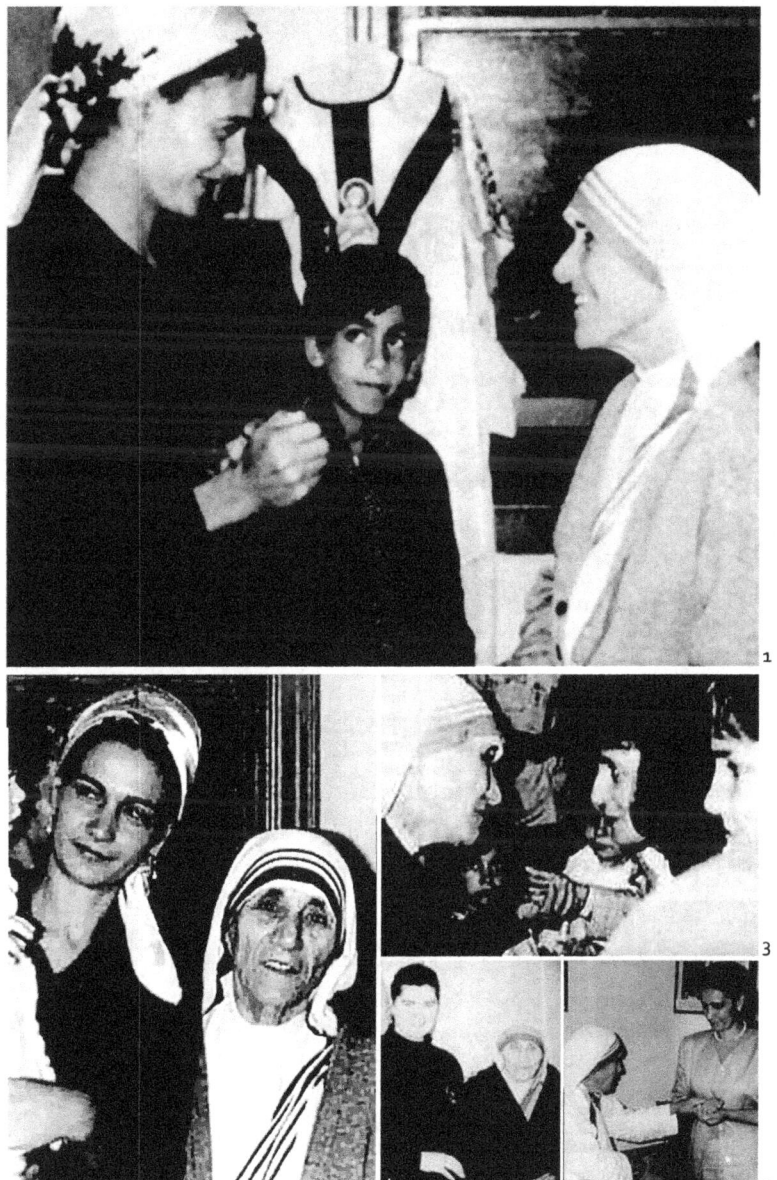

1. Blessed Teresa greets Conchita (1976). 2. With Conchita, who is carrying one of her daughters in her arms (1976). 3. Holding Mari Loli's hand (1987). 4. With Jacinta (1992). 5. With Conchita (1997).

1. The stony surface of the Calleja, the location of many apparitions and numerous dawn rosaries.
2. The slope of Mount Hormazo, including the village and, a little higher up, the plateau of the Pines.
3 & 5. In the 60s, the years of the apparitions, the streets of the village were not asphalted.
4. Corpus Christi procession, Thursday the 17th of June 1965, eve of the publication day of the second message: the Blessed Sacrament is carried by Fr. Laffineur; Ceferino (Mari Loli's father) is holding the palio on the left, and Pepe Díez the one on the right.

The seers: Mari Loli (above, left), Mari Cruz (above, right), Conchita (below, left) and Jacinta (below, right).

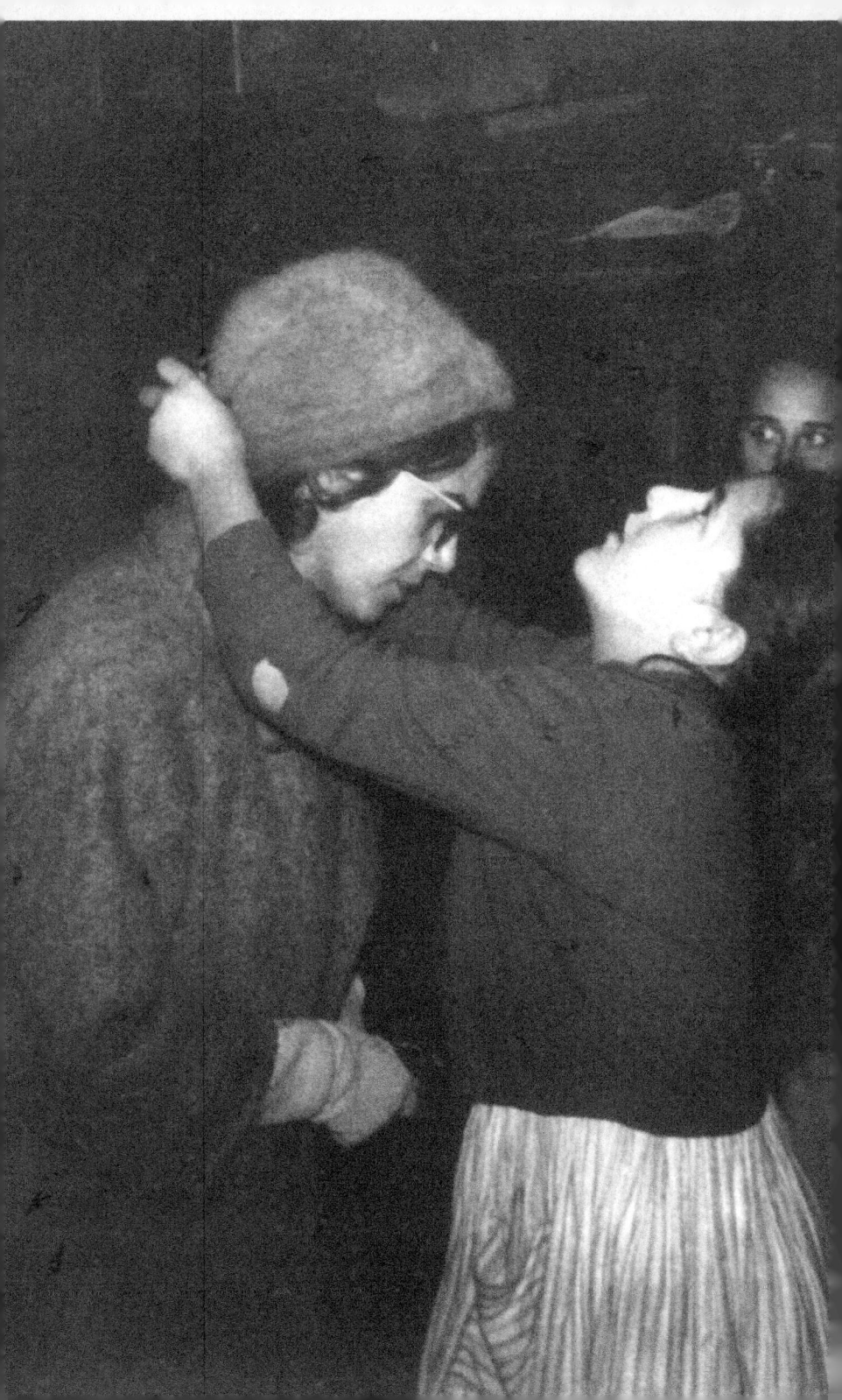

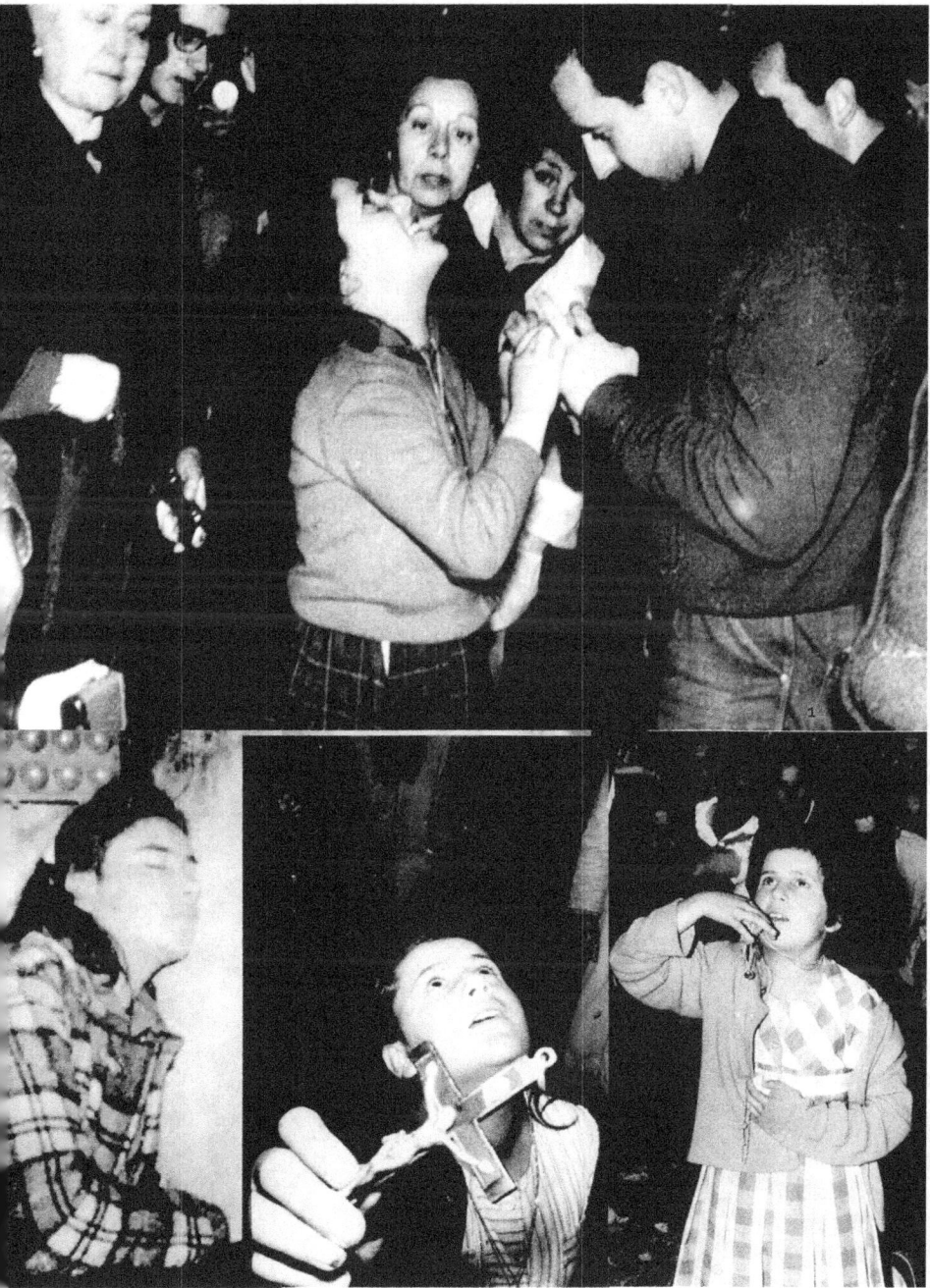

Previous page: Mari Loli in ecstasy returns a medallion to a woman after it has been kissed by the Virgin.

1. Mari Loli returns a marriage ring to its owner.
2. Conchita, awaiting an apparition, asleep in the kitchen of her home.
3. Mari Loli in ecstasy offers her crucifix to pilgrims to be kissed.
4. Loli in ecstasy presents religious objects to the apparition to be kissed.

1. Mari Loli, during an ecstasy, lifted up by Conchita.
2. Mari Loli in ecstasy emerging from a house, in one of the numerous visits to the homes of the village.
3. The four seers in ecstasy. From left to right: Mari Loli, Conchita, Jacinta, and Mari Cruz.

1. Conchita González, the eldest of the seers.

2. The only access to the village is by a six-kilometer path without asphalt from Cosío to Garabandal. Few vehicles were capable of negotiating this path, especially after the rain.

3. The village priest, Fr. Valentín Marichalar, with the four seers.

4. 18 October 1961, the day of the publication of the first public message of the apparitions: heavy and constant rain and even sleet fell unceasingly on the village throughout the day; in the evening there were hailstones. In spite of this, "the crowd reached the figure of 5,000, a really considerable number, bearing in mind how isolated the village is and how difficult the access." Cited in ANDREU, R.M., note in *Conchita's Diary*, 22.

5. Message of 18 October 1962, written by Conchita. The four seers sign the note: "Conchita González, María Dolores Manzón, Jacinta González and María Cruz González."

6. Message of 18 June 1965, redacted and signed by Conchita on the day of its publication.

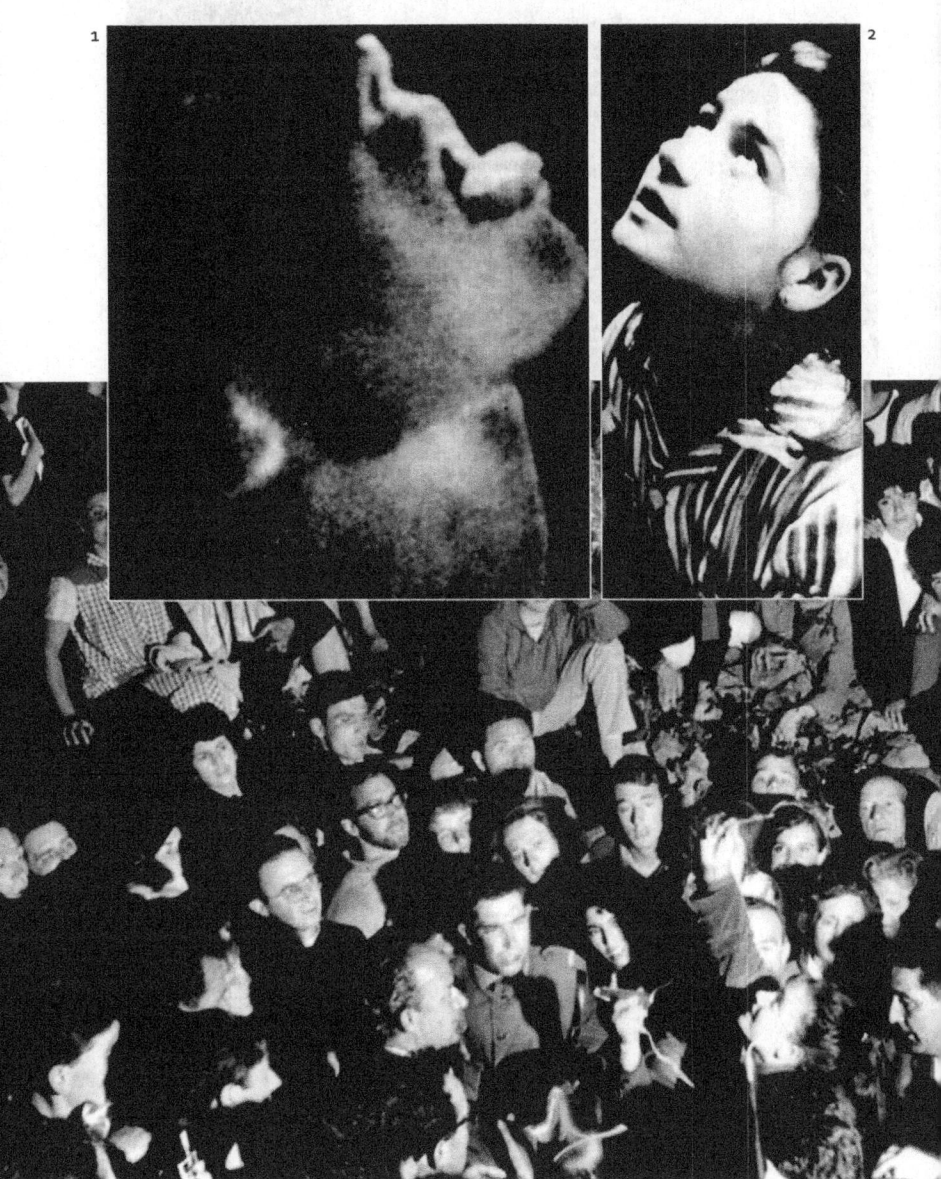

1. One of the 8 mm photograms in black and white from the recording of the Barcelona entrepreneur Alejandro Damians on 18 July 1962, the day of the miracle of the visible communion, the milagruco announced by Conchita. Technically, the image is defective, but is nonetheless sufficiently clear insofar as concerns the event.

2. Conchita in ecstasy.

3. In the midst of the crowd Conchita raises her arm to offer the crucifix to the Lady to kiss on the day of the publication of the second and final public message of Garabandal, 18 June 1965.

Following of the phenomenon

1 & 2. The Calleja, location of numerous apparitions. In the background, in photo 2, "the square" may be seen: a wooden edifice that defended the seers during the ecstasies. Only doctors, priests and members of the girls' families were allowed to pass the barrier.

3. Mari Cruz in ecstasy, surrounded by the public, doctors and agents of public order.

4. The climb from the village to the plateau of the Pines, where many of the phenomena occurred.

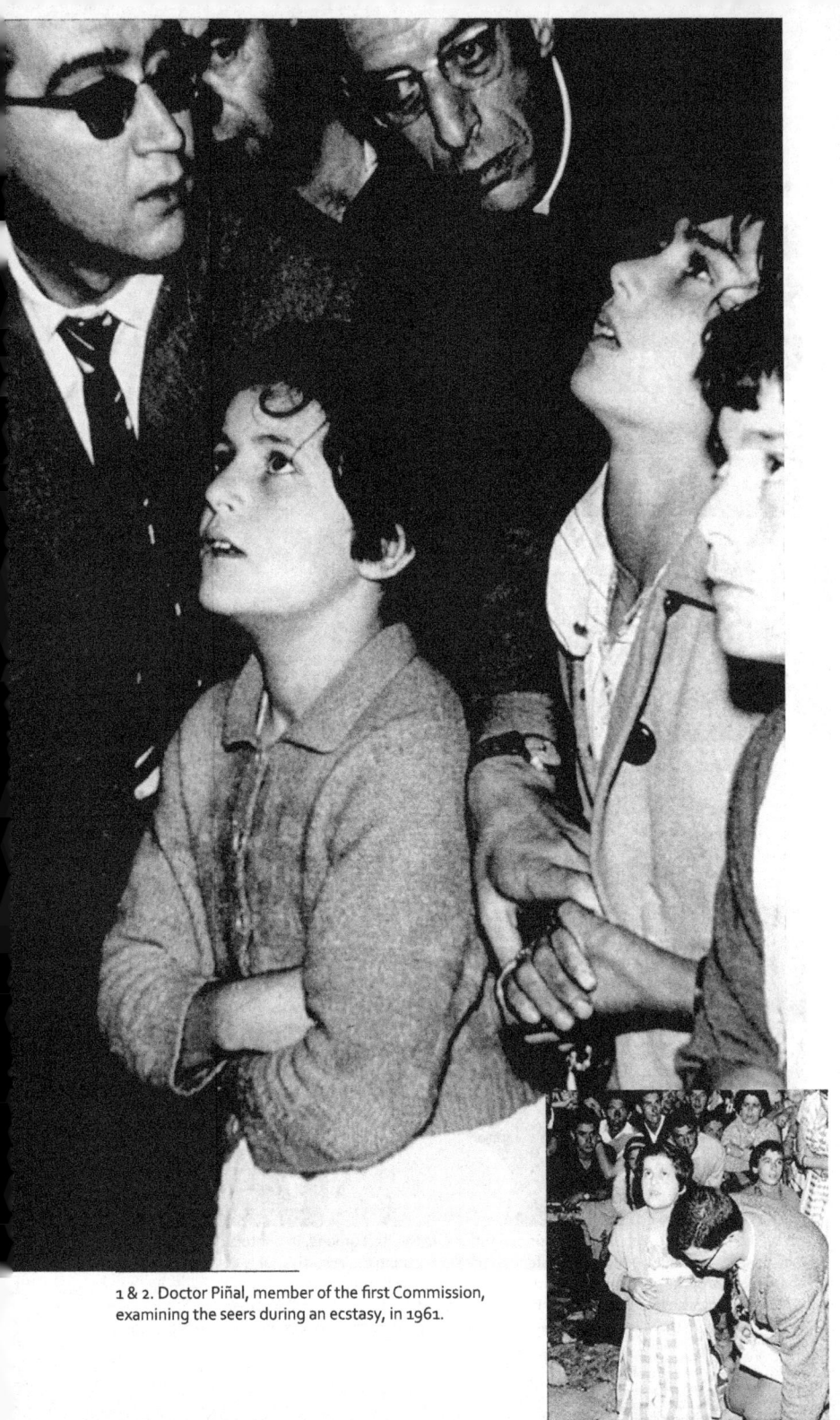

1 & 2. Doctor Piñal, member of the first Commission, examining the seers during an ecstasy, in 1961.

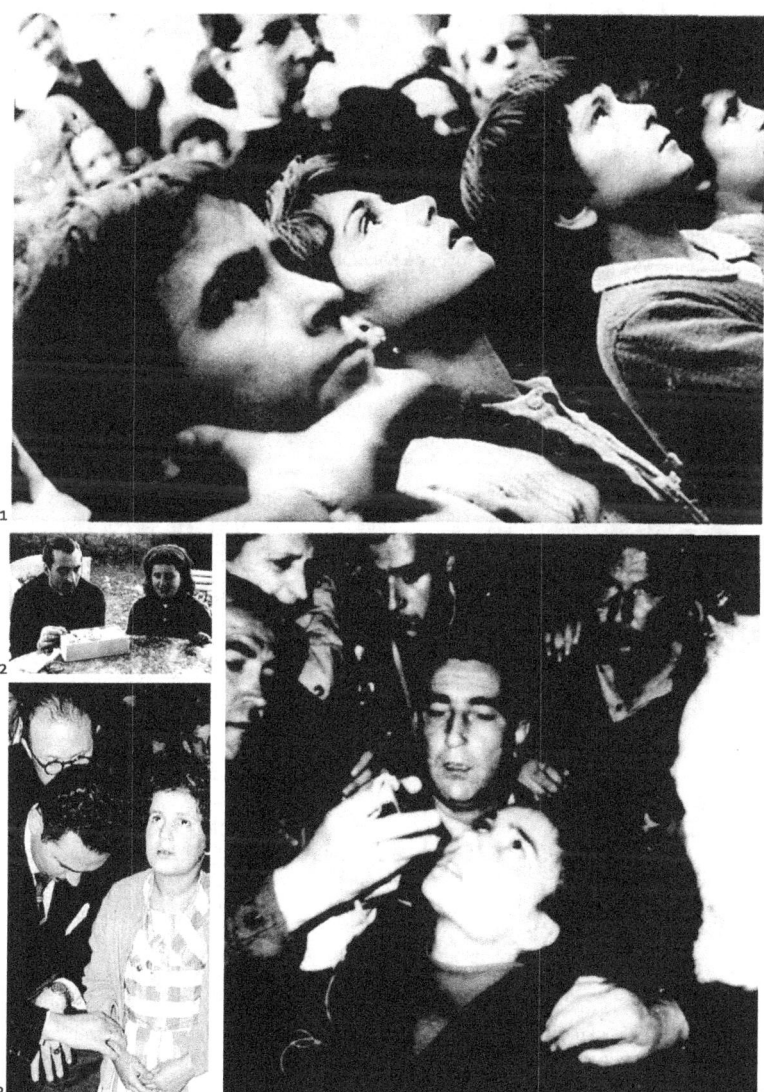

1. From the report of brigadier Álvarez Seco: "[During the trance] the one who cried most was Mari Cruz, whom the doctor grabbed by the lower jaw to twist her face so that she could not stare so fixedly: he was unable to do it, in spite of the force he applied, and I heard a snapping sound and feared he had harmed the child." The girl suffered no after-effects. PESQUERA, 2004, 54.
2. José Ramón García de la Riva, Asturian priest, parish priest of Barro, interrogates Mari Loli
3. A doctor checks the external manifestations of the phenomena in Mari Loli. Just behind the doctor Juan Antonio Del Val, future bishop of Santander, may partially be seen.
4. Conchita under the spotlights, microphones and gaze of doctors and witnesses during the ecstasy of 18 June 1965, when she received the second public message of the apparitions.

De commissie onderzoekt de ziensters in extase

1. From left to right: Fr. Luis J. Luna, Cecilia de Borbón-Parma, Conchita and her mother, Aniceta, in the Coliseum, during the trip to Rome in 1966. Conchita responded to a call from Cardinal Ottaviani. For some time doubts prevailed as to whether this journey took place, until this photograph was published.

2. Conchita (center) and her companions smile as the leave the Vatican buildings after important encounters with Cardinal Ottaviani and Paul VI, who received them positively.

3. Xavier Escalada S.J. discusses Garabandal with Paul VI in a historic interview (1966).

4. Xavier Escalada with Conchita in Mexico during the canonization of the seer of Guadalupe, Saint Juan Diego (2002).

5. The main newspaper of Cantabria, the *Diario Montañés*, highlights the impact of the conference on Garabandal by Dr. Morales on 13 May 1983, in which the Chief Medical Expert of the first episcopal commission admitted manipulating the reports to nullify the apparitions. The subtitle of the news report is significant: "Record attendance at the Ateneo, packed full."

6. Dr. Morales (upper right corner) inspects the Garabandal phenomena in 1961.

7 & 8. Dr. Morales at the conference on Garabandal in the Santander Ateneo (13.V.1983).

PART III

"The Fruits"

What happened with Garabandal?

XII

"The Seers" after the Apparitions

"Lord, do You not love me any more?"

The mystical life is not a spectacle, a show. In God's plan it has a very clear objective: *"not only the sanctification of the one who receives it, but the spiritual benefit of others."*[508] To approve revelations, the Church requires "abundant and constant spiritual fruits (for example, spirit of prayer, conversion, testimonies of charity, etc.)."[509] This being the case, if the mysticism of Garabandal is to be proven authentic, it must necessarily produce *fruits* among the faithful.

This question leads us to assess the phenomena beyond the confined ambit of the village which has been our focus thus far. We have looked at *the facts* (PART I) and *the doctrine* (PART II); it behoves us now to look at *the fruits* as a factor in discerning the authenticity of the events of Garabandal.[510]

The question is an ample one; it ranges from the fruits in the lives of the seers themselves and in the faithful to the reception of the diocesan hierarchy and even several statements by Cardinals like Alfredo Ottaviani, Joseph Ratzinger, and even two Popes. This will give us the global perspective necessary to form a judgment concerning the

---

508 ROYO-MARÍN, A., *Teología de la perfección cristiana*, Madrid, 1958, 792.
509 CDF, *Norms for discernment of presumed apparitions*, 1978, I.1-3
510 *Ib.*

phenomena which have responded so well, thus far, to the requirements of witnesses, theology and the human sciences.

The first of the *"fruits"* required of the apparitions involves the personal trajectory of the seers themselves after the apparitions:

> It is very important to know the personal disposition "of the subjects (mainly their psychological equilibrium, honesty, rectitude of life, sincerity and habitual docility towards the ecclesiastical authority; their capacity to return to a normal regimen of the life of faith).[511]

The rectitude of life of the seers does not constitute a definitive proof; however, according to the *Norms* of the Congregation for the Doctrine of Faith, it is of great importance when it comes to judging apparitions.

"I want you in the midst of the world"
A vocation that defies every prognosis

In Garabandal, none of the seers becomes a nun after the apparitions. All four get married. This differs from the usual known pattern in the Church's history. It will become another source of scandal for Garabandal among many, detractors and believers alike:

> We rejoice that they are honest women and good Christians. But who can deny that [by getting married] they have disappointed everyone or nearly everyone?... The first instruments of God in the work of Garabandal, in the years afterwards, have not been duly faithful... [in terms of] maximal generosity [the consecrated life]... This provides motives for those who opt in favor of doubt or denial.[512]

Without contradicting the most recent pontifical Magisterium, which plainly expounds "the objective excellence -*concreta*

---

[511] *Ib.*

[512] GARCÍA DE PESQUERA, E., (Pseudonym: Dr. Gobelas) *Garabandal: Hora x*, Bilbao, 1983, 7-9.

praestantia- of the consecrated life,"[513] we must however point out an error in this line of argument: all vocations lead to the plenitude of holiness. Thanks to Vatican II (cf. LG 32), this issue does not nowadays present significant difficulties; but it would take time for the Council to be assimilated by the Church; and the seers of Garabandal would suffer the consequences of that delay. They discern their vocation sincerely, but they are pressurized to join the religious life.

After Garabandal, apparitions would be approved in which the seers remained in the lay state; like those of Finca Betania (Venezuela, 1976-1984), officially approved in 1987 by the local Ordinary.[514] In Betania, the Cause of Canonization of the main seer, *María Esperanza Medrano de Bianchini* (+2004), has been initiated in Rome, after its favorable completion at the diocesan level. Esperanza had a great desire to be a religious, but was a laywoman: a wife and mother. Later, she had seven children and twenty grandchildren, and is today recognized as a *Servant of God*. But Esperanza dies in 2004: the *problem* of Garabandal in this sense is, without doubt, that it proclaimed this doctrine too soon, before the Vatican Council II had been assimilated. This entailed, for many people at the time, a literally *"incredible"* novelty.

It is a fact that the seers of Garabandal do not find their vocation in the hiddenness of the cloister. They did attempt that option: Conchita, from the time of the apparitions, expressed desires to be a religious. When the apparitions ended in 1965, "She was taken to a Carmelite [Missionaries of Teaching (Pamplona). While there, on the 13ᵗʰ of February 1966]... *Jesus*

---

513 JOHN PAUL II, Apostolic Exhortation *Vita Consecrata*, *AAS* 88 (1996) 392, 18c.
514 Cf. LAURENTIN, R., *Apariciones actuales de la Virgen María*, Madrid, 1991, 89.

spoke to her in an inner locution... to tell her that her place was in the world, giving a good example":[515]

"Conchita, you have come here to the school to prepare to be My spouse and to follow Me. Do you not say to Me, Conchita, that you wish to do My will? But now you wish to fulfill your own will; do you wish to continue doing so all your life? I have chosen you to be in the world, facing the many troubles you will find there for Me. All this I want for your sanctification and for you to offer for the salvation of the world. You must speak to the world about Mary. Remember that in June you asked Me if you will be a nun. I told you: you will find the Cross in all parts, and suffering. I say this to you again now: Conchita, have you felt My call to be My spouse? No, because I have not called you..."

I said to Him: "Does that mean you do not love me, Jesus?" He said to me: "Conchita, how can you ask Me that? Who has redeemed you? Fulfill My will and you will find my love. Examine yourself closely. Think more of others, don't worry about the temptations; if you are faithful to My love, you will triumph... Be intelligent... Do not cover up the eyes of your own soul; do not let yourself be deceived by anyone. Love humility, simplicity; never think that what you have done is a lot; think of what you must do, not to win Heaven, but so that the world will do My divine will; so that every soul will begin to prepare. Anyone whose soul is ready to listen to Me will know what My will is.

I wish to tell you, Conchita, that before the Miracle, you will suffer greatly, because few will believe you; your own family will think you have deceived them. All of this I desire for your sanctification and so that the world will fulfill the message. I wish to forewarn you that the rest of your life will be a continual suffering; do not be dismayed, for I and Mary, whom you love so much, are present in suffering."

"Of course," Mother Nieves remarks, "this hurts Conchita very much."[516]

[515] CARRIÓN LÓPEZ, G., *El lado oscuro de María. El gran fraude de las apariciones marianas*, Alicante, 1992, 107.
[516] *Diario de Conchita*, 108; MADRE MARÍA DE LAS NIEVES GARCÍA, *"Mis recuerdos sobre Conchita"* in HOGAR DE LA MADRE, *Garabandal*, Santander, October 10, 2013.

But from this moment on she definitively embraces the lay vocation. Jacinta's attempt, having entered a convent of Discalced Carmelites in 1965, ends in a similar way. Jacinta abandons the attempt and becomes a boarding student in the College of Santa Ana de Borja (Zaragoza) run by the Sisters of Charity in September 1965, together with Mari Loli.[517]

There are some who still expect them to enter religious life through their contact with the religious at the school, but this does not happen either.[518] The seers return to their homes after a serious vocational discernment. Their vocation is to the lay state. This distinguishes Garabandal from the usual process of the classical apparitions. In Lourdes, Fatima, Laos or La Salette, all of the seers enter religious communities. Garabandal, on the other hand, reflects the newness of the Vatican Council II.

"Remembering my village makes me suffer"

All four of the Garabandal seers get married and leave the village; three of them even leave Spain. Conchita, tired of the difficulties impeding a peaceful life in her native land, accepts an offer of work in the United States in 1971. The Zamoran Dr. Jeronimo Domínguez, after visiting the village of the apparitions and seeing the suffering of the young woman in that narrow environement, offers her a formation course and a nursing position in his Clinic on Long Island, New York. There, she meets Patrick J. Keena (+ 2013), whom she marries on the 26th of May 1973, establishing her family there also. Conchita and Patrick will have four children, whose names reflect the couple's special devotion to *Our Lady*: *María* Concepción, Fátima *Miriam*, Ana *María* Josefa and Patrick Joseph *María*.

---

517 Cf. PESQUERA, 2004, 578; Cf. LUNA, L. J., *Garabandal*, Zaragoza, 1972, 15.
518 *Ib.*

In 1974, a year after Conchita's wedding, Mari Loli also gets married; in Massachusetts, United States, to Frank Lafleur. The couple will have three children: Francis, María Melanie and María Dolores. But Loli soon falls ill. An auto-immune disease in the respiratory system (*lupus eritematoso*) causes seven long years of suffering until her death at the age of 59 on the 20th of Abril 2009, in Plaistow, Massachusetts. She is the first of the seers to die.

Jacinta gets married on the 21st of February 1976, also to a North-American Jeffrey Moynihan: from California. They settle there, where they continue to live, and have one daughter, whose name is also *María*.

Mari Cruz is the only one who remains in Spain, but she too leaves the village, to marry Ignacio Caballero in Avilés (Asturias), in May 1970. She has four children and, like her companions, returns occasionally to the village. [519]

United States

None of the seers remains in the village, where their roots are. And three of them have a common destination, the United States. Why? Partly to get away from an exhausting environment. Conchita, at the age of 17, provides a good sketch of their difficult situation:

> *Remembering my village makes me suffer; when I'm there I feel constrained. Everyone is constantly advising me and I do everything under orders: "Go to Mass... Pray the Rosary... Do this... Stop doing that..." Sometimes I imagine how happy I would be in a hermitage, far from everyone, doing things for God alone, and seeing what I would be able to do without others always ordering me...*[520]

519 Cf. GALMÉS BELMONTE, R., "*Las niñas*" in FUNDACIÓN HM, *www.garabandal.it*, Lumezzane, 2013.
520 PESQUERA, 2004, 298.

In the village, the seers are besieged by the curious with a thousand questions, requests and requirements. They are sometimes even required to comply with what others think a seer should be and do. This is a daily routine; the people change but the scenario is the same. Their departure from the village was only to be expected. They need serenity, simplicity. And they decisively reject popularity. Conchita hints along these lines in an interview she gave years later in New York (1988):

> When I came here for the first time I was happy. Nursing the poor with Doctor Domínguez I was happy; oh yes! Because now nobody knew me. And here, in America, I feel good, although I also sometimes feel alone.[521]

"*I was happy. Because now nobody knew me....*" Something of what the little ones underwent at the mercy of the curious may be glimpsed here. So, their resolution to leave the village recalls the case of *Saint Catherine Labouré* (1806-1876), the visionary of the Miraculous Medal (1830). The message of the Miraculous Medal was being promulgated by Fr. Aladel, the seer's confessor. He orders the making of the medal and a statue. That way, she succeeds in remaining anonymous. It is true that news filters out that one of the Sisters of Charity has had the apparitions, but not even Saint Catherine's companions ever discover which of the Sisters has been honored by the visit from the Virgin. Catherine confounds every inquiry, to the point that for a long time her companions believe that another nun—the cook of the *Hospice de Reuilly*—is the protagonist of the apparitions. Just two months before dying, Catherine reveals her secret to her superior, Sr. Dufès. Then, on the very night of her death, the 31st of December 1876, Sr. Dufès communicates the great secret to the community,

---

521 Quoted in CARRIÓN LÓPEZ, G., *El lado oscuro de María. El gran fraude de las apariciones marianas*, Alicante, 1992,110.

46 years after the apparitions. The Miraculous Medal had spread throughout France, making a great impact in all of Christendom in the lifetime of the seer; she herself, however, was not known until her death.[522]

Saint Catherine seeks anonymity. This lends more credibility to the apparitions of the *Rue du Bac*, and in Garabandal it is repeated. But why, in their diaspora, do the seers coincide precisely in the United States? This fact should perhaps be qualified simply as fortuitous. When all is said and done, it is a fact that the message of Garabandal has been best received in the English-speaking countries, "particularly in the U.S. and Australia."[523] One proof of this is that *Conchita's Diary*—an indispensable collection of notes written in the time of the apparitions by the eldest of the seers— was published for the first time in North America (Lindenhurst-New York, 1967). Owing to this openness, the children quickly come into contact with pious families of American pilgrims who visit Garabandal. Later on they will integrate their lives with these families, thus distancing themselves from the tensions that, in Spain, were much more difficult to avoid.

Conchita: the focus of everyone's attention

The eldest of the seers, in the midst of all this tension, has a clearly exceptional role. She is the one who has most ecstasies and, above all, it is only to her that the date of the Miracle is revealed, which she must announce eight days beforehand.[524] This means that all eyes are upon her, and, as may easily be imagined,

---

[522] Cf. COLIN-SIMARD, A., *Les apparitions de la Vierge*, Paris, 1981, 91; SESÉ, J., *Historia de la espiritualidad*, Pamplona, 2005, 268.
[523] VIDAL MARTÍNEZ, C., *"...Y los suyos, no la recibieron." Estudio de las epifanías marianas*, Alcalá de Henares, 1988, 57.
[524] Cf. LANÚS, S., *Madre de Dios y Madre Nuestra. Fátima, Ámsterdam y Garabandal*, Madrid, 2013, 255.

it entails no small amount of suffering at the untiring and not always well-intentioned questions of the curious.

From very early on Conchita will try to evade this notoriety brought upon her by the apparitions. On the 20th of July 1963, after Communion, the Lord speaks to her in a locution, instructing her about the Miracle she must announce. In her response, she challenges His choice: *"It would be better if it were all of us, and otherwise, don't make any of us the intercessor* [sic].*"* But Jesus does not enter into debate. The decision is made. And this is put to her in the brevity of his answer: *"No."*[525] Conchita has been chosen for this task and she must accept it. With the mission, she will receive the grace to fulfill it.

Conchita's request is not about seeking to evade responsibility; the cross that she knows will come with this task. Rather, what she is trying to avoid is the privilege of centrality it entails: being the *"intercessor,"* as she puts it, once again employing this word incorrectly, since she clearly does not mean to say that she is the one who will grant the Miracle.

In the end, Conchita accepts, reluctantly, this singular role required of her. And she will always fulfill it, zealously guarding the date of the Miracle, which has been revealed on only one occasion: in Rome, in January of 1966, "very probably to the Pope [Blessed Pope VI] and certainly to Cardinal Ottaviani."[526] Neither did they reveal it. We will return to these interviews later. Conchita did try to reveal the date also to the Bishop of Santander, His Excellency Puchol, in September of 1966, "But in the moment of wishing to say it to him she totally forgot it, and

---

[525] *Diario de Conchita,* 82, note 2.
[526] PÉREZ, R., 1991, 173.

only remembered it again out on the street, having left the Bishop's Palace."[527]

At present, Conchita remains in anonymity. She has been asked many times to make declarations, to appear in public life. In the beginning she acquiesces on a few occasions; over time she ceases to do so:

I fear—she writes in 1971—that what I said in a spoken message to some Americans in 1971, with the only intention of seeing people think more about the message... might have obscured somewhat the authentic message of the Virgin. It must always be understood that those words are mine and not those of the Blessed Virgin. That is why they are worthless. I have noticed that for a time people gave them an importance that they do not have. I am saying this to you to express to you my desire that those words not be published. I continually receive declarations to sign, which I would rather tear up.[528]

Conchita keeps herself busy nowadays in charitable service, tending to the elderly as a volunteer, and directs a prayer group in her own home. In none of these environments has she allowed her identity as a seer to be known. And when, on some occasion or other, the question of Fatima or Lourdes comes up, and in conversation someone mentions Garabandal, she wonders if people might have recognized her, and remains silent. When she is sure she has not been recognized, she smiles to herself, listening to what is said without intervening. She knows that her place now is to wait, to prepare the way with her prayer and a holy life. No doubt, she is very aware of the words that the Lord spoke to her in a locution when she was 14 years old. That day, the 20th of July 1963, when she asked Him *if she would die soon*, Jesus answers her:

527 *Diario de Conchita*, 115.
528 CONCHITA GONZÁLEZ, *Letter to J. Lomangino*, September 8, 1971, in PÉREZ, R., 1991, 63, note 71.

"You will have to stay on earth, to help the world."

"I am very small," she responded, *"I couldn't help in anything."*

"With your prayers and sufferings you will help the world"."[529]

And in that life of family and charity, she continues to this day, the same as her companions.

---

[529] *Diario de Conchita,* 82, note 2.

XIII

The Testimony of the Pilgrims

Conversions and extraordinary healings among the faithful

There were many graces of conversion and healing in Garabandal, during the phenomena and even more so afterwards. We have already seen quite a few. We will focus now on some of the clearer and documented cases. They are absolutely exceptional.

I

The Converts of Garabandal

Maximilian Föeschler
A Protestant in love with the Eucharist

A woman, in deep emotion, approaches one of the seers. It is the summer of 1961, the apparitions are in full fervor, and the girls have seen the Lady with great frequency. The woman wishes to ask the Virgin a question, a question that is for her a cause of anguish:

"Does my husband believe in God?"

When the ecstasy ends, the girl approaches her and transmits to her the answer received: *"In God, he does believe; in the Virgin, very little; but he will believe."* The seer is not aware of the fact that this woman's husband, Maximilian Föeschler Entenmann, is Protestant.[530] The response accurately describes the situation of a totally unknown man. And if this seems little, the prophecy of his conversion is added. For now, though, nothing else happens.

Months later, in October, a few days before the publication of the first message, Ramón María Andreu travels to Garabandal, bringing with him a German engineer: Maximilian Föeschler. Although a Protestant, Maximilian is closely connected to the Andreu family and is a good friend of the priest who is so committed to Garabandal. Maximilian's wife is very devoted to the apparitions and has spoken to him of them with great enthusiasm, but the German does not have the slightest interest in the apparitions.

In the journey, just a few kilometers before Cosío, the two travelers have a tremendous traffic accident. This delays their arrival in Garabandal, although they manage to arrive in time to witness the phenomena that night. But the ecstasies do not impress Maximilian *"in the slightest."* However, at bedtime, "around midnight, Father got very sick, with fainting spells, cold sweats, terrible pains in the left ankle, which seemed inflamed" due to the accident. Two doctors, who are then in the village to study the phenomena, visit the patient, but are only able to apply ice and a bandage to the probably fractured ankle that is causing him such pain. The decision is made to take him to Santander first thing the following morning. Maximilian keeps the patient company throughout the night.[531]

The night wore on until around 3:30 in the morning, when *"we begin to hear noise in the street,"* Maximilian relates, *"and people were shouting at the owner of the house* [Epifania] *to open the door, because Jacinta was there in ecstasy, wanting to enter. She suddenly appeared in the room, went towards Father and gave him the crucifix to kiss."* In the very instant that he kissed the crucifix presented to him by the child, the pains completely disappeared.

Then she suddenly stops—the German writes—*leans backwards, towards where I was standing, and gives me also the crucifix to kiss, twice!*[532]

It seems that after this Maximilian was not quite so *"cold"* as before: *"When the girl left, we naturally reflected on all the details; and Father confessed to me that he had prayed very sincerely in his heart that before leaving, the child would also give me the crucifix to kiss. I had a lot to think about during the few hours that remained of that night."* Hours earlier, Maximilian had followed the seers in their trances without obtaining any show of attention from them; instead, the opposite occurred, in that whenever they gave the crucifix to the bystanders, they always skipped him.

That morning at around eight o'clock, when the doctor arrived, Andreu admits to him that all his pains have disappeared. The doctor does not pay him much heed, but when he inspects the ankle he has no choice but to recognize it: Andreu is cured. Jacinta had returned in ecstasy during the night to tell him so: *"Father, the Virgin has sent me to tell you that you are cured."*[533]

The German engineer, shaken out of his initial coldness, now begins to waver in his convictions. He returns to the village the following 17th of March. And although he is Protestant, this time

[532] Ib.
[533] Ib.

he decides to accompany Andreu on a retreat: he does the Spiritual Exercises of Saint Ignatius in Loyola itself, beginning two days after the visit. In the retreat, Maximilian surrenders:

On the third day, during the Holy Mass we had in the Chapel of the Conversion— he writes—seeing that the other participants were able to receive Jesus (in Eucharistic Communion) and I couldn't, I broke into tears.[534]

He is ready now. Ten days later he is formally received in the Catholic Church. The following day, April 1st, 1962, with deep emotion, he receives his First Communion.

Muriel Catherine
An anticipated baptism

Muriel Catherine is an 18 year old French girl, daughter of a Jewish father and Protestant mother. She has never witnessed any interest on the part of her family in religious matters: neither of her parents profess their faith. Muriel travels to Spain in the summer of 1961 with the intention to study Spanish. She is received in Burgos, in the home of a young single woman, Ascensión de Luis. Ascensión is a deeply religious woman and her example soon awakens the French girl's interest in the supernatural. Observing Muriel's progress, Ascensión proposes a pilgrimage to her. And so, on the 27th of August 1961, they arrive together in Garabandal. But everything seems to go wrong: the village is packed with people who show little interest in things religious. It is the height of the summer, August, and the good weather and vacations have drawn a crowd of curious spectators. The atmosphere is ugly, so much so that a Salesian openly remarks that "it gave the impression that the devil was appearing

---

[534] Ib., 351.

there rather than the Virgin."[535] This statement reaches the ears of the seers and causes them such sorrow that they decide to test the apparitions: they take a jar of holy water and determine to hurl it over the Lady the next time she appears. The opportunity arises the following night, in Jacinta's house. Muriel and Ascensión are present, among either eight or nine other people.

Jacinta and Mari Loli have closely guarded their little jar and remain firm in their resolution.[536] The ecstasy begins and the little ones mention to the vision that the priest's comment has spread the opinion that it is all from the devil. With sadness they tell the Lady their decision about the holy water for her to move away. Quickly, however, their sadness turns to joy. They seem to speak about Muriel, and are heard to say: *"She is not Catholic... She is not baptized... Come, help her... Oh, because of her parents..."* Then they give objects to the apparition to kiss and when it came to one owned by Ascensión, they remark: *"Oh, she learned to pray with this Rosary?... She said her first Hail Mary with it?..."* Ascensión was unable to believe her ears. Effectively, Muriel had not long previously said her first prayers with that Rosary. But how could the seers know this? It is impossible.[537]

And this is not all. Having finished with the kissing of the objects, the girls ask: *"Now? Okay!."* Loli takes the jar of holy water, opens it and hurls the water upwards, in front of her. Now something quite inexplicable occurs:

*The water did not follow a normal course. I was seated right in front of Loli and it did not fall on me—*Ascensión explains. *"Instead, curving mysteriously on its way, it fell like a small shower of rain on Muriel, who was sitting facing Jacinta. Fr. Valentín* [the parish priest], *who was*

---

535 Turner, F., *"Conversión de Muriel Catherine"* in WORKERS OF OUR LADY, Ontario, 2013, www.ourlady.ca.
536 *Ib.*
537 *Ib.*

behind Muriel, assured me that not a single drop had fallen on him. I was holding on to his arm and both of us, stunned, leaned on each other. I too can testify that none of the liquid fell on me. Muriel, on the other hand, felt this mysterious "bath" not only on her head but also on her clothing and even her feet. "Yes, I got soaked," she said. This was truly remarkable, since the jar was very small and wasn't even full.[538]

This experience is definitive for Muriel. She could not act on it immediately because of her parents' opposition, but after a long two-year wait, on reaching legal adulthood—then 21 years of age—she was finally baptized on the 20th of October 1963 in the Cathedral of Burgos by the Jesuit Ramón María Andreu, the witness of so many phenomena. Muriel will choose the baptismal name suggested to her by Conchita: *María del Carmen*, in direct relation to the apparitions which had helped her so much in her conversion.

II

The Testimony of Medicine

The healings of Garabandal

Cristina Wayo
An astonishing cure

Cristina Wayo is a young Nigerian Catholic who in 1968 suffered an unfortunate accident, the consequences of which include atrocious pains. X-rays show that the damage was serious. Several doctors treat her over the following years, but she never finds relief. Her right kneecap is split in two. Cristina's calvary is

---

[538] *Ib.*

prolonged and she has to make several visits to the surgeon, without success. Eventually the doctors decide to extract the kneecap in an operation which ends her hopes of a cure. Her knee is left completely welded, without the possibility of movement.

Years later, Cristina signs up for a pilgrimage to Garabandal. By this point she has been unable to walk without crutches for thirteen years. Arriving on the evening of the 20th of July 1981, she cannot climb the steep slope leading to the Pines. The next morning, with determination and the aid of two companions, she succeeds in reaching the Pines with her group. They pray the Rosary and she experiences the peace and presence of the Virgin. So, she wishes to return there that afternoon, only to discover that her companions have done the climb without waiting for her. Cristina then tries to get there by herself, but it is impossible: she falls down at the beginning of the steep *calleja* and prays to the Virgin. With this, she recovers her courage: "*It was as if an inner strength,*" she writes, "*was helping me.*"[539] She sets off again and reaches the top of the hill all by herself. Once there, she kneels down in deep emotion; this is something she hasn't done for years. Her prayer is one of intense thanksgiving. Her companions are as completely disconcerted as she is.

Cristina is cured. Her recovery has been total and instantaneous. The kneecap extracted by the doctors is mysteriously back in its place, in a perfect state. The members of the group "*were stunned, weeping and shouting: "A miracle! A miracle!" and thanking the Virgin... Ever since then I have been able to kneel without difficulty and to spend long periods in prayer*

---

[539] HANRATTY, B., *"Cristina Wayo´s remarkable cure at Garabandal"* in GARABANDAL JOURNAL, Minnessota, 2004, 10.

without needing help. My right knee is better than ever... and this leg feels stronger than the other."[540]

It is a surprising case: a complete surgical extraction, a crowd of witnesses and an instantaneous and radical healing in which a missing bone *reappears;* the right kneecap had been *removed* years earlier.[541]

Doctor Luis Morales
From fierce enemy to defender of the apparitions

A well-known psychiatrist from Santander, Luis Morales Noriega, stands out in the process of Garabandal. From the beginning of the phenomena in 1961, Morales had been designated by the Apostolic Administrator of the diocese, Msgr. D. Fernández, as the principal doctor of the Committee set up to investigate the apparitions. Morales himself would later confess to not having been up to the task. However, after a preconceived negative position regarding the phenomena, Dr. Morales retracts and radically alters his view. This arises from events of which he is a privileged witness in the *Hospital de Valdecilla* (Santander). His wife, gravely ill with cancer and depressed, "after great pain, recovered her inner peace in the last month of her life through a crucifix *kissed by the Blessed Virgin* in Garabandal; she received the last sacraments and died with great peace."[542] Seeing his wife's change of heart was a big factor in the conversion of Dr. Morales. He knew, moreover, that this same crucifix had a short time earlier been in the hands of Antonio F. Bonín Cavero, also a victim of malignant cancer. Pronounced incurable by the doctors of *Valdecilla,* Antonio had entrusted himself to God: he kissed that

---

[540] *Ib.*

[541] *Ib.*

[542] LANÚS, S., *Madre de Dios y Madre Nuestra. Fátima, Ámsterdam y Garabandal,* Madrid, 2013, 161.

same crucifix which would later awaken the faith of the wife of Morales, and the unthinkable happened: from the moment that Antonio kissed the crucifix, the doctors observed an inexplicable improvement. They declare as much to his family: "*What is happening to Antonio is a miracle.*"[543] Very soon afterwards Antonio is cured and back at home.

Dr. Morales closely follows both cases and, deeply moved, initiates a u-turn in his personal and religious life. Later, taking a further step, he goes so far as to recognize publicly his fraudulent role in the study of Garabandal: he had doctored the Reports of his committee to discredit the apparitions at all costs. Around the figure of this man, three exceptional graces are combined: the healing of a terminal cancer and two authentic conversions. The Lady had pre-announced such occurrences: "*Jesus,*" Conchita wrote, "*will work wonders through the objects kissed by Her.*"[544]

Wonders throughout the world

Matters do not end here. There are numerous cases of healing connected to Garabandal: Mercedes Mendiolea, a young woman from Santander, in August of 1966, was cured of an illness diagnosed as terminal by doctors; Alberto Gutiérrez Orena, also from Santander, was cured instantaneously on the 18th of September 1966 after kissing an object kissed by the Virgin in Garabandal; the same happens to Concepción Peña, in 1995; and to a 6-year-old Canadian boy named Shaun Udovic, who was unable to speak, in 1999, in London (Ontario); and to another Canadian, Angela Bolcic, from Scarborough (1999); and to the

---

543 *Ib.*
544 *Diario de Conchita,* 40.

Ukrainians Michael Rozeluk, from Ivano-Frankivsk (2002) and Maria Sychevska of Zolochiv (2004), etc.[545]

This being said, rigorous medical studies do not yet exist to support all the cases. Reports point in the right direction, but proofs must be established. This has been noted in the diocese of Santander itself by Archbishop Carlos Osoro when, in 2007, he mentioned the need to promote authentic *"studies, so that the events of Garabandal may be examined more profoundly."*[546] All the signs point to Garabandal as a truly interesting case.

---

545 Cf. LAFFINEUR, M. - LE PELLETIER, M.T., *La estrella en la montaña*, Tielt, 1967, 182; cf. UDOVIC, F. (the child's father), *"Shaun begins to speak"* in WORKERS OF OUR LADY, Ontario, 2005, www.ourlady.ca; GARCÍA DE LA RIVA, J. R., *Memorias de un cura de aldea. Garabandal 1961-2011*, Madrid, 2011, 360-383.

546 OSORO SIERRA, C., *"Letter to Edward Kelly* (May 7, 2007)" in GARABANDAL JOURNAL, Minnesota 2007, V—VI, 5; LANÚS, S., *Madre de Dios y Madre Nuestra. Fátima, Ámsterdam y Garabandal*, Madrid, 2013, 174.

XIV

The Testimony of the Saints

*St. Pio of Pietrelcina · Bl. Teresa of Calcuta · St. Josemaría
Escrivá*

There are saints among the faithful drawn to Garabandal,
whose virtue and orthodoxy have been tested and proposed by
the Church. Their testimony should not be seen as a definitive
"*proof*" of the phenomena. They are no such thing. However, the
saints provide a witness authorized by the Church, which requires
that apparitions produce "healthy devotion and abundant and
constant spiritual fruits."[547] The saints are the most perfect
example of this. Several of them feature in the Garabandal story,
as we will now see.

I

Saint Padre Pio of Pietrelcina

In March 1962, a mysterious letter arrives in Garabandal. It is
addressed to the four seers, but is unsigned. It mentions a

---

[547] CDF, *Norms for the discernment of presumed apparitions*, 1978, I.3.

supernatural communication received by the sender in relation to Garabandal, is written in Italian, and is dated the 3rd of March 1962. The sender's identity is soon discovered, giving rise to a close bond with the seers, who will later visit him. It is Saint Pio of Pietralcina (1887-1968). It was Conchita who opened the letter and Félix López, a seminarian from Bilbao who was present, translated it for her:

> Dear girls: at nine o'clock this morning, the Blessed Virgin told me to say to you:
>
> > "Oh blessed girls of San Sebastián de Garabandal! I promise you I will be with you until the end of the times and you will be with me at the end of the world. And afterwards, united to me in the glory of Paradise."
>
> I send you a copy of the holy Rosary of Fatima, which the Virgin has ordered me to send to you. This Rosary has been dictated by the Blessed Virgin and must be propagated for the salvation of sinners and the preservation of humanity from the worst chastisements which the good God is threatening. I give you just one counsel: pray and encourage prayer, because the world is at the beginning of perdition.
>
> They don't believe you, or in your conversations with the White Lady... They will believe when it is too late.[548]

The brief text of the letter contains several references to aspects of the apparitions: the closeness of the Virgin, the importance of prayer... but perhaps the most surprising one is the almost textual quotation of the reiterated response of the Lady to the girls' requests for proof so that people will believe. "*They will believe,*" the Lady always responds. "*They will believe,*" the Capuchin now writes, "*when it is too late.*"[549]

---

[548] PESQUERA, 2004, 337;76.
[549] Ib.

In February 1975, in an interview for the magazine *Needles-Garabandal Journal*, Conchita talks about her reaction to this letter:

> *"I was taken aback by what it said and, since it came unsigned, I kept it in my pocket until the next apparition. When our Holy Mother appeared, I showed her the letter... and asked her who it was from. Our Blessed Mother answered me that it came from Padre Pio. I didn't know at the time who Padre Pio was, and it didn't occur to me to inquire further.*
>
> *"After the apparition, we were discussing the letter; and then a seminarian who was there [Félix López] explained to me who Padre Pio was and where he lived. I wrote to him, telling him that if he ever visited my country I would like very much to see him... He answered me with a short letter, in which he said: 'Do you think that I can climb in and out of chimneys?' At 12 years of age, I had no idea of what a monastery might mean."*
>
> *"Have you kept those two letters?"*
>
> *"Yes."*[550]

Conchita visits the Capuchin with the Stigmata

In February 1966, Conchita travels to Rome. She has been called by the Pro-Prefect of the Congregation for the Doctrine of Faith, Cardinal Ottaviani. She sets out in the company of her mother Aniceta, Luis J. Luna (now parish priest of Garabandal, having substituted Fr. Valentín the previous summer) and an illustrious lady named Cecilia De Borbón-Parma, member of the Royal Carlist famy and "artificer of the journey's eventual success."[551] In this journey, one of the contacts of the little expedition is Dr. Enrico Medi, friend and personal doctor of Blessed Paul VI. Medi suggests availing of the journey to visit San Giovanni Rotondo and to see Padre Pio. Conchita is overjoyed at

---

550 *Ib.*
551 LUNA, L. J., *Garabandal*, Zaragoza, 1972, 18.

this idea, since she vividly remembers the message the Capuchin transmitted to them in his letter on behalf of the Lady: *"I promise you that you will be united to me in the glory of Paradise."* Conchita herself tells the story:

> We arrived at around nine at night and they told us we couldn't see Padre Pio until his Mass at five the next morning. Before Mass, Fr. Luna and the professor [Medi] went to the sacristy. The professor told me afterwards what happened there. He said that Fr. Luna told Padre Pio that the Princess of Spain was there to see him [Cecilia De Borbón-Parma]. Padre Pio said to Fr. Luna: "I don't feel well and won't be able to see her until later today." Professor Medi then said: "There is another person who also wishes to see you. Conchita wishes to speak with you." Then Padre Pio said: "Conchita from Garabandal? Have them come at eight o'clock this morning."
>
> On arrival we were lead to a small room, a cell, which had a bed, a chair and a small table... I remember I had the crucifix kissed by Our Lady, and I said to Padre Pio: "This is the Cross kissed by the Blessed Virgin. Would you like to kiss it?" Padre Pio took the Christ figure and placed it on the palm of his left hand, over the stigma. Then he took my hand, which he placed over the crucifix... He blessed my hand and the cross... as he spoke to me. [552]

Conchita was just 16 at the time and, due to her nervousness and emotion, would not later recall what the stigmatized saint said to her. However, the meeting shows the Capuchin's goodwill and affection toward the phenomena of Garabandal; which he would demonstrate again on other occasions.

In fact, there are several testimonies of people directed towards Garabandal by the stigmatic of Gargano. One who stands out is Joachim Bouflet, Doctor and Professor of Philosophy in the Sorbonne University of Paris and Consultant of the Congregation

---

[552] Cf. WORKERS OF OUR LADY, *Padre Pio and Garabandal*, Ontario, 2005, www.ourlady.ca

for the Causes of the Saints in Rome. Bouflet, on the evening of the 23rd of August 1968, after confessing with Padre Pio in the cloister of the Convent of San Giovanni Rotondo, spoke for a few moments with him. Padre Pio said to him: *"Pray to the Madonna. Consecrate yourself to the Virgin of Mount Carmel who appeared in Garabandal."*[553] Bouflet was taken aback; and Padre Pio insisted: *"Consecrate yourself to the Virgin of Mount Carmel who appeared in Garabandal."* The Frenchman asked: *"The apparitions of Garabandal? So it's true?"* To which the Capuchin effusively responded: *"Certo è vero!"*[554] "Of course it's true!"—Padre Pio shows his appreciation for Garabandal, encouraging devotion to the apparitions among those he directs.

Joey Lomangino and the crisis of Garabandal

Another figure who stands out among those encouraged by Padre Pio to visit Garabandal is Joey Lomangino, a North-American who in his youth had lost sight in both eyes in an unfortunate accident in the workplace. Lomangino was to become one of the best known promoters of the apparitions in America, through the *Workers of Our Lady of Mount Carmel*, an organization founded by him, devoted to spreading the messages.

For many, however, Joey's death (June 18, 2014) would turn him into a proof of the *falsity* of Garabandal. This is because Lomangino always united his testimony with the expectation of a miracle that in the end could seem was not fulfilled: the healing of his blindness. Effectively, in 1964, Conchita transmits to him a few words on behalf of the Virgin which, at least on first sight, are not fulfilled:

---

553 ZAVALA, J. M., *"Padre Pío sobre Garabandal: «¡Certo è vero!»"* in RELIGIÓN EN LIBERTAD, August 31, 2013, www.religionenlibertad.com (October 7, 2014).
554 *Ib.*

"The Virgin told me that you will receive new eyes."[555]

As it turns out, Joey dies in 2014, after more than fifty years of working for Garabandal, without having recovered his sight. And both he and Conchita had tirelessly explained those words of the Lady in terms of a physical healing.

For many, this story entails *"the end of Garabandal"*: Joey, deceased without having *"physically"* received new eyes, proves that the prophecy has failed. Therefore, everything else is equally false.

But this *interpretation* of the prophecy never convinced everyone. Some doubted that this prophecy of *"new eyes"* implied *"necessarily"* a material interpretation, a physical healing. They always advocated in favor of a *spiritual interpretation*. In fact, Joey himself, at the end of his life, without losing peace, opts also for this interpretation, and confesses to having received *new eyes*: *"eyes of faith,"* he says, explaining that his faith no longer rests on a *material* fulfillment of the prophecy.[556] Significantly, Lomangino will never abandon Garabandal or cease to be faithful to the Church, in spite of having spent entire decades waiting for a miracle. He now sees the matter *with new eyes*.

Is it reasonable, Joey's step from the material to the spiritual interpretation of the prophecy? For many it changes nothing. And pages certifying the death of Garabandal multiply on the Internet. However, the material interpretation (of a physical miracle) creates more problems than it solves; because, if everything is false, what response is there to account for all the phenomena between 1961-65 witnessed by thousands of people and qualified

555 LANÚS, S., *Joey Lomangino Dies*, Buenos Aires, 2014, www.virgendegarabandal.com (consulted on:October 7, 2014).
556 LANÚS, S., *Joey Lomangino, Gran apóstol de Garabandal*, Buenos Aires, 2014, www.virgendegarabandal.com.

doctors? The Jesuit Lucio Rodrigo (1885-1973), Doctor and Professor of Theology at the University of Comillas and great studier of the seers, says that:

> These phenomena were not and could not have been invented by the children, nor [could they] be the result of imaginings of pathological origin... No one has reason to destroy [the apparitions] or even to attenuate them simply because of what the children might say in the present or even in the future.
>
> [If that happens] they will be under an illusion, not us.[557]

Rodrigo's position would be that *the Lomangino case* cannot explain the events that have occurred. It is meaningless to try to establish the explanation of those events in what the children say about their visions. If they misinterpret them, *"it is they who are under illusion, not us."* If they interpret the prophecy materially, they may be under an illusion, but this does not undo the facts. The explanation must be objective, since the facts are undoubtedly so. This being the case, the option of a *material interpretation* could explain an error in the prophecy of Lomangino, but it does not overrule the other phenomena.

The *spiritual interpretation*, on the contrary, avoids such problems. If Joey persevered in faith and received *eyes of faith*, the prophecy has been fulfilled.

The question then is: how could Conchita have made a *material interpretation* of the prophecy, confusing so many people of good will? Is there an explanation for this? There certainly is, but it is sad to recognize it: the apparitions of Garabandal have never received, at the time of the events or afterwards, the appropriate attention of theology. *For years*, neither the seers nor the promoters of

---

557 Cited by ANDREU, R. M., *"Puntos principales de la historia de Garabandal"* in *Diario de Conchita*, 118.

Garabandal—such as Joey—have enjoyed the aid of pastors. Lucio Rodrigo himself is a good example of this:

> Silence [about Garabandal] has been imposed upon me, without a prior hearing, and all I can do is remain silent; which is why I cannot say all that I would have to say to you on the matter.[558]

In 1968, Fr. Rodrigo is forbidden by his superiors to discuss Garabandal. Why? Eminent members of the diocesan committee like its chief doctor, Dr. Morales—who will publicly recognize as much in 1983[559]—doctored their *Reports* with the express intention of sinking Garabandal. This leads to widespread suspicion, and the seers are left alone with the challenge to explain what is happening to them. This explains why, in some cases, like that of Lomangino, the little ones venture interpretations which only time has been able to correct. It must be emphasized that their error is only in the interpretation: the fact, the date, remains intact. It also explains why they themselves come to realize very early on that they must keep silent. And they no longer offer interpretations; this is the Church's task.

Padre Pio and the Great Miracle of Garabandal.

Other saints have shown interest in the phenomena of Garabandal, but the way Padre Pio got involved is quite exceptional: Conchita quotes his name in her *Diary*, noting that, according to the apparition, no matter where he would be, he would see the Miracle.[560] So, when the Capuchin dies in 1968, Conchita is puzzled. However, a month after the saint's death, on the 16th of October 1968, she receives a telegram from Lourdes asking her to go there to collect a letter left for her by Padre Pio.

---

[558] RODRIGO, L., *Carta sobre Garabandal*, Comillas, December 16, 1968.
[559] Cf. LÓPEZ DE SAN ROMÁN, *La verdad sobre Garabandal*, Valladolid, 2012.
[560] Cf. *Diario de Conchita*, 70.

Two Frenchmen who happen to be in Garabandal at the time, Father Alfred Combe and Bernard L'Huiller, offer to take Conchita and her mother to Lourdes. They set out that same night. Father Bernardino Cennamo O.F.M. is waiting for them in Lourdes. He explains that Father Pellegrino, the priest who took care of Padre Pio during his last years, had written down a note for her dictated by the saint.

Father Cennamo admits not having believed in Garabandal at first, but also admits to Conchita that when Padre Pio asked him to give Conchita the veil that covered his face after his death, his opinion changed. That day, in Lourdes, "the veil and the letter were delivered to Conchita."[561] But she is more interested in another matter, which she swiftly brings up to Father Cennamo: *"Why did the Virgin tell me that Padre Pio was going to see the Miracle and now he has died?"* To which the Capuchin responds: *"He saw the Miracle before dying. He himself told me so."*[562] If this was so, the saint of the stigmata thus joins the tight circle of protagonists of Garabandal who see the foretold Miracle shortly before dying. This connects Padre Pio to Garabandal beyond the level of a pious spiritual interest in its message, given that, supernaturally, he experiences in advance *a vision of the Miracle,* which not even the seers themselves have had.

Luis María Andreu: the fifth seer of Garabandal

However, Padre Pio does not exclusively occupy this extraordinary place in the story of Garabandal. We know of someone else, another priest, who receives *the same grace:* Luis María Andreu (1923-1961). Luis María is a young Jesuit and brother

---

561 LANÚS, S., *Madre de Dios y Madre Nuestra. Fátima, Ámsterdam y Garabandal,* Madrid, 2013, 182.
562 *Ib.*

of one of the most outstanding analysts of the phenomena; Ramón María Andreu, also a Jesuit. On the night of the 8th of August 1961, Luis finds himself in Garabandal, notebook in hand, meticulously examining an ecstasy of the girls in the Pines. He suddenly begins to weep. Both brothers, Conchita recalls, *"had come with many, believing nothing."*[563] Now Luis is "visibly impressed."[564] The spectators discover that, like the girls, he too seems to be in ecstasy. In fact, the seers see him within their ecstasy: "It was the first and only time that a stranger to the seers fully entered their field of vision; during the ecstasies the girls usually only saw the apparition." Suddenly Luis cries out: *"Miracle!"*[565] Four times he repeated that cry. He has not seen *a miracle* but, in advance, *"the Miracle"* of Garabandal, the foretold wonder. After the ecstasy, Fr. Luis descended from the Pines among the other people, without revealing the details of his experience, acting with simplicity, trying to divert attention from himself.

Shortly afterwards, after nightfall, he set out with his group on the return journey to Aguilar de Campoo, whence he had come that morning. During the journey, the Jesuit, absorbed in the experience of the day, didn't speak much until he uttered the words that constitute the only testimony of what he might have seen that day:

> *I feel truly filled with joy, with happiness. What a gift the Virgin has given me! What a blessing to have such a Mother in heaven!... We must have no fear of the supernatural life... We must learn to relate to the Virgin like the girls do. They have given us an example!... I cannot have*

---

[563] *Diario de Conchita,* 98; PÉREZ, R., 1991, 49.
[564] PESQUERA, 2004, 156.
[565] *Ib.*

the slightest doubt about the truth of their visions... Why has the Holy Virgin chosen us? Today is the happiest day of my life.[566]

These turn out to be the last words spoken by Luis in his life. Having uttered them, Luis María Andreu falls peacefully asleep in the car seat, and dies. No one expected it: he was only 38 years old and in good health. His brother Ramón, who would later study Garabandal in depth, is deeply shaken.

Luis thus became a protagonist in the events of Garabandal; he is *"the fifth seer."* He would later be joined by Padre Pio, who probably had a similar experience. Both take the experience of the Miracle to the tomb. Neither of them told anyone what he saw. All we know is that it made a deep impression on them both: Padre Pio reveals as much with his gift to Conchita, Luis with his words: *"Today is the happiest day of my life."*

II

Blessed Mother Teresa of Calcutta

It won't be easy to find another saint whose relationship with Garabandal is as close as that of Saint Pio of Pietralcina. And yet there are solid testimonies of saints who have manifested a clear and decisive support towards these apparitions. Among them, the close bond between Blessed Teresa of Calcutta and the seers of Garabandal, even in the most difficult moments for the phenomena, undoubtedly stands out. Mother Teresa (1910-1997) first learned of the phenomena in 1970: *"From the beginning,"* she

---

[566] *Ib.*, 160.

later writes, *"I felt that the events were authentic."*[567] The Albanese founder followed the events of Garabandal with interest and knew three of the seers personally, maintaining a particularly close and prolonged contact with Conchita. Whenever she traveled to New York, she would meet with the seer, who lived there.[568]

And Mother Teresa, intimately familiar with the events and even with their protagonists, did not hesitate to support the apparitions as far as she could in their ecclesiastical process, to the extent that her commitment to Garabandal is today beyond question. She counseled Conchita on repeated occasions in her decisions, even leaving a written testimony: in 1980, Mother Teresa wrote a note to Conchita with a question for the Bishop of Santander about the licitude of making the messages known. Mother encouraged Conchita to express total submission to the Bishop, no matter what he might ask. Mother Teresa of Calcutta demands blind obedience to the Hierarchy, reminding her that to obey the Bishop in all things was the best way to assist the canonical process of the apparitions. Conchita, who had always made sure to conduct herself in that way, faithfully follows the nun's advice; she presents to the Bishop at the time His Excellency Del Val, the question in the note written by the founder of the Missionaries of Charity, asking his view regarding the promulgation of the events. Specifically, she asked for direction regarding an interview, which the British television station, the BBC, had requested of Conchita concerning Garabandal. His Excellency Del Val granted the permission, asking the seer also to send him Mother Teresa's note, which is conserved ever since in the archives of the Bishop of Santander as proof of Conchita's

---

[567] ZAVALA, J.M., *"Teresa de Calcuta sobre Garabandal"* in RELIGIÓN EN LIBERTAD, *www.religionenlibertad.com*, August 23, 2013, http://www.religionenlibertad.com/articulo.asp?idarticulo=30784 (October 1, 2013).
[568] *Ib.*

fidelity and obedience towards the legitimate authority and the involvement and interest of Blessed Mother Teresa in Garabandal.[569]

III

Saint Josemaría Escrivá de Balaguer

The founder of Opus Dei (1902-1975) personally visited Garabandal. However, his position on the events is not known. In the summer of 1962, availing of a few days of rest in Cantabria: "He visited Garabandal in the company of several boys... He spent time chatting cheerfully and in depth with the girls, which they remember with affection."[570] Mari Cruz, the youngest of the four seers, remembers Saint Josemaría, who visited the village several times, as a particularly friendly priest: "Very sociable, always surrounded by young people."[571] Saint Josemaría always had candy for the seers and stood out among the visitors for his good humor. Santiago Lanús affirms that Msgr. Escrivá visited Garabandal up to three times, expressing great interest in the phenomena.[572]

Unfortunately, the details of those visits to Garabandal are not well known even today. We do know, however, that several members of the institution founded by Saint Josemaría will play a sometimes crucial part in Garabandal. Such is the case of Manuel

[569] Cf. LANÚS, S., *Madre de Dios y Madre Nuestra. Fátima, Ámsterdam y Garabandal,* Madrid, 2013, 183-186.
[570] YAGÜE, A., *San Josemaría y Garabandal,* Badajoz, 2011,
http://www.garabandal.org.es/index.php/hechos/45-opiniones-relevantes/92-san-josemaria-y-garabandal (December 29, 2013).
[571] MADRE MARÍA DE LAS NIEVES GARCÍA, *Letter to the author,* October 29, 2013.
[572] Cf. LANÚS, S., *Letter to the author,* June 11, 2013.

Guerra, theologian and priest later received in the Holy Cross, who was Conchita's confessor during the time she spent in Burgos after the apparitions ended (1966-67). Guerra will always defend the young woman's integrity and the authenticity of Garabandal.[573]

Other Saints Connected with Garabandal

There are many valuable testimonies about Garabandal from saints who have since been canonized. We will not spend much time on them, since their contributions, of openness to and interest in the apparitions, are similar. Their contribution is merely external, providing nothing theologically new apart from the suggestive detail that an abundance of saints are connected to Garabandal, directly or indirectly. We will, however, focus on two such cases, not so "external," in the next chapter: when discussing the attitude of the Popes towards Garabandal, we will see the interest shown by Blessed Paul VI and Saint John Paul II. There is also the testimony of Saint Maravillas of Jesus (1891-1974), reformer of the Discalced Carmel, who encourages her daughters to appreciate the messages of Garabandal,[574] and that of Venerable Marta Robin (1902-1981), mystic and founder of the *Foyers de Carité,* from whom there are several testimonies relating to Garabandal. It was she whom Alfred Combe consulted in the first months of 1971. This French priest, soon after the death of Fr. Laffineur (1970), one of the most documented and convinced defenders of Garabandal, was in doubt about continuing this task. Deeply worried, he presents to the Servant of God that "He was exposing himself to great incomprehension and many blows from priests, general vicars and bishops..." She listens to him and encourages him to continue in his commitment, *"without fear of*

---

573 Cf. LANÚS, S., *Madre de Dios y Madre Nuestra. Fátima, Ámsterdam y Garabandal,* Madrid, 2013, 298.
574 Cf. GARABANDAL JOURNAL, Minnesota, 2003, VII-VIII.

the blows." She was well informed about the facts of Garabandal. At the end of the conversation she says to Fr. Combe:

"Tell the four little ones that I pray for them every day."[575]

Venerable Mother Esperanza of Jesus (1893-1983), founder of two religious congregations of *Merciful Love* in Madrid in the thirties, was also "convinced of the supernatural character of the apparitions of Garabandal."[576]

Two other cases are also worthy of mention; Jesuits of recognized virtue, namely the Servant of God Manuel García Nieto (1894-1974), confessor and spiritual director of Conchita after the apparitions, especially between 1968 and 1970, but later than that too, and Fr. Lucio Rodrigo.

Fr. Nieto is especially attentive towards Conchita "during her difficult years, after the battles of her adolescence and early youth, when she was sometimes frivolous and vain. The letters from him that Conchita kept are brief and sober, but manifest the high opinion he had of her and indicate that he recognized the authenticity of the gifts she received." In fact, "There is a formal testimony of Fr. Nieto's faith in the divine origin of Garabandal... In the course of an interview in 1969, Fr. Nieto assured Juan Bosco Ramos, *Hospitalary Brother of Saint John of God*, who was interested in Garabandal, with a few brief but significant words, that:

"Yes, Garabandal is true."[577]

Lucio Rodrigo (1885-1973), Doctor in Moral Theology and Professor of the University of Comillas, where Fr. Nieto also

---

575 OCHAYTA PIÑEIRO, F., *Estudio sobre Garabandal*, Sigüenza, 2001, IV.9; SERRE, J.-CAUX, B., *Garabandal. Apparitions prophétiques de Marié*, Paris, 1996, 224-225.
576 *Ib.*
577 OCHAYTA PIÑEIRO, F., *Estudio sobre Garabandal*, Sigüenza, 2001, IV.6-7; SERRE, J.-CAUX, B., *Garabandal: Apparitions prophétiques de Marié*, Paris, 1996, 220.

resides,[578] knows and has personal dealings with the seers. Fr. Rodrigo expresses a favorable judgement of Garabandal in numerous writings:

> Our belief is not based on what the girls said about their visions in those times, be it in the moments of ecstasy or afterwards, but rather on the consideration of the combination of phenomena which we have witnessed, or which other thoroughly reliable persons affirm they have seen; we have submitted this accumulation of facts to a severe critical analysis and have reached the conclusion that these phenomena were not and could not have been invented by the children, nor could be the result of imaginings of a pathological or demonic origin... [That is why] we concluded with belief in the divine supernatural character of these phenomena.[579]

Fr. Rodrigo shows firm conviction concerning the supernatural nature of Garabandal, contributing the prestige and authority of a recognized theology. There are other testimonies accompanying his: Mother María Naya, Mother Marie de la Croix, Father Pel, Father Walter Ciszek, all of whom have the fame of sanctity, believed Garabandal to be true.[580]

There is no need to spend more time on this; we have shown that, even though their belief is not a factor that definitively resolves the question, many theologians and saints provide an added indicator in favor of Garabandal. The confidence shown by such eminent figures of faith points to a "healthy devotion and abundant and constant fruits,"[581] as required by the Church.

---

578 Cf. PESQUERA, 2004, 194; cf. http://www.mensagemdegarabandal.com/products/priest-manuel-garcia-nieto/ (October 1, 2013).
579 Cited by ANDREU, R. M., "Puntos principales de la historia de Garabandal" in Diario de Conchita, 118.
580 OCHAYTA PIÑEIRO, F., Estudio sobre Garabandal, Sigüenza, 2001, IV.9; SERRE, J.-CAUX, B., Garabandal: Apparitions prophétiques de Marié, Paris, 1996.
581 CDF, Norms for the discernment of presumed apparitions, 1978, I.3.

It is an undeniable fact: there are saints associated with Garabandal.

XV

Unofficial Gestures of the Popes

Blessed Paul VI and Saint John Paul II

"Defying hail, rain and snow, Conchita, her mother and I travelled together to Rome in response to the call of Cardinal Ottaviani, in January of 1966."[582] Thus begins the sincere account of Luis Jesús Luna, the priest who succeeded in presenting Conchita to none other than Pope Paul VI.

I

Blessed Paul VI

Chronicle of a historic journey to Rome

"Towards the end of August [of 1965] I offered to put the new Bishop of Santander, His Excellency Vicente Puchol, in direct contact with the children."[583] Luna urgently desires to enable Bishop Puchol to form an objective judgment concerning the apparitions. The reason for this is that the seers are about to leave

---

582 LUNA, L. J., *Garabandal,* Zaragoza, 1972, 16-17.
583 *Ib.*

the diocese to study elsewhere, and His Excellency Puchol, who has been bishop for scarcely two weeks, does not yet know them. However, the devastating *Report of the Committee*, doctored—as would be revealed later by Dr. Morales, its chief medical expert—now diverts all of the Prelate's attention:

"[The Bishop] told me," Luna writes, "that he did not deem it necessary or even prudent to meet them. He assured me he was well informed [by the Committee] and confided in me his plan: to put a young priest, José Olano, in charge of the village, and the girls should remain there; he would indoctrinate them. I told him that I thought it an excellent idea to send a chosen priest there; but that when it came to the children neither he nor I had the authority to decide where they should go; Aniceta—Conchita's mother—had authorized her daughter to study in Pamplona and Loli's and Jacinta's parents had also consented to their departure to Borja. I remember he asked me: '[Is that authorized] *in writing?,*' and I answered: '*Yes, your lordship, in writing. I have the signed permission forms.*'"[584] Fr. Luna had been the acting parish priest of Garabandal for some time (assigned by the previous bishop), and helped the families to register the girls for the academic year of 1965-66 so that they could study and get a good formation, as effectively happened.

> Mari Cruz did not leave the village that year—*Luna continues*—because her parents were elderly and unwell and couldn't be left alone.
> For me it has always been a rule to respect the Hierarchy and to demand respect for it. I have been conscientiously noble in my dealings with God's representatives; but not weak. That day in late August, I said to Bishop Vicente:

---

584 *Ib.*

*"I do not wish to do things behind your back; that is why I have offered
to introduce you to the children. Now I will confide to you a secret. A
gentleman of high standing is arranging for them to be received in Rome
by the Pope."*

The lord Bishop smiled broadly, with characteristic optimism. We
were seated alone, each on opposite sides of the desk, in a lecture hall
on the first floor of the seminary of Santander. I withdrew two
telegrams from my wallet, unfolded them and presented them to
him, open. *"You are from Áragon,"* he said. *"From Zaragoza, your
lordship,"* I said, to be precise.

News of the arrangements filtered out and attempts were made to
impede the meeting. It wasn't until mid-December that I received a
telephone call from Santander informing me of the arrival of
someone from Rome with a letter from Cardinal Ottaviani, which
said:

"With or without the lord Bishop's permission, bring the children to me."

I would have flown there, but Christmas was near and we didn't have
tickets. I asked my illustrious mediator to give the lord Bishop the
letter to read secretly and personally and assured him that I would
prepare the trip for the second week of January. But a lot of patience
and charity is needed—as I know from experience—not to give up in
the face of the barricaded doors of a prelate: the Vicar General [Javier
Azagra] received the copy of the letter. When I met the lord Bishop
again after returning from Rome, he assured me that it had not been
delivered to him. I believed he was being sincere.[585]

In the presence of Paul VI

Between the 12th and 19th of January 1966, Conchita finds
herself in Rome. The 16-year-old makes the journey with great
expectations. In her heart she nurtures the hope of finding in
Rome the comprehension of the Church, which has taken an
interest in her case, but she cannot avoid also feeling a certain

---

[585] *Ib.*

trepidation. Called by the Pro-prefect of the Congregation for the Doctrine of Faith, Cardinal Ottaviani, and accompanied by her mother Aniceta, Fr. Luna and Cecilia De Borbón-Parma, with these feelings she is introduced to Cardinal Ottaviani on the first day of the trip.

For over two hours, the Cardinal himself, together with two other members of his Congregation, personally interrogates her.[586] With the *Diocesan Report* in hand, the Pro-prefect listens attentively to the girl, focusing particularly on the points he finds most obscure in the diocesan document.[587] Conchita tells the Cardinal absolutely everything. She would have liked to do the same before the bishop of her diocese, but it has not been possible to organize a meeting. She knows, therefore, that this is perhaps her only opportunity to testify before the Church. And she tells all: the experiences, her mistakes, her fears, her sins, what she sees in the people... and even something that she has never revealed to any other person, neither to the other girls nor even to her closest family members: the date of the *Miracle*.[588] The Cardinal is satisfied. Fr. Luna, who accompanied her, expresses as much:

> Conchita was two and a half hours making her declaration—Luna writes—before three monsignors of the Roman Curia. The Cardinal came out several times to manifest to us how impressed he was by all that Conchita was saying. I remember he said to me, and later he repeated it:
> *"Bring me the other girls; bring them to me."*
> If Jacinta and Loli did not go to Rome it was because their respective parents refused; and they were in their rights to do so, but it was also

---

[586] LANÚS, S., *Madre de Dios y Madre Nuestra. Fátima, Ámsterdam y Garabandal*, Madrid, 2013, 167.
[587] Cf. PESQUERA, 2004, 303.
[588] PÉREZ, R., 1991, 173; Cf. ch. VI, Actuación de la Santa Sede.

because someone influenced them; and that someone did not have the right. The Cardinal seemed content. Among the twenty or so apparitions of the Blessed Virgin being studied at that time in the Holy Office, those of Garabandal seemed to him [particularly interesting] *'molto interesanti,'* to use his exact words.[589]

The Cardinal must have been very satisfied indeed, given that, when Conchita daringly requested to meet the Holy Father, Ottaviani assented. This is a very revealing detail: when all is said and done, Conchita is the 16-year-old presumed seer of unapproved apparitions unfavorably viewed by the diocesan committee. But Ottaviani has found Conchita to be sincere.

> The next day—*Luna continues*—he [Ottaviani] told us that the Holy Father, after being updated, had expressed the wish to receive us. *"Go, he said, to the Apostolic Palace and ask the audiences secretary for a day and hour."* We did so; but rumors travel fast and we were greeted with hostility: *"The Pope won't receive you; he never will."* *"But, monsignor,"* I argued, *"His Eminence has just told us that the Holy Father has manifested to him, face to face, that he wishes to receive us."* *"Let Cardinal Ottaviani stick to his own Dicastery; I'm in charge here."* And that was the end of that; a knockout punch.
>
> The Cardinal listened impassively to my account. He was evidently used to dealing with such shenanigans. That evening the message of the 18th of June came up in conversation, and when I recalled the statement about *"Bishops, Cardinals are on the way of perdition,"* he expressed agreement with a notable movement of the head, giving credence to the words of the Angel. He did not give up; neither did I.
>
> Before going on, I should clarify that Conchita and I promised to be discreet and have acted accordingly. I cannot reveal who it was that intervened or the methods used; but I can and do testify, before God, that Paul VI, updated on everything, and in spite of everything, blessed Conchita with these transcendental words:
>
> *"I bless you and with me the whole Church blesses you."*

---

589 LUNA, L. J., *Garabandal,* Zaragoza, 1972, 17.

The Pope is with us.[590]

Father Luna, faithful to his promise, cannot tell us who made that historic meeting possible. We know, however, from other sources. It was Professor Enrico Medi—the man who had interceded for Conchita before Padre Pio—who succeeded in arranging, *in extremis,* the interview with Blessed Paul VI:

Wednesday, 19th of January 1966:

The Pope, in the gestatorial chair, leaves the hall of the General Audience. He observes Professor Medi, his personal physician [that is the sign]. The Pope calls him: *"Professor, professor."* Then he says to the bearers of the chair: *"Fermi tutti"* [stop], indicating that they leave the gestatorial chair on the floor and withdraw. The Pope remains alone with Dr. Medi's little group which includes Conchita, her mother and Father Luna, and thus the *audience* takes place, unprogrammed. They have been able to speak with perfect tranquility. Conchita spoke personally with the Pope... Then the little group, with unspeakable joy, headed towards the car to go directly to the airport for the return journey to Spain.[591]

This encounter is unquestionably significant. Nevertheless, it would be erroneous to see it as an approval of the apparitions. The Pope trusts in his collaborators. This gesture of Paul VI does not therefore contain such high pretensions; it is not the result of a completed process, or a papal approval. However, his words do express a certain fact: the will of the Holy Father to encourage the young lady to persevere in the arduous business of seeking approval in the Church. They must persevere in the positive resolutions of that trip. Father Luna is therefore justified in saying: *"The Pope is with us."* Garabandal is from the outset seen by Rome

---

590 LUNA, L. J., *Garabandal,* Zaragoza, 1972, 18.
591 GARCÍA INZA, J., *"Garabandal, Pablo VI y Juan Pablo II"* in RELIGIÓN EN LIBERTAD, February 25, 2013, http://www.religionenlibertad.com/articulo.asp?idarticulo=27863 (September 19, 2013); Cf. *Diario de Conchita,* 108, note 3.

as something *"molto interesante"* in the eyes of Cardinal Ottaviani and those of the Holy Father.

Xavier Escalada, Paul VI and the Phenomena of Garabandal

The Navarran Jesuit Xavier Escalada (Pamplona 1934-México 2006), journalist, investigator and historian, has done outstanding work in the field of Marian apparitions. The Mexican Bishops' Conference has stated as much: "Thanks to Escalada we have discovered an infinity of historical data and evidence that confirm and augment our vision of the life of Saint Juan Diego Cuauhtlatoatzin, especially by the study of the 1548 Codex or Escalada Codex, the oldest document on the Marian apparition [of Guadalupe]."[592] The name of this renowned Jesuit historian will be linked forever to the apparitions of Guadalupe and also, as we will now see, to Garabandal.

In 1966, Escalada, accompanied by his Superior General, Father Pedro Arrupe, is received by His Holiness Paul VI. The investigator has a brief but significant conversation with the Pope. He presents to him the results of his study of the recent phenomena of Garabandal. Previously, the Pope "had read with great interest the history of the apparitions [by Laffineur-Pelletier], the circulars of Dr. Bonance [articles by the same M. Laffineur] and the *Report* of Cardinal Ottaviani, after the interview with Conchita in January of 1966, so that Fr. Escalada only needed to give a quick presentation of the facts... He spoke to the Pope of his work [promoting the

---

592 LAS NOTICIAS. MÉXICO, http://www.lasnoticiasmexico.com/39262.html (September 20, 2013).

messages of Garabandal] in Mexico."[593] And Paul VI interrupted with vigor:

Those messages must be made known.[594]

So, the Pope encourages him to continue his work. Escalada, boosted by the encouraging words of the Pontiff, replies with candor: "*Yes, Holiness, but there are many people who oppose it, even among our own.*" Then the Pope raised his voice:

That doesn't matter; tell those people that it is the Pope who says it, that it is urgent to make these messages known to the world.[595]

Paul VI encourages the work of promoting Garabandal with surprising decisiveness. The Pope went on to say more. With typical Italian eloquence, Pope Montini in two brief sentences provides the most authorized synthesis ever made about Garabandal:

It is the most beautiful story of Humanity since the Birth of Christ. It is like the second life of the Most Holy Virgin on Earth, and there are no words to express thanks for it.[596]

With these words, the Pope highlights the extraordinary frequency of the ecstasies that distinguished the apparitions (roughly "*two thousand heavenly encounters*"[597]): "*It is like a second life of the Virgin on Earth.*" The expression begins to be quoted at a very early stage (1967 and 1968) in places as distant as Spain and Peru. Two extremely early sources reproduce the remark in an identical form: the first testimony is that of another renowned

---

[593] Cf. GARCÍA INZA, J., "*Garabandal, Pablo VI y Juan Pablo II*" in RELIGIÓN EN LIBERTAD, February 25, 2013, http://www.religionenlibertad.com/articulo.asp?idarticulo=27863 (September 19, 2013).

[594] LANÚS, S., *Madre de Dios y Madre Nuestra. Fátima, Ámsterdam y Garabandal*, Madrid, 2013, 179.

[595] *Ib.*

[596] Cited in PESQUERA, 2004, 7.

[597] YAGÜE BALLESTER, A., *Garabandal, 50 años después*, Badajoz, 2011, 9; Cf. PESQUERA, 2004, 233, note 3.

Jesuit, Ramón María Andreu, who, ever attentive to works on Garabandal, refers to this interview of Escalada with Paul VI in a letter signed on the 13th of April 1967 in Valladolid.[598] The following year, on the 7th of November 1968, the same quotation is published for the first time in the city of Tacna (Peru) by the *White Peruvian Legion*; and it is done with the *"imprimatur"* of the diocesan Bishop, His Excellency Alfonso Zaplana Belliza.[599] From then on, this expression reappears in a multitude of media and publications, maintaining the same form.

These are all indications of credibility. Even so, Santiago Lanús, unable personally to verify the fact that the Holy Father made this statement, does not dare in 2013[600] to give assurance that the Pope spoke these exact words, and he separates them from Paul VI's other two expressions to Escalada (concerning the value and urgency of spreading the messages of Garabandal), which enjoy a more *"accessible"* credibility. At that time, the Argentinian lacked a direct confirmation from someone in Escalada's immediate circle. This reservation moved Lanús to check one other detail:

> Through a relative of Fr. Morelos, [a well-known promoter of Garabandal in Mexico], who knew Fr. Escalada, we found out that effectively the words attributed to Pope Paul VI were exact [that is, in conformity with the words untiringly transmitted by the Jesuit]. And they are very inspired: providential. They totally fit the apparitions of Garabandal. They describe and summarize them to perfection.[601]

The Pope's expressive words, *"Garabandal is like a second life of the Virgin,"* point to a distinctive feature of Garabandal: the great frequency and duration of the apparitions (1961-1965). René

---

598 GARCÍA INZA, J., *"Garabandal, Pablo VI y Juan Pablo II"* in RELIGIÓN EN LIBERTAD, February 25, 2013, http://www.religionenlibertad.com/articulo.asp?idarticulo=27863 (September 19, 2013).
599 Cited in PESQUERA, 2004, 7.
600 Cf. LANÚS, S., *Madre de Dios y Madre Nuestra. Fátima, Ámsterdam y Garabandal*, Madrid, 2013, 179.
601 LANÚS, *Letter to the author*, September 18, 2013.

Laurentin, expert in the matter, expresses amazement at "the abundance of extraordinary occurrences that took place in Garabandal from 1961 to 1965."[602] This, in 1966—when the Pope mentions it—was something new: Fatima had had only six apparitions, Guadalupe four, Lourdes eighteen. Today, however, apparitions much more similar to Garabandal have been approved: Akita (1973-1981), Betania (1976-1984) or Kibeho (1981-1983).[603]

This "extraordinary multiplication of signs"[604] entails for Lucas F. Mateo-Seco an undeniable theological category that unites the contemporary Marian apparitions. Garabandal stands out among them by virtue of preceding them all. So, among the "modern Marian apparitions," if it is authenticated, our case presents itself as the first. This is what Blessed Paul VI expressed in referring to the events of Garabandal with that significant confidence in 1966: "It is like the second life of the Virgin and there are no words to express thanks for it."

The Ill-fated "Document" of Paul VI

The words of Paul VI that we have just seen cannot be construed as the Holy Father's definitive judgment. They are far from "magisterium" in any real sense of the word; to be magisterium, a declaration must be "public and solemn," "presented as definitive" or "at least as certain."[605] Such definitions are the fruit of a juridical process that gives the Pope the support of studies previously solicited from diverse experts. The words of Paul VI to Conchita, Escalada and other persons, therefore,

[602] LAURENTIN, R., Apariciones actuales de la Virgen María, Madrid, 1991, 244.
[603] Cf. LAURENTIN, R.(dir.), Dictionnaire des apparitions de la Vierge Marie: Inventaire des origins à nos jours: Méthodologie, bilan interdisciplinaire, prospective, Paris, 2007.
[604] MATEO-SECO, L. F., Fe y visiones en la literatura espiritual del Siglo de Oro español," Estudios Marianos 75 (2009) 133.
[605] Cf. IZQUIERDO, C., Teología Fundamental, Barañain, 2009, 129-130.

though positive, do not constitute a formal pronouncement on Garabandal. The Pontiff does not say them with this intention. They simply contain a desire, an interest, even perhaps a personal opinion on the issue, which is no small thing in itself. However, the poor formation of some supporters of Garabandal will provoke a head-on clash on this point in the ecclesiastical processing of the apparitions.

The spark is ignited in April 1970. The Bishop of Santander, His Excellency Cirarda, publishes a note expressing his sorrow at the fact that some members of the faithful, a group of pilgrims in Rome ("*Legión Garabandal*"), on the basis of being included on a list of groups that received the *Pontifical Blessing*, claim that the Pope has thus given a kind of *implicit approval* to the events.[606] They allege that the said Pontifical Blessings, addressed to a movement that is explicitly *Garabandalist*, are an unequivocal proof of the Pope's decision.

The argument is sadly mistaken because, as is known, these blessings are prepared by secretaries without any involvement of the Holy Father. This group draws the conclusion that the Blessings entail nothing less than official pontifical approval. His Excellency Cirarda, Bishop of Santander, in an official note, denounces the claim: "Literature has been published saying that the Pope has blessed the apparitions of San Sebastián de Garabandal on the basis of one of these cited blessings."[607] These members of the faithful, with this action, demonstrate a fanatical, abusive and biased disposition. The bishop finds himself obliged to put the faithful on guard against this group which has no fear of spreading quite erroneous opinions.

---

[606] Cf. OBISPADO DE SANTANDER, *Declaraciones oficiales de la Jerarquía sobre Garabandal*, Santander, 1970, 17.
[607] *Ib.*

The Pope awaits, perhaps with interest, but *awaits* the result of the diocesan studies. And he had done so because, as His Excellency Cirarda would explain very well, "the Holy Father identifies himself wholly with his Congregation and leaves the judgment of the matter in the hands of the Bishop of Santander, who is responsible, unless the Holy See reserves the matter to itself."[608] From this moment on, all attempts at communication with the Bishop of Santander concerning Garabandal will be entombed beneath this strange conflict. Everyone, prudent and imprudent, finds themselves equally discredited by the sad affair of the ill-fated *"document"* of Paul VI. Both sides could have proceeded with greater discretion.

II

Saint John Paul II

The doorbell rings. It is early, but Albrecht Weber is already seated at his desk, revising some papers. The writer rises wearily to go and see who it is:

"Good morning. May I speak with Albrecht Weber, please?"
"Yes, speaking."
"I bring you a certified letter from the Vatican. Sign here please."

Weber, although he shows no exterior sign of it, is shaken. He signs the confirmation, takes the letter and, dismissing the messenger with a smile, makes his way somewhat nervously back to his desk. He is used to receiving letters from abroad, especially from Spain, because many of his travels and studies throughout the past thirty years have involved investigations in that country

---

[608] *Ib.*

of the apparitions of Garabandal. He has published a multitude of articles and several books on the subject. But from the Vatican? He has never received a letter from there and has no idea what it might be about. He walks hurriedly, worriedly even, and as soon as he reaches his desk he carefully opens the elegant envelope bearing the insignias of the internal Secretary of the Pontifical Household. Albrecht gets more nervous by the minute. Inside there is just one sheet, bearing few letters. The German's eyes leap directly to the end of the page. There he finds handwritten words, an affectionate greeting and, underneath it, a name, a signature: *John Paul II*. Albrecht cannot believe his own eyes. Excited now, he directs his gaze to the beginning of the letter and begins to read it with total attention; from beginning to end, several times. He is particularly struck by these lines:

> *May God reward you for everything; especially for the deep love with which you are making known the events related to Garabandal. May the Message of the Mother of God be received in people's hearts before it is too late... Expressing joy and gratitude, the Holy Father wishes to bestow upon you his Apostolic Blessing.*[609]

This written testimony demonstrates that, as well as Blessed Paul VI, another Pope, Saint John Paul II knew of Garabandal and was positively interested in it. The Pontiff himself, having read Weber's book, *"Garabandal: Der Zeigefinger Gottes"* (1992), wished to send a note to the author. The note is brief and without formal pretensions. And yet, it is of great interest as an expression of *"joy and gratitude."*

The note, reproduced in the second edition of Weber's own book, is redacted by the Pope's personal secretary, Stanislaw

---

[609] WEBER, A., *Garabandal. Der Zeigefinger Gottes*, Meersburg 2000, 19

Dziwisz; but the Holy Father, at the end of it, adds a personal greeting and his signature in his own handwriting.[610]

Evaluation of the Unofficial Gestures of Paul VI and John Paul II

It seems difficult to dismiss the interest of both Blessed Paul VI and Saint John Paul II in Garabandal, since the testimonies supporting it, in both cases, are quite solid. However, in order to avoid confusion, we must recall that such affirmations by the Popes do not entail approval of any kind.

Paul VI's comments to Xavier Escalada and to Conchita, or John Paul II's note to the writer Albrecht Weber, remain on the level of personal remarks; and this in no way involves their judgment as Pontiffs. Certainly, though, their words show their goodwill towards Garabandal, a hope in it, by virtue of its *messages*, their recognition of its *opportuneness*.

They constitute an irrefutable proof that both Popes consider Garabandal to be of interest to the Church. This is what motivates them to encourage the seer and the investigators to work on it with *"urgency."* However, the Popes in no way seek to skip due process with their words of encouragement; rather, they encourage their interlocutors to persevere with tenacity in the arduous process they have scarcely begun.

---

[610] *Ib.*

XVI

Official Pronouncement

Official Notes of the Church Concerning the Events of Garabandal

The village of the apparitions belongs to the diocese of Santander. Its Ordinaries have made official declarations on several occasions throughout the years. These *Notes* are very important, since it is they who have "the duty to oversee and intervene first of all."[611] Outside of Rome, only the local Ordinary has authority in the matter. Ultimately, Rome's responsibility is "to judge the actions of the Ordinary" and the authenticity of the apparitions.[612] And in Garabandal we find extensive communication between the diocese and the Holy See. This issue is of the greatest interest   .

---

[611] CDF, *Norms for the discernment of presumed apparitions*, 1978, III.1.
[612] *Ib.*, IV.2.

Bishop Doroteo Fernández: Garabandal *"is not clear"*

"It would be premature to pronounce a definitive judgment"

When the phenomena of Garabandal begin, the diocese lacked an appointed Bishop. It is run by His Excellency Fernández (1913-1989) as Apostolic Administrator, after the death of its Ordinary, Bishop Eguino y Trecu, in early 1961. In the few months that his responsibility lasts, the Apostolic Administrator makes decisions of great importance, which make him a key figure in the history of the apparitions. He establishes the first Committee to study the phenomena, encouraged by the customary practice of the Congregation for the Doctrine of Faith, "to suggest to the competent Bishop the setting up of a Committee of analysts which should include experts in theology, Canon Law and psychology."[613] Bishop Fernández puts the matter in the hands of Francisco Odriozola, professor of theology and canon of the cathedral. The Bishop does not declare an official nomination; rather, "it seems that Bishop Fernández told Odriozola to choose competent people and that they set to work."[614] So, still in the month of July 1961, Odriozola completes the group with several priests, as experts in theology, and two laypersons, experts in medical sciences.

The priests chosen are Juan Antonio Del Val (later Bishop of Santander), José María Saiz, professor of respected theological formation in the diocese, and Agapito Amieva, vicar of the diocese of Santander, although his participation in the works of the Committee was more limited. The medical experts are Luis

---

[613] PONTIFICAL INTERNATIONAL MARIAN ACADEMY, *Doctrinal orientations and competencies of the Diocesan Bishop and the Congregation for the Doctrine of the Faith in the discernment of Marian apparitions*, Lourdes, 2008, 12.
[614] PESQUERA, 2004, 112, note 32.

Morales Noriega and José Luis Piñal Ruiz Huidobro, the first being a very renowned psychiatrist and the second an anaethesist; both have a residence and clinic in Santander. The Committee occasionally used the services of experts like, for example, Dr. Peláez, a physician from Valladolid.

As soon as he receives the first *Report of the Committee*, Bishop Fernández published the first Episcopal *Note* on the phenomena of Garabandal, on the 26th of August 1961, scarcely two months after the first apparition. That early *Note*, as one would expect, considers "any definitive judgment premature."[615] A prudent and balanced position, in line with the usual practice of the Church. Nothing is defined in this *Note*, beyond the manifestation of the Apostolic Administrator's attentive attitude to the apparitions.

Garabandal "Is not clear" ("non constat")

Two short months later, Bishop Fernardez publishes the *second Note* concerning the apparitions. Although he still does not consider it prudent "to give a definitive verdict,"[616] he now pronounces a judgment on Garabandal, adopting as his own the verdict of the Committee he has established:

> It is not clear that the aforementioned apparitions or revelations may at this point be presented or taken with a serious basis to be true and authentic.[617]

---

[615] Mons. FERNANDEZ, D., *"Nota sobre los sucesos de San Sebastián de Garabandal (August 26, 1961)"* in OBISPADO DE SANTANDER, *Boletín Oficial de la Diócesis de Santander*, Santander, 1961, VIII, 154; OBISPADO DE SANTANDER, *Declaraciones oficiales de la Jerarquía sobre Garabandal*, Santander, 1970, 21.

[616] MONS. FERNANDEZ, D., *"Nota sobre los sucesos de San Sebastián de Garabandal (XI.1961)"* in OBISPADO DE SANTANDER, *Boletín Oficial de la Diócesis de Santander*, Santander, 1961, XI, 214; OBISPADO DE SANTANDER, *Declaraciones oficiales de la Jerarquía sobre Garabandal*, Santander, 1970, 22.

[617] *Ib.*, 23

"Non constat" is the position of this first diocesan verdict. What does this mean? The North-American theologian Michael B. Donovan explains: "This expression corresponds to the third of the categories employed by the Church in evaluating a possible case of apparitions:

· [Approval:] *Constat de supernaturalitate* (the supernatural origin is confirmed)
· [Rejection:] *Constat de non supernaturalitate* (the non-supernatural origin is confirmed)
· [Doubt:] *Non constat de supernaturalitate* (the supernatural origin is not confirmed).["618]

So, the expression *"it is not clear"* chosen by His Excellency Fernández, "although negative in its form, only expresses a doubt of the committee (notably where opinions are most frequently divided), which has not been able to reach a majority conclusion; this neither clarifies the situation nor provides clarity to the faithful seeking discernment. In this way, the diocesan authority, to put it more clearly, remains in a state of ambiguity."[619]

His Excellency Fernández has not yet formed a judgment. It is very soon, and the Bishop is aware that nowadays, "the exigencies of a critical scientific investigation make it more difficult or almost impossible to pronounce that [definitive] judgment with the appropriate swiftness."[620] We do not know the information on which D. Doroteo relies for his *Note*; he presents no argument. He only manifests prudence towards the events so widely discussed in the province's capital city.

---

618 DONOVAN, M.B., *The Alleged Apparitions at Garabandal, Spain,*
http://www.ewtn.com/library/bishops/garaband.htm (September 9, 2013).
619 GUTIÉRREZ GONZÁLEZ, J., "*Las apariciones de la Virgen María en la vida de la Iglesia y en la vida del Cristiano,*" *Estudios Marianos* 75 (2009) 428.
620 CDF, *Norms for the discernment of presumed apparitions,* 1978, II.1.

Bishop Beitia
"I have never closed my folder about this matter"

His Excellency Eugenio Beitia (1902-1985), Bishop of Santander between January 1962 and January 1965, publishes the *third Note* on the apparitions on the 7th of October 1962. In it he states that the investigating Committee, in a recent report (October 4, 1962), has expressed to him that for them the phenomena lack any sign of the supernatural and clearly have a natural explanation.[621] This judgment of the Committee, mentioned by the Bishop in the *Note*, provokes severe disciplinary measures: as of now it is forbidden for priests and religious to visit the village. This measure provokes a major rumpus.

However, the Committee itself was still far from scientifically concluding its studies. One of its members, Msgr. Juan Antonio Del Val, would later recognize as much after becoming Bishop of Santander, by setting up the second Garabandal Committee in 1989, without the existence of new elements to justify a new study: the objective of the new Committee is solely to complete the reports of the first one. Therefore, the verdict which justifies the prohibition in the *Note* was very premature.

Bishop Beitia seems to realize promptly that *"something"* is not right in the Committee. So, he publishes another *Note*, the *fourth*, on the apparitions. In the new communication, now in the role of Apostolic Administrator having resigned as Bishop, he states that he has never "closed his *"folder"* on this matter."[622] This is important, since for many, the disciplinary measure of the previous *Note* entailed an implicit condemnation of the events and

---

[621] Cf. MONS. BEITIA ALDAZÁBAL, E., *"Nota Oficial sobre los sucesos de San Sebastián de Garabandal* (October 7, 1962).

[622] Cf. MONS. BEITIA ALDAZÁBAL, E., *"Nota Oficial sobre los sucesos de San Sebastián de Garabandal* (July 8, 1965).

a closing of the case. In the new *Note*, the Bishop makes it explicit that the Church's verdict is still not formed, is ambiguous (*"non constat"*); for this reason he asks the faithful to abstain and to wait.

Bishop Beitia avails of the *Note* to affirm the full orthodoxy which, in his judgment, is to be found in Garabandal, showing profound knowledge of the phenomena:

> We have not found material for condemnatory ecclesiastic censure, either in the doctrine or in the spiritual recommendations which have been promulgated on this occasion, addressed to the Christian faithful; given that they contain an exhortation to prayer and sacrifice, to Eucharistic devotion, to devotion to Our Lady in the laudable traditional forms and to the holy fear of God, offended by our sins. They simply repeat the current doctrine of the Church in this matter.[623]

This judgment by the Prelate is of great importance, because, given in July of 1965, it encompasses the two messages, the prophecy and, practically, the totality of the phenomena, which will conclude shortly afterwards.

At the end of Bishop Beitia's mandate, the matter remains as it was at the beginning: unresolved. For the moment, Garabandal "is not clear": *"non constat."* The investigation must go on.

Bishop Puchol: *"The Denials"*

His Excellency Vicente Puchol Montis (1915-1967) succeeds Bishop Beitia from July 1965 until his sudden death on the 6th of May 1967. Bishop Puchol "believed that everything was clear and took the decision to publish a *Note* [the fifth], seemingly definitive, concerning the non-supernatural [origin] and natural

---

[623] *Ib.*

explanation of those events."[624] His verdict is categorical:

> [In Garabandal] there has been no apparition... there has been no message... [It is simply a matter of] a girls' innocent game.[625]

Before publishing his *Note*, Bishop Puchol had sent to Rome, on the 27th of October 1966, the *Reports* of the Committee and the norms that he intended to give concerning the apparitions. In his letter he shows such resolve that Rome, in its response to him (March 7, 1968), distances itself from the matter:

> [Given that] this matter has been examined and decided upon by Your Excellency, there is no reason for this Sacred Congregation to intervene in it.[626]

The Sacred Congregation makes no statement. Since the Prelate, *in situ*, sees the matter with such clarity, Rome leaves it in his hands.

But how does the Bishop achieve such firm certainty, so beyond the position of his predecessors who had always spoken so sparingly? Bishop Puchol does what the previous bishops had not done: he personally interviews the seers. Between the 30th of August and the 11th of October of 1966, the Bishop has five encounters with the girls. From them he obtains a new detail which moves him to act swiftly: the four seers deny to him that they have ever seen the Virgin.[627] He himself declares as much in his *Note*:

> From the declarations of the interested parties [the *denials*] it follows... that there has been no apparition... there has been no message; all of the events that have occurred in the said locality have

624 OCHAYTA PIÑEIRO, F., *Estudio sobre Garabandal*, Sigüenza, 2001, I.23.
625 PUCHOL MONTIS, V., "*Note on the events of San Sebastián de Garabandal* (March 17, 1967)" in OBISPADO DE SANTANDER, *Boletín Oficial de la Diócesis de Santander*, Santander 1962, I/III, 35.
626 OBISPADO DE SANTANDER, *Declaraciones oficiales de la Jerarquía sobre Garabandal*, Santander, 1970, 33.
627 Cf. OCHAYTA PIÑEIRO, F., *Estudio sobre Garabandal*, Sigüenza, 2001, I.22.

a natural explanation.[628]

Just ten days after the signing of the letter in Rome leaving the matter in the hands of His Excellency Puchol, the Bishop publishes his *Note*, on the 17th of March 1967. In it, he certifies the end of the apparitions: *"All of the events that have occurred in the said locality have a natural explanation."*[629] Garabandal is dead.

"Now I'm always going to look bad"

Those who had rejected the apparitions from the beginning now see themselves totally vindicated: the denials of the seers before Bishop Puchol are absolutely devastating. Conchita herself tells what happened:

> [On the 15th of August 1966] *I went to tell a priest* [José Olano] *that I hadn't seen the Virgin, that I wanted to tell the Bishop that it was all an illusion, a dream or a lie. Later on, in Pamplona, I said to the Bishop* [Puchol] *that I had never seen the Virgin, and that I had deceived everyone, the whole time.*[630]

At the end of the summer, Conchita returns to the Carmelite Missionaries' College in Pamplona, where she is studying as a boarder. Just two days after arriving there, on the 30th of August, the Bishop of Santander turns up in the school. Bishop Puchol, having learned of Conchita's doubts, wishes to question her personally. She had desired to go to Santander to be introduced to her Bishop many times and for many years, but it happens only now, in the moment of her darkest doubts, which began just 15

---

[628] MONS. PUCHOL MONTIS, V., *"Nota sobre los sucesos de San Sebastián de Garabandal* (March 17, 1967)" in OBISPADO DE SANTANDER, *Boletín Oficial de la Diócesis de Santander,* Santander, 1962, I/III, 35.

[629] MONS. PUCHOL MONTIS, V., *"Nota sobre los sucesos de San Sebastián de Garabandal* (March 17, 1967)" in OBISPADO DE SANTANDER, *Boletín Oficial de la Diócesis de Santander,* Santander, 1962, I/III, 35.

[630] LAURENTIN, R., *Apariciones actuales de la Virgen María,* Madrid, 1991, 243; DALEY, H., *Miracle at Garabandal,* Dublin, 1985, 189.

days earlier. The other three girls will also be questioned in the following days—the 2nd, 7th and 27th of September and the 11th of October—with a similar result.[631]

Bishop Puchol believes in good faith that the seers sincerely make a "*spontaneous retraction.*"[632] He expresses as much in a letter to René Laurentin; and so signs his *Note* pronouncing the end of the apparitions. However, today we possess more data which allow us to affirm that those retractions were far from being *spontaneous*:

The new parish priest of Garabandal, José Olano, having arrived at the end of the summer of 1965 substituting Fr. Valentín, takes on the apparitions with the firm objective of removing the whole business from the minds of the seers.[633] Very soon the seers, who, foreseeably, were fully and trustingly open with him, begin to doubt. Conchita and Loli experience strong doubts about the apparitions; doubts which extend to the real presence of Christ in the Eucharist. Furthermore, during her time in the school in Pamplona, a young priest from the city who gave a retreat to the students of her school, threatens not to give her absolution if she does not deny the apparitions:

> *If you do not promise to say in the village and to those who go there that you have deceived them, I will refuse you absolution.*[634]

In this same time period Jacinta is also threatened with excommunication: "*If we didn't deny, they told us they would discommunicate us.*" Eventually, the Bishop's visit to the school in Pamplona on the 30th of August would change the course of events. Conchita's mother, Aniceta, had forbidden that anyone

631 OCHAYTA PIÑEIRO, F., *Estudio sobre Garabandal*, Sigüenza, 2001, I.22; Cf. PORRO CARDEÑOSO, J., *El misterio de Garabandal en la teología católica*, Zaragoza, 1970, 69-70.
632 LAURENTIN, R., *Apariciones actuales de la Virgen María*, Madrid, 1991, 243.
633 Cf. OCHAYTA PIÑEIRO, F., *Estudio sobre Garabandal*, Sigüenza 2001, I.22
634 GARCÍA DE LA RIVA, J. R., *Memorias de un cura de aldea en Garabandal*, Santander, 2011, 64.

visit her daughter without her personal authorization in relation to the apparitions, which must remain a secret: no one must know of it. But the Superior of the school, who does not believe in the apparitions, is surprised by the arrival, without prior warning, of four prelates, to interrogate the supposed seer. The group is headed by the bishop himself, His Excellency Puchol, and with him are his Vicar General, Javier Azagra, the parish priest of Garabandal, José Olano, and the secretary, Agapito Amieva. This tribunal interrogates Conchita for a duration of seven hours, the only pause consisting of a brief interruption for lunch. When Aniceta learns of all this, she is quite indignant at the manner of proceeding and the lack of respect for her authority.[635]

But the declaration has been made. Conchita hoped to recover by this retraction the peace she had lost on the 15th of August, but it is useless. And in the following months she will live in torment not knowing which way to turn:

> *"Now I only have one desire: that the date of the Miracle come, not for the Miracle itself, but to see once and for all if this is true or not. If it has been the Virgin, the Miracle will happen, because what She said always happened. As for me, whether the Miracle happens or not, now I'm always going to look bad."* "Why?"— Mother Nieves, her spiritual guide, asks her—*"If the thing is true, for having behaved badly, denying and not being generous. And if it's not... well, for everything!"*[636]

"To deny and not to deny"

These interrogations with the answers of the girls provide the basis of the episcopal *Note* of March 1967. The historian—*writes Félix Ochayta, theologian of the Spanish Mariological Society*—cannot ignore the circumstances of those interrogations of four girls in full adolescence, troubled, pressurized; especially Conchita. I have had

---

[635] *Ib.*
[636] PESQUERA, 2004, 302.

the opportunity to read the photocopies of the replies—*Ochayta affirms*—and the longest of them is Conchita's: 6-7 pages. She recognizes that they came up with it all, but sometimes speaks with naturalness of the visions, messages... That of Jacinta is even more hesitant, since she says that, if they weren't true for the others, they mustn't have been true for her either.[637]

That the seers do not make a complete retraction is a significant fact. And if it is not complete, this means that they remain firm, at least partially, in the truth of the apparitions. They declare it all a lie; all, that is, except *"the callings and the miracle of the Sacred Host; that part was true."*[638] In these words Conchita will always remain unmovable, even before Bishop Puchol. Under the influence of authority, the eldest of the seers goes no further than this incoherent denial; as Santiago Lanús has put it, it is *"denial and non-denial."*[639]

Jacinta will be the first to retract the denials of 1966 in writing to the authorities. Conchita, Loli and Mari Cruz will follow her steps having recovered their calm. The Virgin had foretold them from the beginning that they would deny her.[640]

The "Denials" in Perspective

Today we possess more details than Bishop Puchol had available to him, to interpret the *retractions*. He, in all honesty, judged the retraction to be "spontanous,"[641] and therefore considered the doubts and denials of the girls to be definitive. He expressed this by letter to René Laurentin a few days before his

[637] OCHAYTA PIÑEIRO, F., *Estudio sobre Garabandal,* Sigüenza, 2001, I.22.
[638] *Diario de Conchita,* 71.
[639] LANÚS, S., *Madre de Dios y Madre Nuestra. Fátima, Ámsterdam y Garabandal,* Madrid, 2013, 137.
[640] Cf. MARI CRUZ GONZÁLEZ, *Carta a la Madre Nieves García,* El Escorial, May 5, 2005; OCHAYTA PIÑEIRO, F., *Estudio sobre Garabandal,* Sigüenza, 2001, V.4; Cf. *Diario de Conchita,* 70.
[641] LAURENTIN, R., *Apariciones actuales de la Virgen María,* Madrid, 1991, 243.

death, on the 6th of May 1967, in a tragic accident. His sudden death prevents the prelate from observing the subsequent change in the girls: the seers will not remain for long in their retractions. This is an important point: the fact that the girls disown them as soon as they recover serenity and feel free to speak demonstrates the instability of the denials.

· Casimir Barthas, recognized author in the area of apparitions, considers these denials as *"momentary vacillations,"* similar to those of Lucia in Fatima:[642] "Those denials were not absolute; nor did they occur in propitious circumstances but in moments of doubts, fears and some pressures from persons with authority."[643]

· Lucio Rodrigo, S.J., writes: "Our belief in the supernatural character of the phenomena of Garabandal is not founded upon what the children have said... but on the real and concrete facts checked by me [personally] and by many other witnesses. No one has reason to destroy them or even to attenuate them simply because of what the children might say [the denials] in the present or even in the future. They will be under an illusion, but we will not."[644]

· Antonio Royo-Marín, O.P., after witnessing in Garabandal the ecstasy of the 8th of August 1961, affirms: "I am not infallible; but I am a specialist in these matters, and *the children's visions seem to me to be true.*"[645]

Ample medical studies reach the same conclusions:

· Dr. Honorio Sanjuan Nadal, microbiologist and neuro-psychiatrist from Barcelona, having shared his study with diverse *Scientific Societies and Congresses,* affirms: "The greater part of the judgments coincide in *finding no explanation* in accordance with the known laws of nature for the combination of occurrences, a point of view shared

---

[642] Cf. TURNER, F., *"El problema de las dudas y negaciones o contradicciones en las videntes de Garabandal"* in OCHAYTA PIÑEIRO, F., *Estudio sobre Garabandal,* Sigüenza, 2001, V.10.
[643] OCHAYTA PIÑEIRO, F., *Estudio sobre Garabandal,* Sigüenza, 2001, II.2.
[644] Citado por ANDREU, R. M., *"Puntos principales de la historia de Garabandal,"* in *Diario de Conchita,* 118.
[645] In 1958, he had published his *Teología de la Perfección Cristiana,* frequently cited in this study. PESQUERA, 2004, 158.

as much by believers as by the incredulous."[646]

· Dr. Serge Fournier, family doctor from in Uzerche (France) states that, in his opinion, *"there is no natural explanation for the events of Garabandal."*[647]

The arguments of these and other authors do not admit an explanation of the phenomena founded upon *"the denials"* of the seers: it is necessary to explain the events, which no longer *"belong"* to the children.

Bishop Puchol, however, considered the retraction of the seers to be so solid that he felt there was no need for further investigations, with the result that in the end, as the *Note* reflects, the denials became the sole basis of his conclusions: *"From the declarations* [denials] *of the interested parties it is clear that...."*[648] As a result, important questions are not addressed:

The *Note* affirms that those occurrences *"have a natural explanation,"* but does not explain what this is, not even in a general way. It could be said of some, without doubt, but not of many others. [In summary,] the statement that it all began as an *"innocent little girls' game"* does not withstand the statements and examinations of innumerable witnesses.[649]

Cardinal Ratzinger supports this perspective when he explains that, "When it comes to the question of interventions in the prudential order, it could happen that some Magisterial documents might not be free from all deficiencies... because while the pronouncements contained true assertions and others which were not sure, both types were inextricably connected. Only time

---

[646] La Sociedad internacional de Sofrología y de Medicina psicosomática, el VI y VII Encuentros de Poblet, el II Congreso Internacional de Psicodrama y Psicoterapia. Cf. PÉREZ, R., 1991, 186.
[647] *Ib.*
[648] OBISPADO DE SANTANDER, *Declaraciones oficiales de la Jerarquía sobre Garabandal,* Santander, 1970, 33; cf. OCHAYTA PIÑEIRO, F., *Estudio sobre Garabandal,* Sigüenza, 2001, I.23.
[649] OCHAYTA PIÑEIRO, F., *Estudio sobre Garabandal,* Sigüenza, 2001, I.24.

has permitted discernment and, after deeper study, the attainment of true doctrinal progress."[650] This sheds light on our case: declarations of a prudential or disciplinary order—like Bishop Puchol's *Note*—seem to have been based upon *"pronouncements not... free from all deficiencies"* in the form of objectively inconsistent denials.

"Denials" in the History of the Church

At this point, the denials of Garabandal have over time been clarified, but another difficulty arises; if the falsity of the denials is accepted, wouldn't Garabandal become the first case of apparitions to be approved after having been denied by its own seers? Certainly not. The similar cases are many; it is common among seers to undergo moments of doubt:

1) Saint Teresa of Jesus, the *mystical doctor*, writes of her visions that she,

"remembered them only as a dream... I had a thousand doubts and suspicions whether I had ever understood matters aright, thinking that perhaps all was my imagination, and that it was enough for me to have deceived myself, without also deceiving good men. I looked upon myself as so wicked...."[651]

2) Blessed Bernardo de Hoyos—receiver of the *Great Promise of the Heart of Jesus* (1733)—often said to his superior and spiritual director: "[I am] *the greatest liar, who has deceived everyone, who has never seen the Most Sacred Heart and who himself has invented everything he has said.*"[652]

3) Saint Bernadette Soubirous, in Lourdes, also for a time loses the confidence in her visions.[653]

---

[650] CDF, Instruction *Donum Veritatis*, Rome, 1990, 24c.
[651] SAINT TERESA OF JESUS, *Life*, ch. XXX, 10.
[652] TURNER, F., *"El problema de las dudas y negaciones o contradicciones en las videntes de Garabandal"* in OCHAYTA PIÑEIRO, F., *Estudio sobre Garabandal*, Sigüenza, 2001, V.9.
[653] Cf. PÉREZ, R., 1991, 169.

4) Saint Catherine Labouré—the seer of the Miraculous Medal—affirms the same: *"I thought I was deceived."*[654]

5) Saint Thérèse of Lisieux, after trying to respond to her sisters' questions about a vision of the Virgin that was crucial for her life, confesses: *"I imagined I had lied. Ah! Only in heaven will I be able to tell what I suffered."*[655]

The examples of doubts in canonized saints are multiple. However, Bishop Puchol is perplexed and overwhelmed by the confession of the seers of Garabandal and sees himself duty bound to act, making this situation public and definitive.

The Bishop is not the only one who is disconcerted by the denials. In fact, during this agitated period, Conchita's identity is concealed (she goes by her second name, María) in the school in Burgos, to avoid further complications. Conchita herself acts with such discretion among her companions that, in spite of her fame, it would be over a year before she is discovered.

One of the few persons with permission to visit the teenager in this time of secrecy in Burgos is Fr. Laffineur. In his efforts to help her, in 1967 he consults Fr. Casimir Barthas, a noted expert in studies on Fatima. The disconsolate Belgian priest outlines to him the whole affair of the denials. The response of Barthas is illuminating:

Do not be surprised at the momentary darknesses of the girls of Garabandal, at the failures of their memory. This was the mysterious case of Lucia; from 1925 to 1930 she too doubted her apparitions. And she has recovered total light precisely in the moment that they were recognized by the Church[656]

---

[654] CRAPEZ, E., *La venerable Catherine Labouré*, Gabalda, 1911, 41.

[655] SAINT THÉRÈSE OF THE CHILD JESUS, *Story of a Soul*, ch. III.

[656] TURNER, F., *"El problema de las dudas y negaciones o contradicciones en las videntes de Garabandal"* in OCHAYTA PIÑEIRO, F., *Estudio sobre Garabandal*, Sigüenza, 2001, V.10.

The experience of so many saints could have offered Bishop Puchol a valuable instrument for interpreting the denials of the seers, so relativized in the context of the whole story. In the light of the events, we know today that the retractions of Garabandal, as received and presented by Bishop Puchol in 1967, do not offer a conclusive objective basis for judging the phenomena:

> No one can doubt the good faith and good intentions of the interrogators, but nor should one forget the methods employed and the pressures to which those [16-17 year old] girls were subjected in the early flush of youth. In the end of the day, there was no process, properly speaking. So many witnesses of the events were never called, many of them persons of prestige, like priests, medical and other experts... and many others who were simple people, incapable of deceit or of denying what they had seen... The haste and insufficiency of the methods used to get to the truth of those events is surprising.[657]

The *Note* will be revised with the passing of time. However, the damage to the due process of the apparitions was already done.

Bishop Cirarda
"The solid judgment of my predecessor"

His Excellency José María Cirarda (1917-2008) will be Bishop of Santander between July of 1968 and December of 1971. It seemed that after Bishop Puchol's *Note*, it was all ended. And yet, through his secretary, Bishop Cirarda feels impelled to publish a new official *Note* about the Garabandal affair, the *sixth* on the apparitions (October 9, 1968). In reality, Bishop Cirarda does not contribute any new details. Trusting in the sureness of his predecessor's position and without carrying out new inquiries, the *Note* limits itself to reaffirm what had already been said; it is

---

[657] Cf. OCHAYTA PIÑEIRO, F., *Estudio sobre Garabandal*, Sigüenza, 2001, I.23.

simply of a disciplinary nature.[658]

A little over a year later, on the 25th of April 1970, Bishop Cirarda publishes yet another *Note, the seventh*. The new *Note*, once again disciplinary in nature, does evaluate the content of the apparitions. Bishop Cirarda affirms—as Bishop Beitia had done in 1965—that in the message of Garabandal "there is nothing contrary to dogma and morals."[659] However, at the same time, he relies on the conclusions of Puchol, for whom—Cirarda recalls— the phenomena of Garabandal "had a natural explanation."[660]

The problem arises when the *Note* itself presents the basis of its conclusions: "the solid basis of my predecessor's judgment."[661] Cirarda flatly relies on his predecessor's judgment, from which he draws his conclusion. Sadly, Bishop Cirarda has not yet discovered that, apart from Puchol's judgment, exclusively based on the retractions of the *interested parties*, the whole matter possesses important precedents in the history of mysticism and theological arguments that impede the closure of the question based solely on the reality of the said *retractions*, even if made before the Bishop in person.

The confusion refuses to go away. And only the passing of time will succeed in returning to the *"denials"* their relative value.

Bishop Del Val
A New Investigation Committee

In December 1971, Bishop Juan Antonio Del Val (1916-2002) is appointed to the See of Santander. Del Val has a profound

[658] *Ib.*
[659] OBISPADO DE SANTANDER, *Declaraciones oficiales de la Jerarquía sobre Garabandal,* Santander, 1970, 15-16.
[660] *Ib.*
[661] *Ib.*

knowledge of the case of Garabandal: he had been a member of the investigating Committee in the years of the phenomena. He personally saw two ecstasies and, before being Bishop, had recognized that the Committee's work had not been sufficient.[662]

Bishop Del Val is very familiar with the most difficult points of the issue. He performs an official gesture that recognizes that his precedessors' *Notes*, by which the case had apparently been closed (Puchol in 1967 and Cirarda in 1970), do not have the last word. In 1989, Del Val sets up a new Episcopal Committee.[663] This decision draws no little criticism because it is made without new events to justify it, thereby contradicting the earlier *Notes* that had closed the case. If there are no new events and the case is closed, why create a second Committee? This is the question many people put to Del Val. Although he cannot make them public, the Bishop has the benefit of very objective arguments which fully justify his decision and he does not pull back: his experience as member of the first Committee equips him with a thorough knowledge of the limitations of those *Reports*, upon which the present situation is based; a situation so unjust for those four poor children, whose testimony has been processed without the application of genuine criteria of discernment. Del Val knows this very well, and he is the only person who can establish a new Committee: he is now the bishop.

But if Del Val, as bishop, cannot speak of the errors of the first Committee, another of its members, Dr. Luis Morales, psychiatrist and main medical expert of the same, can do so. On the 30th of May 1983, with His Excellency Del Val's blessing, Dr. Morales gives a conference in the Athenaeum of Santander, publicly admitting

---

[662] PÉREZ, R., 1991, 163.
[663] LANÚS, S., *Madre de Dios y Madre Nuestra. Fátima, Ámsterdam y Garabandal*, Madrid, 2013, 172.

that he directly intervened to impede the studies of the Committee and direct them towards negative and preconceived conclusions. Before a packed auditorium, Morales retracts his negative opinion and recognizes the authenticity of the apparitions of Garabandal.[664]

This retraction, made with the authorized approval of the Bishop, along with the creation of a new investigating Committee, publicly confirms the inconclusive and therefore insufficient nature of the first Committee's study. The Episcopal *Notes*, which judged the apparitions on the basis of that study, are thus deprived of the argumentative foundation upon which they expressly purport to be based. This fact affects the first four *Notes*. Then, the three more recent *Notes*, which are no longer based "on the report of the technical Committee but on the declaration [retraction] of the seers,"[665] equally lack a definitive foundation. A study of the said *"retractions"* clearly shows that, in spite of the good intention of their respective authors, they are unfit to sustain objective judgment.[666] So, in the nineties—thirty years after the events—the episcopal evaluation of the apparitions of Garabandal once again seems indeterminate.

Undoubtedly, Bishop Del Val expects positive results from the new committee, because as the new reports are being elaborated he progressively relaxes or cancels the disciplinary measures dictated against Garabandal by his predecessors. He allows priests to visit; he gives express permission to Conchita to present the message of Garabandal in a BBC documentary that draws international attention to the apparitions. Thereafter, Bishop Del

---

[664] Cf. OCHAYTA PIÑEIRO, F., *Estudio sobre Garabandal*, Sigüenza, 2001, I.34; Cf. LANÚS, S., *Madre de Dios y Madre Nuestra. Fátima, Ámsterdam y Garabandal*, Madrid, 2013, 172.
[665] GALMÉS BELMONTE, R., *"Posición de la Iglesia respecto a Garabandal"* in FUNDACIÓN HM, *www.garabandal.it*, Lumezzane, 2013.
[666] CDF, Instruction *Donum Veritatis*, Rome, 1990, 24c.

Val will not sign any further documentation concerning Garabandal, because the conclusions of the new Committee are delayed until the time of his retirement (in August 1991), and the matter is left in the hands of his successor.

However, Del Val does perform an important public gesture: "As he retired, he said in an interview that the message of Garabandal was *'important'* and *'theologically correct.'"*[667] These simple words are of great importance: Del Val says them with full knowledge of the *Report* of the second Committee, despite the fact that this was negative. There is, therefore, a clear discord between the words of the retiring Bishop and the result of the recent *Report* of the Committee he himself had established, a discord that indicates that the Bishop is not satisfied with the new studies. Effectively, the new *Report* is not impartial either. It succumbs to defects like those of the first Committee: new investigations are not carried out; there is no genuine attempt to document the facts; no significant inquiries are made *in situ*; witnesses are not questioned... The result is that, in the end, the previous *Report* is simply repeated.[668] Later on, Bishop Del Val's disagreement with the new *Report* will be corroborated by Archbishop Carlos Osoro, in his role as Apostolic Administrator of Santander. The widespread confusion in the process of Garabandal will not disappear.

---

[667] DONOVAN, M.B., *"Garabandal"* in *EWTN*,
http://www.ewtn.com/expert/answers/garabandal.htm (September 8, 2013).
[668] Cf. PÉREZ, R., 1991, 158.

XVII

Current State of the Question

· Latest episcopal declarations · Role of the Holy See ·
· The Diocesan Committees ·

The story goes on after Bishop Del Val's departure from the scene, having published no document on the apparitions. He does expressly allow the seers to make the events known; he encourages Dr. Morales in his public retraction; he officially sets up the second Committee and positively evaluates the phenomena after the negative *Report* of the new Committee. His gestures are encouraging, but he has not taken any definitive or conclusive stand. The incoming Bishop will have to deal with the new situation.

I

The Letters of Bishop Vilaplana and Carlos Osoro

1993. Bishop Vilaplana
"I consider the matter closed," "Garabandal is not clear"

The Committee instituted by Bishop Del Val decrees in 1991 that "the supernatural character of said apparitions is not clear."[669]

---

[669] VILAPLANA, *Letter to Richard Paul Salbato,* Santander November 7, 2001, nos. 1, 3 and 5.

"Not clear" was the decree of Bishop Doroteo Fernández in 1961. So, after Bishop Del Val, the situation has been left at the same point as it was thirty years before, prior to the devastating reports of the first Committee. Effectively, the expression *"it is not clear,"* "though negative in its form, only expresses the Committee's doubt... To put it more clearly, the diocesan authority remains in ambiguity"[670]: *"It is not clear;" "We don't know."*

The new Bishop, His Excellency Vilaplana (1944-), on his arrival in the diocese in August of 1991, writes a letter to the Congregation for the Doctrine of Faith (November 12, 1991). In it he presents the conclusion of the new Committee and asks for a declaration from Rome on the matter. Soon afterwards, in his first visit *ad limina*, Bishop Vilaplana renews his request to the Congregation personally. Finally, in a letter of the 28th of November 1992, the Cardinal Prefect himself, Joseph Ratzinger, responds:

> [By] letter—and, subsequently, on the occasion of a recent visit to this Congregation—Your Excellency expressed the wish to count on the Holy See's support in the matter of an eventual declaration on the abovementioned events [of Garabandal].
>
> The Congregation for the Doctrine of the Faith, having attentively examined the documentation, does not consider it opportune to intervene directly... This Dicastery suggests that, if you deem it necessary, you publish a declaration reaffirming that the supernatural nature of the said apparitions "is not clear."[671]

In the *Diocesan Report*, Cardinal Ratzinger does not find reasons to intervene. And so, like his predecessors, he leaves the

---

[670] GUTIÉRREZ GONZÁLEZ, J., *"Las apariciones de la Virgen María en la vida de la Iglesia y en la vida del Cristiano,"* Estudios Marianos 75 (2009) 428.

[671] CARD. RATZINGER, *Letter of the Congregation for the Doctrine of Faith to His Excellency Vilaplana,* November 28, 1992, cited in OCHAYTA PIÑEIRO, F., *Estudio sobre Garabandal,* Sigüenza, 2001, I.34.

matter in the hands of the diocese.[672] With this response, Bishop Vilaplana gives up the idea of making an official proclamation. He will prepare something simpler: an informative letter that will not be published officially, to be delivered to those who approach the Bishop's offices from this time on (1993) requesting information on the apparitions. It is the *eighth* episcopal document on the phenomena. Bishop Vilaplana does not present new data or studies of the matter:

> Given that the declarations of my predecessors, who studied the case, have been clear and unanimous, I have not considered it opportune to make a new public declaration to avoid giving notoriety to events now too distant in time. However, I have considered it opportune to redact this report as a direct response to the persons who seek orientation on the matter, which I consider closed, accepting the decisions of my predecessors, which I make my own, and the orientations of the Holy See.[673]

The complications are perpetuated: Bishop Vilaplana, as he himself affirms, once again bases the matter solely and exclusively on the incomplete reports he has inherited (*"Given that my predecessors, who studied the case..."*). So, he superimposes a new document upon the basis which, as we have seen, Del Val had carefully begun to revise. The letter, furthermore, contains some statements that must today be qualified:

1) The opinions of successive Ordinaries of Santander—as we have seen—had certainly not been *"unanimous"*;
2) The Holy See, rather than *intervening*, carefully avoided making any declaration every time it had been consulted. We will return to this point;
3) The events were not distant in time, given that the four seers, now adults, were still alive (Mari Loli, the first to die, does not die until

---

[672] *Ib.*
[673] VILAPLANA, *Letter to Richard Paul Salbato,* Santander, November 7, 2001.

2009).

Bishop Vilaplana's action seeks, no doubt, to restore equilibrium, to remain in continuity with the positions of Bishops Puchol and Cirarda. To do this, he bases himself on the fact that the new Committee coincides substantially with the decrees of the first one.

In the end, his verdict is: *"The supernatural nature is not clear,"* as Rome had advised: the text repeats this as many as three times (nos. 1, 3 and 5). But this *verdict* does not express a definitive judgment; it is ambiguous, saying that the authority is *in doubt.* Therefore, as Félix Ochayta remarks, "the matter remains open, as is always the case when the Hierarchy speaks in that way."[674] And yet, Bishop Vilaplana affirms in this letter, *"I consider the matter closed."*

On the one hand he declares the matter open, saying *"it is still not clear,"* as Rome recommends, and on the other hand *"I consider it closed."* This means that the matter is archived unconcluded. Vilaplana, then, departing the diocese in 2006, leaves the matter entirely open, in the hands of his successor.

2007. Archbishop Carlos Osoro
"I am open to all information about Garabandal"

In September of 2006, the diocese of Santander receives directly from Rome an Apostolic Administrator who will remain in charge for just under a year, until July of 2007: His Excellency Carlos Osoro (1945-). The future Archbishop of Madrid is at that time Archbishop of the neighboring See of Oviedo. He is a native of the Santander diocese where he has been Rector of the Seminary, Dean of the Cathedral and Vicar General. Like Del Val,

---

674 OCHAYTA PIÑEIRO, F., *Estudio sobre Garabandal,* Sigüenza, 2001, I.37.

he knows the diocese well and the intricacy of the studies about Garabandal.

On the 7th of May 2007, the new Apostolic Administrator signs the *ninth* episcopal communication on the apparitions and gives a new twist to the story. Osoro declares that the events "*Are not so distant in time,*" and merit attention. As Bishop Vilaplana had done, he writes a letter to express his perspective without imposing. To do so, he avails of the interest in the apparitions shown by Edward Kelly, a North-American layman who consults him, on behalf of numerous members of the faithful in the U.S., concerning the delicate matter of the studies of the second Committee, which had been called into question in an indirect but public way by Del Val in a televised interview, at the end of his time serving as Bishop.

While not settling the question, Archbishop Osoro's letter constitutes the most recent episcopal testimony and demonstrates the Prelate's interest in Garabandal. If his predecessor stated "*I consider the matter closed,*" Osoro now writes the contrary: "*I am open to all information, to all considerations about Garabandal.*" The text, furthermore, adopts Bishop Del Val's delicate suggestion: that the study of the second Committee had been—like the first one—incomplete and insufficient:

> *I am sure that the next Bishop will promote the studies, so that the events of Garabandal may be examined in greater depth.*[675]

With these words ("*may be examined in greater depth*"), the Apostolic Administrator succinctly recognizes the insufficiency of the previous studies, specifically the most recent ones, of the

---

[675] OSORO SIERRA, C., "*Letter to Edward Kelly* (May 7, 2007)" in GARABANDAL JOURNAL, Minnesota 2007, V-VI, 5; LANÚS, S., *Madre de Dios y Madre Nuestra. Fátima, Ámsterdam y Garabandal,* Madrid, 2013, 174.

second Committee, upon which rests the last episcopal declaration, the letter of Bishop Vilaplana, in which many still invested hopes of a definite decision.

Without personally taking a position on the phenomena, the Apostolic Administrator recognizes that the case is not closed: Garabandal must be studied *"in greater depth."* This is because the second Committee, like the first, halted its investigations before concluding its task.[676] Numerous voices have affirmed this over time with abundant proofs. The Bishop now puts this in writing, and even adds a new argument. Osoro points to the *fruits* surrounding the apparitions:

I have known authentic conversions [in Garabandal]. *In the face of these events, how can we not feel the need to open our hearts always to our Mother Mary... I encourage you to continue to maintain this devotion.*[677]

With this most recent document on the apparitions, Osoro re-opens the subject, prudently but clearly. His words do not consist of a judgment on the events, but they do show the Prelate's decided openness towards the phenomena. However, given the provisional nature of his position, the Apostolic Administrator does not set further measures in motion; he leaves the matter, as is customary, in the hands of the incoming Bishop, who at the time of writing is the last one before the Bishop currently in charge.

---

[676] Cf. PÉREZ, R., 1991, 158; Cf. ch. VI, *Valoración de los Informes de las Comisiones técnicas.*
[677] OSORO SIERRA, C., *"Letter to Edward Kelly* (May 7, 2007)" in GARABANDAL JOURNAL, Minnesota 2007, V—VI, 5; LANÚS, S., *Madre de Dios y Madre Nuestra. Fátima, Ámsterdam y Garabandal,* Madrid, 2013, 174

Bishop Vicente Jiménez Zamora
Recent history

In July of 2007, His Excellency Vicente Jiménez (1944-) takes possession of the diocese of Santander. Bishop Jiménez will not show any special interest in Garabandal: he signs no document, taking the line of referring back to the approach adopted by his predecessors.

Bishop Jiménez will make no public references to Garabandal. He visits the village of the apparitions in 2012, and many will attempt to interpret this visit as openness to the apparitions. However, the Prelate carefully avoids any reference to the phenomena during the visit. That day the restoration of the parish church is celebrated, a restoration made possible largely by donations proceeding from abroad, from pilgrims devoted to the apparitions. The silence of Bishop Jiménez, who makes no reference to the phenomena in the whole day, manifests his decision not to address the phenomena.[678]

The current parish priest, Fr. José Rolando Cabeza Fuentes (1944 -), however, is addressing the issue. In 2012 Fr. Rolando publishes a website of the little rural church of Garabandal. In it he provides ample coverage of the phenomena: the messages, their development and, in particular, their reception. The parish priest advocates an open attitude towards the possibility of approval of the apparitions:

> *Radical positions of rejection or mockery cannot be adopted towards the phenomenon of Garabandal; it is very easy to express unfounded and casual opinions or perhaps mawkish euphoria. But this is wrong, all the more so when the facts and their long history are not known. An*

---

[678] Cf. LANÚS, S., *Madre de Dios y Madre Nuestra. Fátima, Ámsterdam y Garabandal*, Madrid, 2013, 174.

attitude of fraternal respect must be cultivated, before the religious and believing sentiment of so many persons who throughout these years have... found an inner strength in this place.

It is very easy to label such people with condescending adjectives or with our own personal concepts; it is more difficult to respect and comprehend that each one lives his faith with different personal motivations. The people of the village and from elsewhere, who actually lived through the "events" express themselves as follows: "What we have lived and experienced, nothing and no one can ever erase from our hearts." Nothing and no one can oblige us to pray or not to pray here or there (Lourdes, Fatima, Garabandal or anywhere else), and this is especially so when the position of these faithful is not contrary to the doctrine of the Church.[679]

Fr. Rolando awaits the authorized judgment that can only come from the Church, but points to the beneficial impact of Garabandal in those who approach its messages, "having realized that its words (the messages transmitted by the children) are coming true."[680]

II

Intervention by the Holy See

Up to this point in time, Rome has responded to the Garabandal question on four occasions. In response to the reiterated request by successive bishops of Santander for a pontifical declaration, up to three different Cardinals communicate with the diocese of the apparitions: Cardinal Alfredo Ottaviani (1967), Cardinal Franjo Šeper (1969 and 1970) and

---

[679] CABEZA FUENTES, J. R., *"Un antes, un después y un hoy"* en www.garabandalparroquia.com (September 8, 2013).
[680] *Ib.*

CURRENT STATE OF THE QUESTION

Cardinal Joseph Ratzinger (1992). The four documents approach the matter with reiterative unity: "The Congregation maintains a zealous silence on its opinion regarding the events of Garabandal. The first two letters say that the Sacred Congregation has emitted no judgment concerning Garabandal... The third says that the Congregation has always procured to abstain from any declaration on the matter of the supernatural character of the events of Garabandal."[681] The most recent letter, avoiding a declaration for the fourth consecutive time, delegates the study of the matter to the diocesan authorities.

The Dicastery evidently does not wish to enter into the matter. Cardinal Franjo Šeper indicates as much to the Archbishop of New Orleans, His Excellency Philip M. Hannan (in whose territory it seems the Garabandalista movement was very active): "This Sacred Congregation has not up to now wished... to take the matter in its hands."[682] In the *"up to now"* of the translation published by Bishop Cirarda, the Santander Bishop's sense of the *provisional* nature of the diocesan judgment on the apparitions may be noted. Rome has the last word. But the Holy See does not wish to intervene.

The cause of this long silence seems to be the markedly prophetic nature of the message of Garabandal, which would incline the Roman dicastery to defer any declaration.[683] Rome is better informed on the matter than might be supposed: it is known that "Conchita [in January of 1966, in Rome] told the Pope very probably and Cardinal Ottaviani certainly, the date of the

---

[681] GALMÉS BELMONTE, R., *"Posición de la Iglesia respecto a Garabandal"* in FUNDACIÓN HM, www.garabandal.it, Lumezzane, 2013 (September 8, 2013).
[682] CARD. ŠEPER, F., *Letter of the Congregation for the Doctrine of Faith to the Archbishop of New Orleans*, Vatican, 1969; Spanish translation: OBISPADO DE SANTANDER, *Declaraciones oficiales de la Jerarquía sobre Garabandal*, Santander, 1970, 43.
[683] GALMÉS BELMONTE, R., *"Position of the Church regarding Garabandal"* in FUNDACIÓN HM, www.garabandal.it, Lumezzane, 2013.

great Miracle."[684] However, at the diocesan level Bishops have been expressing a sense of displeasure regarding Garabandal., This situation leads Rome to maintain a distance and wait. It is the Bishop of Santander's responsibility—*"up to now"*—to discern the matter.

Rome, following its own norms, sees no reason to intervene: "In doubtful cases that clearly do not put the good of the Church at risk, the competent Ecclesiastical Authority is to refrain from any judgment and from any direct action (because it can also happen that, after a certain period of time, the presumed supernatural fact falls into oblivion); it must not however cease from being vigilant by intervening if necessary, with promptness and prudence."[685] Rome attentively observes and waits. This attitude is applied to Garabandal; as Cardinal Ratzinger expresses in his letter to Bishop Vilaplana in 1992:

> The Congregation for the Doctrine of Faith, having attentively examined the cited documentation [sent by Bishop Vilaplana: the *Reports* of the second Committee], does not consider it opportune to intervene directly, appropriating from Your Excellency's ordinary jurisdiction a matter that corresponds to you by right. Therefore, this Dicastery suggests that, if you deem it necessary, you publish a declaration reaffirming that the supernatural nature of the said apparitions is not clear.[686]

The 1978 *Norms for evaluating presumed apparitions* outline clearly that, "Above all, the duty of vigilance and intervention falls to the Ordinary of the place."[687] This being true, it is also true that

---

[684] PÉREZ, R., 1991, 173.

[685] CDF, *Norms regarding the manner of proceeding in discernment of presumed apparitions*, 1978, II, 4.

[686] CARD. RATZINGER, *Letter of the Congregation for the Doctrine of Faith to His Excellency Vilaplana*, November, 28, 1992, cited in OCHAYTA PIÑEIRO, F., *Estudio sobre Garabandal*, Sigüenza, 2001, I.34.

[687] CDF, *Norms for the discernment of presumed apparitions*, 1978, III.1.

the Sacred Congregation's responsibility is: "To judge and approve the Ordinary's way of proceeding or, in so far as it be possible and fitting, to initiate a new examination of the matter, distinct from that undertaken by the Ordinary."[688]

In Garabandal, given the complications arising from the diocesan study, entrenched afterwards by successive official *Notes* in which the Ordinaries quote one another in good faith, the Holy See must from a distance have intuited some inaccuracy, given that as many as three Prefects have repeatedly opted to abstain from intervening in support of a negative diocesan decree, which with its backing would have been irrevocable. To avoid this, Rome decides not to commit to a judgment on Garabandal; it carefully avoids pronouncing in favor or against, always manifesting an attitude of waiting for eventual new information. Meanwhile, the diocesan handling of the matter will follow its course with the subsequent documents that we have already seen. In the final analysis, the cited letter of Cardinal Ratzinger permits Félix Ochayta to draw four significant conclusions:

1) The very fact that the Bishop of Santander [Vilaplana] made that consultation indicates that this is not a closed case.

2) The Holy See has *"attentively examined"* the documentation sent, which indicates that the matter is an important one, which is not yet resolved.

3) The Holy See does not consider it opportune to intervene directly, appropriating from the jurisdiction of the Bishop of Santander *"a matter that corresponds to you by right."* This entails that the matter is not yet resolved and that the Holy See could reserve it to itself, but prefers not to do so.

4) The Holy See suggests to the Bishop that, if he deems it necessary, he make a declaration: *"Reaffirming that the supernatural nature of the said apparitions is not clear."* The phenomena are not rejected, it is

---

[688] *Ib.,* IV.2.

not stated that they have a natural explanation, or that they are of diabolical origin. Put another way, the Holy See leaves things as they are, which implies openness to a future recognition of their supernatural character, if heretofore unknown elements for judgment appear.[689]

So then, officially, both at the diocesan level and at the level of the Holy See, the case remains *"open"* pending new information.

Xalapa of the Immaculate, 8ᵗʰ of July 1966

In the summer of 1966, the Archbishop of Xalapa, Mexico, His Excellency Manuel Pio López (1939-1968), after consulting Rome and Santander, approves the promotion of Garabandal in his Archdiocese:

> Bearing in mind the indications of the Holy See and of His Excellency, the Ordinary of Santander (Spain), together with the norms prescribed by the *Code of Canon Law*, we approve and bless the publication of the Message of the Blessed Virgin Mary in San Sebastián de Garabandal in our Archdiocese.... The prudence of the Holy Church in this important matter has been manifested in attentive study and pastoral vigilance, and absolutely not in prohibition and rejection thereof.[690]

"We approve the publication of the message of Garabandal." This positive judgment of Archbishop López possesses no canonical value; this resides solely with the Ordinary of Santander and Rome.[691] Nonetheless, it is authoritative. And as the Archbishop himself affirms, the *obedience* of the seers to the Hierarchy in every moment "is a sure sign for all that God is here."[692]

[689] OCHAYTA PIÑEIRO, F., *Estudio sobre Garabandal*, Sigüenza, 2001, I.35.
[690] MONS. LÓPEZ, M. P., *"Carta al P. Gustavo Morelos (July 8, 1966)"* in *Diario de Conchita*, 14; cf. GARCÍA DE LA RIVA, J. R., *Memorias de un cura de aldea en Garabandal*, Santander, 2011, 399.
[691] CDF, *Norms for the discernment of presumed apparitions*, 1978, III.1.
[692] MONS. LÓPEZ, M. P., *"Carta al P. Gustavo Morelos (July 8, 1966)"* in *Diario de Conchita*, 14.

"God is here." This statement, made in 1966 after consultation with Rome and Santander, provides a positive key for interpreting Garabandal. It proves that both Rome and Santander expressed themselves to this Archbishop with openness towards Garabandal, as he himself outlines in his letter (*"Bearing in mind the indications of the Holy See and the Ordinary of Santander... absolutely not in prohibition and rejection... we approve the publication of the Message of the Blessed Virgin in San Sebastián de Garabandal"*).

This testimony may be added to the declarations of other prelates like His Excellency Roman Danlak of Toronto (Canada), and His Excellency Francisco Garmendia, Auxiliary Bishop of New York, who personally interviewed Conchita, was her spiritual director in that city and whose testimony in favor of the phenomena of Garabandal is publicly known, or His Excellency Luis Guízar Barragán, Bishop of Saltillo (Mexico), who reiterates a statement repeated by several bishops:

> The doctrine expounded there or arising from the events that occurred is entirely in accord with the teachings of the Church.[693]

These and other prelates, without anticipating the judgment of the competent authority, provide a unified testimony of real openness of the Hierarchy towards Garabandal. This sheds a consoling light on the drawn out ecclesiastical process of Garabandal tarnished by the incomplete reports of two successive technical investigative Committees.

---

[693] GARCÍA DE LA RIVA, J. R., *Memorias de un cura de aldea en Garabandal,* Santander, 2011, 396-400.

III

The Garabandal Committees

Bishop Del Val considered the work of the first Committee of the apparitions insufficient. For that reason he institutes the second one in 1989. Two years later, when the new reports are ready, everyone asks where they have come from. The new documents do not proceed from on the ground investigations. The witnesses are not interrogated, the seers are not interviewed. It seems that the new Committee, to the scandal of the public and the experts, only carries out a re-elaboration of the previous material.

The new Committee, like the first one, proceeds surreptitiously. Attempting to avoid every possible obstacle to its objectivity, investigations are carried out in absolute secrecy; avoiding the multiplication of witnesses and consultations. This secrecy, according to the Vatican, entails two major limitations in its findings. The Vatican evaluates the procedure as follows:

> While the committees consist very frequently of enclosed and secret groups, the Congregation [for the Doctrine of Faith] recommends that they be more open to information; be it to avail of works already carried out, or be it to provide clarity to the faithful who seek discernment.[694]

In our case, since the *Reports* emitted by the two diocesan Committees after their labors on the phenomena of Garabandal are not even in the public domain, it is not possible, at least for the moment, to study them directly. However, some the circumstances of those labors *are* in the public domain, thanks to

---

[694] GUTIÉRREZ GONZÁLEZ, J., "*Las apariciones de la Virgen María en la vida de la Iglesia y en la vida del Cristiano,*" *Estudios Marianos* 75 (2009) 428.

testimonies—sometimes very authoritative—of contemporaries of the Committee members during the time of their inquiries. These testimonies reveal the limitations and shortcomings of the first study (done during the apparitions) by the Committee nominated by Bishop Fernández, and even of the second one commissioned by Bishop Del Val to correct the shortcomings of the first. Some of the testimonies possess an authority that is difficult to question, and, all together, they acquire a solidity that is difficult to refute:

1. Brigadier Juan Álvarez Seco, that "ringside witness of many events,"[695] so precise in his notes of the events, writes of the Committee that: *"I testify that throughout the year 1961, I have seen the doctors of the Committee in Garabandal three times. One, when Mr. Rocha, from Saltos del Nansa, told me that that day* [2 July] *the seers would not come to the 'cuadro,' because Dr. Morales* [a Committee member] *would stop them and hypnotize them in the Calleja, with the outcome everyone knows...* [Aware of the doctor's intention, the girls avoided him and had the first vision of the Virgin].[696] *Another was the 18th of October, the day of the first message; by that time they* [the Committee members] *were being forceably policed to keep them from bothering them* [the children], *because the villagers were so indignant at their behavior."*[697]

The third visit, Álvarez concludes, was *"the night they spent in Garabandal when the entire neighborhood was asleep, to see if they could take the seers with them clandestinely to Santander* [August 22, 1961].*"*[698] Álvarez here leaves a record of a truly sad fact, borne out by a multitude of witnesses and experts. This distant attitude of the Committee would not be limited to the first year, on which

[695] ROJAS, A. M., *Letter to the author*, September 12, 2013.
[696] Cf. Ch. I.
[697] GALMÉS BELMONTE, R., *"Position of the Church regarding Garabandal"* in FUNDACIÓN HM, *www.garabandal.it*, Lumezzane, 2013.
[698] PESQUERA, 2004, 194.

Álvarez focuses in his account. "According to references from reliable witnesses, the one [Committee member] who was most often present [in Garabandal; Dr. Morales], was there a maximum of six times [in the four years of the phenomena], always displaying clearly and openly a preconceived contrary attitude. There are records of numerous expressions and incidents demonstrating this preconceived position of the Committee members."[699]

2. The Committee's inactivity is a public and notorious fact for all, villagers and visitors alike. The Jesuit Ángel María Rojas, after years of studying the phenomena, concludes that "Rather than carry out an investigation or a study, they [the Committee members] badly misbehaved with those children, who were then very little, threatening them and behaving against them in such a way that they succeeded in alienating not only the villagers who were in favor of the supernatural reality of the events but even those who were not... [In fact,] the Bishop was given prior notice that there was going to be a miracle [that of the visible Communion: June 18, 1962], so that the Committee members could study it, but none of them showed up."[700] Only a delegate was sent to witness this episode, so pre-announced and relevant, and he was not a specialist in the field: Regino Matio, a solicitor of the Council of Santander, who, furthermore, saw nothing; the people were so indignant at the situation that the lawyer was not granted any preferential position among the public.[701]

---

699 GALMÉS BELMONTE, R., "Position of the Church regarding Garabandal" in FUNDACIÓN HM, www.garabandal.it, Lumezzane, 2013.
700 ROJAS, A. M., Letter to the author, September 12, 2013.
701 Cf. GARCÍA DE LA RIVA, J. R., Memorias de un cura de aldea en Garabandal, Santander, 2011, 197.

3. On the 27th of July 1961, at the very beginning of the phenomena, the diocesan Committee intervenes to withdraw Conchita from the village. *"They said I was the one who was obsessing the others,"* Conchita writes, *"and then they led me away to do tests and the first day I had an apparition beside a church, the Consolation* [in Santander, near the quay]."[702] She relates the tenor of that day's interrogations: *"They said to me: 'Stand up straight, look at my nose... I'm going to hypnotize you.' When he said: 'Look at my nose,' I laughed... And he said: 'Stop laughing, this is no laughing matter.'"*[703]

In Santander, Conchita was taken by the nieces of one of the Committee members—Fr. Odriozola—to the beach, the shops and the fairgrounds; and even to a fortune-teller. One authority on Garabandal indignantly observes that "Conchita was submitted to an extremely effective therapy, it seems, of beaches and carnivals, to *distract her.*"[704] When Conchita's mother found out what they were doing with the child, she hastened indignantly to Santander to bring her home. Conchita twice refuses to comply with her mother's intention. Later on, in the village, s--he will remember all of that with different eyes: *"After about a week a man intervened to take me* [home to the village] *and my mom came to get me, and I came home; his name is Mr. Emilio del Valle Egocheaga: I will be grateful to him for it my whole life."*[705]

The child had not seen the Virgin again in Santander since the first day, and on her return, writes: *"The Virgin told me that She didn't come to see me more often* [in Santander] *because I was*

---

[702] *Diario de Conchita*, 46.
[703] *Ib.*
[704] DE DIOS, J. M., *El gran portento de Garabandal: Teología, opiniones críticas y puntualizaciones*, Zaragoza, 1969, 81.
[705] *Diario de Conchita*, 47.

going to the beach. But now I've confessed that."[706] The Committee, thinking that the 12-year-old, the eldest of the girls, was orchestrating *the whole deception*, figured that by removing her from the village everything would fall apart and that, *distracted*, she would *get better*. A complete error: in her absence the phenomena continued *as normal*.[707]

4. Referring specifically to the day of the publication of the first message, the 18th of October 1961, Dr. Celestino Ortiz writes: "Despite the atmosphere, so favorable to the power of suggestion, given that most of the people were excited and expecting a great miracle, I was unable to discover a single case of that kind... A very important fact! Bearing in mind that some of my colleagues [concretely Dr. Morales, main medical expert of the Committee], along with other members of the Committee, have argued that we are dealing with *phenomena of collective suggestion.*"[708] For Dr. Ortiz—among many other experts—the accusation of suggestion has no objective basis. Rather, the facts indicate normality, sincerity and good health in the seers.

5. Materne Laffineur delivers a conference in Lisieux, on the 1st of May 1969, in which he provides details of the interview that the Committee carried out with him on the 24th of June 1965, as a witness and an expert in the phenomena: "All of my replies were subjected to *a priori* interpretations, giving them a meaning that could only be unfavorable to Garabandal... When I had finished my declarations (which took place in a restaurant; the ultimate scandal in canonical material!), I was told: *'Sign here.'* I answered: *'I'm not going to sign that.'* But then I saw something that none of

---

[706] PESQUERA, 2004, 127.
[707] Cf. *Ib.*, 124.
[708] LANÚS, S., *Madre de Dios y Madre Nuestra. Fátima, Ámsterdam y Garabandal*, Madrid, 2013, 129.

you could imagine: with his fountain pen, underneath what he himself [Francisco Odriozola] had written, he put my name and surname in capital letters, without blinking an eye... What is that called in Law?"[709] According to the present *Code of Canon Law*, this procedural vice is called "*Falsity*" (*CIC* 1645 §2.1). And, if proved to be true, the same Code demands a *Restitutio In Integrum* of the case: new documentation, a new study. In fact, it seems there are proofs that all of this happened, at least with the testimony of Materne Laffineur:

> When some friends of mine from Germany visited Santander some time later, they were assured that I had given a sworn statement against Garabandal to the Committee—*writes Laffineur*—and that the declaration bore my signature.[710]

Laffineur's story is illuminating. He also testifies from the time he spent in the village that, after four long years of phenomena, in 1965 "the Committee had not yet had time to interview, appropriately, the seers, or their families, or even the parish priest (or any of the witnesses, no matter how qualified, who might have spoken favorably of the supernatural character of the phenomena)."[711] The Committee, it seems, had already concluded its study a long time before: *a priori*.

6. Julio Porro Cardeñoso, canon of Tarragona and native of Santander, affirms: "I know of concrete instances of lying on the part of members of the Committee."[712] He is referring to Conchita's repeated failed attempts to meet the Bishop, His Excellency Eugenio Beitia Aldazábal (1962-1965). She never got

---

[709] PESQUERA, 2004, 566; cf. LAFFINEUR, M. - LE PELLETIER, M.T., *La estrella en la montaña*, Tielt, 1967, 97.

[710] *Ib.*

[711] *Ib.*

[712] PORRO CARDEÑOSO, J., *El misterio de Garabandal en la teología católica*, Zaragoza, 1970, 69-70.

an appointment; it seems there was a *breakdown* in communication.

7. Dr. Morales, psychiatrist and main medical expert of the Committee, in a conference delivered in the Athenaeum of Santander in 1983, publicly declares what everyone already knows: "In Garabandal there was neither a Committee nor an investigation. It was a sham."[713] He admitted that during the events he had acted as a bitter enemy of the apparitions. Totally incredulous at the beginning, he now becomes a defender of Garabandal. As we know, behind this change there is a strong personal experience and even a miraculous healing, that of Antonio F. Bonín Cavero. Morales would go so far as to state that, in his opinion: "The events of Garabandal were of the same nature as Lourdes and Fatima."[714]

8. Antonio Palacios, professor of the University of Barcelona, testifies to the bias in the work of both Committees (the first, in 1961, and the second set up to correct its errors in 1991). Palacios affirms: "Neither of the Committees that pronounced on whether what happened in Garabandal was supernatural ever sought any statement, or even deigned to interview the official reporter [Commandant Álvarez] of the recognized authority [the Civil Guard]. This detail is enough for anyone to deduce the level of true and total impartiality with which the episcopal committees sought information: they were open not to witnesses who were believers, but to the incredulous. The desire was to discredit the events at all costs, and to achieve that it was necessary to

713 LÓPEZ DE SAN ROMÁN, *La verdad sobre Garabandal,* Valladolid, 2012.
714 LANÚS, S., *Madre de Dios y Madre Nuestra. Fátima, Ámsterdam y Garabandal,* Madrid, 2013, 161; LÓPEZ DE SAN ROMÁN, *La verdad sobre Garabandal,* Valladolid, 2012.

eliminate any witness who might be favorable, no matter how qualified."[715]

IV

"New studies"

The above testimonies, together with many others, sufficiently demonstrate the difficulty: the nature of the *Reports* at the disposal of the Hierarchy has so far prevented an objective decision of any kind. This is precisely the problem that led to Bishop Del Val's institution of a second Committee in 1989, and Archbishop Carlos Osoro alludes to the dilemma in 2007 when he augurs *"New studies, so that the events of Garabandal may be examined in greater depth"*:

> I am open to all information, to every consideration about Garabandal.[716]

In effect, the *Official Notes* of the successive Bishops, which explicitly rely on the *Reports* of the said committees, "Suffer a lack of serious and impartial information."[717] This fact deprives their conclusions of rigor. What Canon Law calls a *"Restitutio In Integrum"* of the process is necessary; that is, a new, objective and competent study (*CIC* 1645 §2.1).

There is nothing new in this for the Church. Cardinal Ratzinger, in 1990, affirmed that even the Pontifical Magisterium can waver

---

[715] PÉREZ, R., 1991, 158.

[716] OSORO SIERRA, C., *"Letter to Edward Kelly (May 7, 2007)"* in GARABANDAL JOURNAL, Minnesota 2007, V-VI, 5; LANÚS, S., *Madre de Dios y Madre Nuestra. Fátima, Ámsterdam y Garabandal,* Madrid, 2013, 174.

[717] GALMÉS BELMONTE, R., *"Position of the Church regarding Garabandal"* in FUNDACIÓN HM, *www.garabandal.it,* Lumezzane, 2013.

somewhat at times, initially and in disciplinary matters, as in our case:

> When it comes to the question of interventions in the prudential order, it could happen that some Magisterial documents might not be free from all deficiencies. Bishops and their advisors have not always taken into immediate consideration every aspect or the entire complexity of a question... [T]he theologian, who cannot pursue his discipline well without a certain competence in history, is aware of the filtering that occurs with the passage of time. This is not to be understood in the sense of a relativization of the tenets of the faith. The theologian knows that some judgments of the Magisterium could be justified at the time in which they were made, because while the pronouncements contained true assertions and others which were not sure, both types were inextricably connected. Only time has permitted discernment and, after deeper study, the attainment of true doctrinal progress.[718]

Three of Ratzinger's arguments converge in our case:

1) *"True assertions and others which were not sure... were inextricably connected."* The successive *Reports* of the Committee are useful to a certain extent: the gathering of the fundamental *"content"* of the apparitions (the messages) with fewer deficiencies than *"the phenomena"* (*ecstasies, levitations, miracles*), provided the Bishops with material by which they could truly come to know *"the message"* of Garabandal. Thanks to this, the Bishops, when it came to judging the content of the apparitions, could do so with objectivity, and in evaluating them positively did so with integrity of judgment. The Committee had not distorted the content but the explanation of the phenomena, upon which they exhaustively based their investigations.

It is justifiable, therefore, to recover the value of the Bishops' judgment on the content of the apparitions, which is positive time

---

[718] CDF, Instruction *Donum Veritatis*, Rome, 1990, 24c.

after time (His Excellency Beitia in 1965, Cirarda in 1970, Del Val in 1991, Osoro in 2007), and which encourages the continued study of the phenomena, disparaged *a priori* by the limited *Reports* of the aforementioned Committees.

2) The successive Bishops of Santander have confined themselves to "*interventions of a prudential order.*" The process of one of these disciplinary interventions, perhaps the most widely spoken of in Garabandal, is interesting. Bishop Beitia, in his early *Note* of October 7, 1962, forbade priests and religious "to visit the abovementioned place [Garabandal], without express permission from the diocesan authority."[719] This prohibition is revoked in 1986 by Bishop Del Val Gallo,[720] although Bishop Vilaplana will later insist, in 2001, that Masses in Garabandal only "be celebrated in the parish church without reference to the supposed apparitions and with the authorization of the parish priest."[721] In 2007, with the letter of Archbishop Carlos Osoro, this *disciplinary disposition* is revised again. In effect, in his letter, the Apostolic Administrator encourages pilgrims: "I have now authorized priests to visit Garabandal and to celebrate the Eucharist there in the parish church at whatever hour they wish and to administer the sacrament of reconcilication there to whomever they wish."[722] The passage of time softens tensions.

3) In fact, as Cardinal Ratzinger affirms: "*Time has permitted discernment.*" In the case just cited, this seems to happen in Garabandal also.

[719] MONS. BEITIA ALDAZÁBAL, E., "*Nota sobre los sucesos de San Sebastián de Garabandal* (October 7, 1962)" in OBISPADO DE SANTANDER, *Boletín Oficial de la Diócesis de Santander,* Santander, 1962, XI, 242.
[720] Cf. LANÚS, S., *Madre de Dios y Madre Nuestra. Fátima, Ámsterdam y Garabandal,* Madrid, 2013, 172.
[721] VILAPLANA, *Letter to Richard Paul Salbato,* Santander November 7, 2001.
[722] OSORO SIERRA, C., "*Letter to Edward Kelly* (May 7, 2007)" in GARABANDAL JOURNAL, Minnesota, 2007, V-VI, 5; LANÚS, S., *Madre de Dios y Madre Nuestra. Fátima, Ámsterdam y Garabandal,* Madrid, 2013, 174.

And yet, the solution will not come by itself; a renewed commitment is necessary, a new and rigorous study and an objective discernment. The elements for judgment and the working instruments already exist and are at the disposition of the Church. Their application, and the extent thereof, is something that corresponds solely to the authority of the Church.

Conclusion

This glance at the teaching Church's attitude in relation to the phenomena of Garabandal is illuminating. Even though the successive Bishops have not for the moment deemed it opportune to affirm the supernatural character of the events of Garabandal, their *non constat* expresses only *"ambiguity"*:[723] Garabandal is not yet clear. This verdict is perfectly open to revision in the light of a more solid scientific study or new information, such as we possess today. Successive Bishops have repeatedly affirmed the perfect orthodoxy of the messages: in Garabandal "There is nothing contrary to dogma and morals."[724] To this it must be added that Archbishop Osoro has recently recommended the apparitions as a positive influence for the faithful (*"I encourage you to continue to maintain this devotion to Our Mother"*) pointing to the fruits of Garabandal: there *"I have known authentic conversions."*

Fermín Labarga, Professor of Theology in the University of Navarre, offers another significant detail: of the more than thirty cases of presumed apparitions in Spain since 1960, all but two have been discounted by the ecclesiastical authority. One of these is Garabandal; the other, El Escorial (1981-2002). In both cases, "Confirmation of their supernatural character continues to await confirmation."[725] With the word *"waiting"* Labarga indicates the

---

[723] GUTIÉRREZ GONZÁLEZ, J., *"Las apariciones de la Virgen María en la vida de la Iglesia y en la vida del Cristiano,"* Estudios Marianos 75 (2009) 428.
[724] OBISPADO DE SANTANDER, *Declaraciones oficiales de la Jerarquía sobre Garabandal,* Santander, 1970, 15.
[725] LABARGA GARCÍA, F., *"La tradición mariofánica española,"* Estudios Marianos 72 (2009) 55.

quiet expectation that Garabandal provokes. The case certainly possesses today as never before the indispensable stability and knowledge required for bringing to an end that long *"wait"* for approval mentioned by Labarga. The signs are positive:

· The integrity of its content.
· The impossibility of explaining the phenomena with the human sciences.
· The seers' rectitude of life and perseverance in good.
· The numerous healings reported from the five continents.
· The beneficial and widespread reception of its message among the faithful.
· The clarification of the complicated process of two ineffective Committees.
· The express will of the Hierarchy to clarify the events.

In any event, in the absence of clarifying studies that go into the matter *"in depth,"* as Osoro puts it, Garabandal, fifty years after the facts, is still awaiting a response.

* * *

A final question: what is the meaning of the apparitions of Garabandal? For some, all that remains at the end of the story is a prophetic announcement. But this is not the whole story, nor even the center of Garabandal. Garabandal was not necessary to announce that when a person turns his back on God, or a society turns away from Him, damage is done: the person or society *"self-chastises."* This is a clear biblical teaching in the stories of Noah and Jonah and even in the Passion of Christ, *pierced for our transgressions,* chastised for our salvation (cf. Is 53:2-12).

But if the message of Garabandal is not about telling us the obvious—even though it is a reminder—then what is it about? It seems that in these difficult times for the Church, these moments of a *"terrible crisis,"*[726] spiritual and human, Garabandal appears as an illustration of the infinite power of God's love, of his closeness to and interest in man and in modern society. Garabandal is a declaration that no matter how much man distances himself from God, there is always a way back. Owing precisely to the lack of sure belief in God's power and mercy, many Christians have lost hope in the midst of a world that seems to have found fulfillment without the need of God.

Pope Francis points to this ecclesial crisis with concern. In *Evangelii Gaudium—The Joy of the Gospel—*(2013), he says that the difficulties that the Church is undergoing today proceed to a great extent from an *inner* crisis, of forgetfulness or distrust of God among the faithful, who have given themselves over to the search for "personal freedom, as though the task of evangelization was a dangerous poison rather than *a joyful response to God's love* which summons us to mission and *makes us fulfilled and productive."*[727] The Pope denounces the sickly spirit of autonomy and distrust and summons the faithful to a spirit of faith, freedom and confidence in God's power and love. His diagnosis of the contemporary situation is clear:

Lack of deep spirituality which turns into pessimism, fatalism, and mistrust.[728]

"Deep spirituality." In the work of healing, the Pope continues, the Virgin Mary fulfills *"a special saving mission."*[729] Vatican Council II already enunciated this idea:

---

[726] SESÉ, J., *Historia de la Espiritualidad,* Pamplona, 2005, n. 300.
[727] FRANCISCO, Apostolic Exhortation *Evangelii Gaudium,* n. 81.
[728] *Ib.,* n. 275.

The Mother of Jesus... is the image and beginning of the Church as it is to be perfected in the world to come... a sign of sure hope and solace to the people of God during its sojourn on earth... This maternity of Mary in the order of grace... lasts until the eternal fulfillment of all the elect. Taken up to heaven she did not lay aside this salvific duty, but by her constant intercession continued to bring us the gifts of eternal salvation.[730]

Garabandal, from beginning to end, is an illustration of these words of the Council, a spark of light against the dark autonomy of secularism, a clear aperture to the ambit of the supernatural, *"with Mary"* and *"from Mary."* The message of Garabandal is thus situated in close and clear continuity with the most recent theology and Pontifical Magisterium. It is a disconcerting and exciting case, with a multitude of novelties and propositions capable of enriching the Church's present path.

In the end, the question that the Lady put to Conchita on the day of the last apparition remains standing :

"I love you very much and I desire your salvation...
You, Conchita, will surely respond to me?"

---

[729] *Ib.*, n. 285.
[730] VATICAN COUNCIL II, Dogmatic Constitution on the Church, *"Lumen Gentium"* (November 21, 1964), 68: *AAS* 57 (1965), 66; n. 62: *AAS* 57 (1965), 63.